The Irish Novel at the End
of the Twentieth Century 🔹

The Irish Novel at the End of the Twentieth Century

Gender, Bodies, and Power

Jennifer M. Jeffers

palgrave

First published 2002 by PALGRAVE™
175 Fifth Avenue, New York, N.Y.10010 and
Houndmills, Basingstoke, Hampshire RG21 6XS.
Companies and representatives throughout the world.

PALGRAVE is the new global publishing imprint of St. Martin's Press LLC
Scholarly and Reference Division and Palgrave Publishers Ltd. (formerly
Macmillan Press Ltd.).

ISBN 0–312–23839–8 hardback

Library of Congress Cataloging-in-Publication Data
Jeffers, Jennifer M.
The Irish novel at the end of the twentieth century : gender, bodies, and
power / by Jennifer M. Jeffers.
    p.   cm.
  Includes bibliographical references and index.
  ISBN 0–312–23839–8
  1. English fiction—Irish authors—History and criticism. 2. English
fiction—20th century—History and criticism. 3. Power (Social sciences)
in literature. 4. Northern Ireland—In literature. 5. Body, Human, in
literature. 6. Ireland—In literature. 7. Sex role in literature. I. Title.

PR8803.J44   2002
823'.914099417—dc21

                                                          2001053132

A catalogue record for this book is available from the British Library.

Design by Letra Libre, Inc.

First edition: March 2002
10 9 8 7 6 5 4 3 2 1

Printed in the United States of America.

For Beckett, Samuel, and Gene

Contents

Acknowledgments

Funding to research this book was provided in part by Dean John Carlson, College of Arts and Sciences at the University of South Dakota, the English Department at the University of South Dakota, and Dean Royce Engstrom, Office of Research, University of South Dakota. I would like to thank Bill Rolston for permission to reproduce a photograph from *Drawing Support: Murals in the North of Ireland,* and Chris Riddell for permission to reproduce a cartoon that originally appeared in *The Observer,* July 18, 1999, and is reprinted in the collection *Tribal Politics.* I would also like to thank Erin Chan, Donna Cherry, Seamus Deane, Mary Jeffers, Roee Raz, Lynn Todd-Crawford, Kevin Whelan, Susan Wolfe, Bill Hart (for the use of his camera), Kristi Long (my ever-patient editor at Palgrave), and Gene Blocker for tasks too numerous to mention.

The Irish Novel at the End of the Twentieth Century

Introduction ▓

Irish Culture in a State of Becoming

The 1990s was a boom period for the Irish novel as a group of young Irish novelists came to the fore to create an entirely new agenda for the genre of the novel. Young novelists, mostly in their thirties or younger, include Tom Lennon, Robert McLiam Wilson, Laura Harte, Joseph O'Connor, Emma Donoghue, Glenn Patterson, Anne Enright, and Kate O'Riordan. Born in the 1950s, Roddy Doyle and Patrick McCabe represent the "senior" class of this young group of novelists. Many of the novels produced in the 1990s are concerned with the body as it is linked to a grid of power that is partly preestablished and partly rapidly changing in contemporary Ireland. For several of these novels the demarcating line of identity—that perennial Irish problem—can be gauged at the basic level of sexual and gender identity in contrast to or in alliance with political, social, religious, or cultural norms. Also, judging from novels written in the last decade of the twentieth century, Irish identity is in large part a matter of economics (replacing the traditionally political) as the Republic of Ireland's postmodern place in the Eurocommunity becomes more important than its postcoloniality. Perhaps one distinguishing characteristic of these novelists is their departure from themes long considered "Irish." In *The Secret World of the Irish Male,* for example, Joseph O'Connor (born in 1963 and pop singer Sinead O'Connor's younger brother) audaciously states that Irish literary history is of little concern to him: "[W]hen I started to write fiction myself, the fact of Joyce's existence—or Wilde's or Yeats's or Synge's for that matter—never bothered me much."[1] Yet, in twentieth century Irish novel writing, Joyce is typically portrayed as the quintessential or primal "father" who must be "killed" in order for the "son" to assert himself. While Beckett is fondly mentioned, Joyce, who wrote such *Irish* novels, can simply be ignored by O'Connor:

The problem for those of us who write "Irish" fiction is that Joyce is so frequently described in superlatives. The greatest, the deepest, the most obsessive, the craziest, the funniest. He is always there, the line goes, always peeking over your shoulder, the monolithic spectacular superstar Joyce who tore up the rulebook and wrote the novel out of existence. But the notion that young Irish writers are lying awake in their beds worrying about James Joyce or Irish history is simply untrue. Young Irish writers are busy telling stories, writing sentences, busy with the grim and unglamorous work of writing fiction which says something to readers about their lives. When they are doing this, they are worried about their German publishing rights, and who is making the movie of their first novel, and will the tax-free scheme for artists remain in place even under a Progressive Democrat government. For a young writer now, James Joyce is probably the biggest irrelevance in a history that is best ignored.[2]

Traditionalists would be shocked to learn that "James Joyce is probably the biggest irrelevance" in a young writer's life; O'Connor's view reflects the young novelist's capitalistic and economic needs; his lack of romanticism may be a turnoff for some readers who wish Irish literature to continue in the vein of Yeats or Synge. Dermot Bolger, another contemporary writer, takes up O'Connor's line of anti-romanticism in regard to Dublin:

This folksy nostalgia has created an isolation that somehow the real Dublin is dead, the real Dubliners scattered and dying and some alien city is rising in its place. To me, at least, a real Dubliner is anyone who has been born or has chosen to live there and now regards the city as his or her home, the real Dublin is wherever they stake their claim to that home. Rather than being dead it is alive and vibrant with new people, with new blood, new streets, new place names. Its history is not finished but yet to be written by the masses of children who are still living it.[3]

This attitude, that whoever lives in Dublin or Ireland is a Dubliner or Irish, may be one of strongest characteristics of the new generation of Irish writers which, in turn, depicts the norm in Irish society as mobile with abundant economic opportunity. Reviewer Damian Smyth, however, faults this attitude in Bolger, stating that Bolger wants to have his cake and eat it, too: "Bolger's insistence that 'Irish' fiction has achieved a mature, contemporary voice which can no longer be adequately described by 'pre-decimal' notions of identity is a heartening one; but the problem is that all the features to which he ascribes the term 'Irish' with such abandon are actually anational—obsessions with childhood, estrangement, sexual *mores*." Smyth concludes, "Hollywood, television, fashion etc. serve to signal a new direction in the writing certainly, but in so doing they render the soubriquet 'Irish' redundant and rather quaint, an example of having one's cake and eating it."[4] As we will see, this charge of the "soubriquet 'Irish'" is found at all levels of Irish society and culture, not only in contemporary writers. The accusation that people now living in Ireland want to be Irish and yet "hip," European, or "urban" is the price, in part, for modernization and a higher standard of living.

Predictably, even the image of the "new Ireland" has quickly gelled into a "standard." Where once there was the clichéd rural Ireland, now there is the clichéd urban Ireland. While Scotland has Irvine Welsh's *Trainspotting* and the collection of short fiction, *Acid Plaid,* Ireland's analogous collection, *Shenanigans,* features an urbane scene where drugs, punk rock (revival), and hopelessness form the desperately cool "Irish" *menage à trois.* In a recent book review, Mick Heaney points out that the older set of writers, Bolger and Doyle, is more responsible for the "dirty realism" in Irish fiction than the younger writers supposedly portraying their generation: "So why is the stereotype of the edgy twentysomething novelist still hyped? The past ten years have seen a crop of books that went against the idyllic, soulful image of the largely rural Ireland, novels that concentrated on the working-class city dwellers, more ravaged by drugs and deprivation than perfidious Albion.*"*[5] Urbanization is obviously a result of modernization that has worked to render any contemporary characterization of rural Ireland passé. Even in Roddy Doyle's last novel of the decade, *A Star Called Henry* (1999), which is set early in the twentieth century before modernization and contains many scenes set in the country where Henry Smart trains his rebel soldiers, there is no trace of rural nostalgia; there is no feeling that the real Ireland is "beyond the pale," rather, "real" Ireland is Dublin, where from 1916 to 1922 everything Irish and important happens.

This urban trend in novels written in the last ten years finds its mirror image in Northern Ireland. Northern Ireland is dominated by two cities, Derry and Belfast, and the differences between the two, according to critic Eamonn Hughes, is more interesting than the usual differences separating the Unionists and Nationalists:

> The divisions between nationalist and unionist, catholic and protestant, Irish and British, in the North tend to obscure other, potentially more interesting, though still largely unexpressed, divisions such as that between Belfast and Derry; these are the twin poles towards which everything in between is oriented. For the Belfastard the country is inhabited by culchies with Derriers being a species of super-culchie. For Derriers, meanwhile, the universe is Derrycentric, and everything outside Derry is but a (beyond the) pale imitation of the real thing. . . . It is also a prejudice which must be seen in the context of the valorisation of the rural in Irish culture which gives rise to an overarching prejudice against the urban.[6]

Hughes, it would seem, has a point; often Northern Irish novelists do seem to privilege one city over the other. For example, Seamus Deane's *Reading in the Dark* is solidly "Derrier," while Glenn Patterson's *Burning Your Own* and *Fat Lad* are true-blue "Belfastards." The only exception from the north that I will discuss is Deirdre Madden's *One by One in the Dark,* set in rural Northern Ireland. The shift away from Ireland's rural past in contemporary literature is based on the shift in population from its agrarian economy to its entry into the European economy.

The historical and economic changes are important to the contemporary scene in Ireland, yet the focus of my book is the representation and *enactment* of gender, bodies, and the manifestation of power in the contemporary Irish novel. There is a critical awareness in these novels that is much like the edgy post-postmodern quality found in innovative British and American novels. In terms of gender, 1980s critical studies saw a shift away from feminism and feminist agendas to the wider area of gender. Gender is viewed as a patriarchal construction that distributes, regulates and represses bodies and power. Gender, bodies and power continue to be regulated by the patriarchal machine, or, as Judith Butler terms it, the heterosexual matrix, which has female as well as male representatives who police society and culture. *Gender in Irish Writing* (1991) was one of the first studies to focus on gender in the Irish context; influenced by continental theory, the editors recognize their considerable task in breaking new ground:

> It should be no surprise if deconstructing gender in the texts of a culture should meet with resistance from those who are in command and advantaged by the *status quo.* Such resistance to "seeing" is inbuilt in the very dynamics of the construction of gender, where the unconscious plays such a crucial role. . . . It sometimes also comes from male-identified women, who have learnt all too well to accept a role that masculinism authorizes, and who resist the uncovering of the personal and psychological price they pay for such role-restriction.[7]

O'Brien Johnson and Cairns concur with Butler's "heterosexual matrix" and the view that in the 1990s the topic will be not the repression of women but the more broadly defined social and cultural matrix that normalizes the very idea of a sexual and gender binary.

Irish novels in the last decade of the twentieth century push the heterosexualist culture to see its "inbuilt" gender identifications, and needless to say, this is not a comfortable or easy process. Irish religious, gender, sexual, and material precedents in fiction that overtly challenge heterosexual culture and regulation are basically nonexistent. And so in terms of tradition or context the problem of interpretation, or how to *read* these novels, arises. Contemporary Irish novelists have produced meaning through form in their texts. Language may or may not refer to the material world; all that we can be certain of is that language can tell us something about *itself.* Discourse comments on the world, but more importantly, discourse comments on discourse. Therefore we are interested in *how* discourse is produced in the novels as well as what is referentially posited. We become more engaged in this "meta" level of reading with each successive chapter because the novels themselves begin to blur, begin to slip off the page. The work of contemporary French philosopher Gilles Deleuze can help us map the trajectory of the novels' events and bodies forcing the action. For it is only through a charting or gauging of *movement* of bodies in fiction that we can begin to see the truly thought-provoking and different, however seemingly bizarre, realm of bodies in space that populate Irish fictional texts.

At the end of the twentieth century, Irish Studies has been in a state of critical ferment because of the centeredness of the "post": postcolonialism, postmodernism, post-revisionism, post-nationalism, to mention only the most prevalent "post" discourses. These discourses have greatly increased the critical sophistication of Irish Studies by initiating new approaches. The supplementarity of meaning created by these theories, however, has aroused suspicions that the method has become a ruse for airing political grievances. Appropriating Gayatri Chakravorty Spivak's theoretical position, Colin Graham denounces monolithic Irish postcolonial readings that subalternize the national cause: "Spivak's comments point to a specific danger in an Irish context: a complex, contorted intellectual nativism, rehearsing the idioms and rejuvenating the discourses of an essentialist Irishness which is always oppressed, and yet is itself oppressive of the heterogeneity with which it is confronted."[8] Basically, Graham points out that "intellectual nativism" is trading one form of homogeneity in for another form: trading "British" for "Irish." However, putting the proliferation of critical sophistication another way, Brenda Maddox states, "Irish Studies is riding the crest of a larger, more sinister wave known as 'post-colonial studies.' This is a politically correct vogue for elevating the grievances of newly independent nations to academic status."[9]

While some critics do not welcome theory into the field, it would seem that the "real" uneasiness is actually to be found within Irish Studies itself. What is Irish Studies? Who is Irish? Who has the right to speak on the behalf of Ireland? Is Gerry Adams more Irish than Ian Paisley? Is Bertie Ahern more Irish than John Hume? Is Mary Robinson more Irish than Martin McGuinness? Is the Republic more authentically Irish than the North? Is the generation coming of age now more Irish than its grandparents? Any attempt to answer these questions, or even one of these questions, immediately lands us in complex web of linguistic, historical, religious, gendered, geographical, political, and economic entanglements. One hundred years ago, at the beginning of the twentieth century, Lionel Johnson in "Poetry and Patriotism in Ireland" also wrestled with the problem of defining and distinguishing Irishness: "After all, who is to decide what is, absolutely and definitely, the Celtic and Irish note? Many a time I have shown my English friends Irish poems, which Irish critics have declared to be un-Irish; and the English verdict has constantly been: 'How un-English! how Celtic! What a strange, remote far-away beauty in the music and in the colour!'"[10] More currently, Benedict Anderson's often cited *Imagined Communities* reminds us that links that build and eventually become the community are temporally constructed: "The idea of a sociological organism moving calendrically through homogeneous, empty time is a precise analogue of the idea of the nation, which is also conceived as a solid community moving steadily down (or up) history."[11] In the Irish context, a contemporary Irish person may look up the hill to Maeve's tomb and across the way to Carrowmore and think, "Ah, my Irish ancestors were great spiritual landscape builders." Anderson would say that there is a naïveté on the part of the contemporary to believe that the builders of, what we now call Carrowmore, would have even the slightest affinity, racially, culturally, or linguistically, with the present day inhabitants of Ireland. This imagined community, according to Anderson, is also prevalent in twentieth century attempts for postcolonial or new republican nations to bond on imagined pre-national racial, cultural, or linguistic bonds that give the new nation a kind of "born again" status: "One could be middle-aged and still part of Young Ireland; one could be illiterate and still part of Young Italy. The reason, of course, was that the language of these nationalisms was either a vernacular mother-tongue to which the members had spoken from the cradle, or, as in the case of Ireland, a metropolitan language which had sunk such deeps roots in sections of the population over centuries of conquest that it too could manifest itself, creole-style, as a vernacular," to which Anderson concludes, "There was thus no necessary connection between language, age, class, and status."[12]

Another attempt at a complex understanding of an imagined community is Graham's abovementioned article, "Subalternity and Gender," which problematizes Irish identity in the context of gender and subalternity. Graham, quoting Ailbhe Smyth, states that "'the question of Irish women's place within but without culture and identity' certainly constitutes a 'running sore on the body politic of Ireland.'" Smyth challenges the complacency of traditional Irish identity as an essentially universal national affiliation that ignores gender difference:

> the position of women in Irish society, bound to constitutional and institutionally religious issues of abortion, contraception and divorce, has invoked

serious examination of how gender and femininity relate to the notion of an Irish identity. And it has been the specifics of the category of "Irish" which has necessitated a debate which can envisage alternative placings "within but without culture and identity" in an Irish context—Irishness, variously understood, may encapsulate or expunge the female, denying or seeking to define and legitimise what the "Irish woman" may be.[13]

Part of the aim of *The Irish Novel at the End of the Twentieth Century* is to analyze and pull apart the power matrix that has constructed the Irish woman. By focusing on the particularities of gender, the body, and the power matrix of the given situation instead of resorting to overgeneralizations ("subalternity"), we can begin to reformulate the Irish identity as a complex and indeterminable entity. This constitutes the "real" uneasiness that emerges in Irish Studies: if the very question cannot be defined, then how can we arrive at any kind of "answer"? I propose two answers. The first answer is that we cannot arrive at any absolute answers; absolute answers are not possible and it is naive to think that we can fix meaning or finally nail down "Irish Studies": Irish culture is in a state of becoming. And so, my second answer is evident: it is for that very reason that we must continuously create new contexts and new ways of understanding texts, historical situations, and cultural change.

Without continual reevaluation and renewed understanding these issues will harden into some kind of anachronistic formula. Intellectual nationalism or national isolation is never a valid alternative in any arena. An example is Peter Neary, an Irish economist who believes we should utilize all possible avenues and ideas in all areas of Irish Studies. In terms of economic policy, Neary argues convincingly "that economic nationalism has failed us in a number of different ways. In the area of international trade and investment, the Sinn Fein approach failed to promote economic development. . . . Finally, in the realm of ideas, our tendency to look for Irish solutions to Irish problems fails to draw on the economic ideas and experiences of other countries."[14] With this example in mind, the following chapters initiate a perspective that does not adhere to any "post" position, though it does utilize theoretical tools in order to open up reading strategies that will provide a different way of thinking about "What is Irish"? and, moreover, a way to discuss gender, bodies, and power in the contemporary Irish novel.

In chapter 1, "The Politics of Gender, Bodies, and Power," I open up a theoretical discussion of the site of the body. I also provide a short historical overview focusing on the *contemporary* scene in Northern Ireland and the Republic of Ireland. The socioeconomic changes in the north and the south have radically altered everyday life through media communication and greater mobility. The Republic's entry into a global economy, for example, has irrevocably changed Irish culture. The contested sites of gender and sexuality, the success of women's rights and gay/lesbian rights are manifested in the novels in the last decade of the twentieth century; this manifestation has no precedent in the history of the Irish novel written in English. These changes, along with the 1990s Northern Peace talks, are imperative to understanding the last decade of Irish novels. Chapter 2, "Irish Identity: Heterosexual Norms," concentrates on novels that depict the norms by (re)producing them and/or encroaching on the regulatory norm and thus, clearly demarcating the boundary. This chapter looks at a wide range of novels from the Republic and from the North in order see how the body is typically presented and functions, how gender is typically established and regulated, and how these functions and regulations socially and culturally construct the "Irish Identity." With the novels in chapter 3, "Bodies over the Boundary," the body crosses the line of gender norms and regulated sex as the novels in this chapter break down both prose standards and heterosexual norms. This chapter interprets some of the most exciting examples of the novel in contemporary Ireland because there have never been novels that are so "out of the closet," so blatantly flaunting their *difference* in terms of cultural expectations and norms.

As we go successively farther out on the grid of becoming—and of difference—interpretation is less and less reliant on traditional readings. In chapter 4, "Immeasurable Distance: Discourse, Bodies, and Power," the novels become more difficult to read along traditional heterosexual lines. "Immeasurable Distance" refers to one's ability to "measure" the distance between, say, point A and point B. If, however, A and B cannot be clearly distinguished, demarcated, or identified, then there is no way to measure the distance between one point and the other. The novels discussed in this chapter have a unique ability to slip off the page, to impair our ability to construct clear lines of thought. At this point, we will attempt to follow Deleuze and "grasp movement only as the displacement of a moving body or the development of a form. Movements, becomings, in other words, pure relations of speed and slowness, pure affects, are below and above the threshold of perception." The body becomes still more difficult to chart in chapter 5, "Discourse and the Body: Velocity and Power," which focuses on novels in which fictional bodies whirl out of control and, in turn, produce another kind of sense. The body blurs the power grid, challenges our ability to understand, and makes non-sense out of accepted or normal ways of acting and agency. Meaning in this final chapter is produced by what de Man calls "literariness" and Foucault terms "discourse." From a Deleuzian view, the movement or becoming of the prose on the page is what is paramount and what we must gauge: bodies, gender, and power operate at the referential level at the same time the discourse itself tells us about the power matrix in contemporary Ireland.

Chapter One ▨

The Politics of Gender, Bodies, and Power

In this chapter I wish to broach two issues that will enable us to better understand, theorize about, and critique Irish novels from the last decade (1989–1999) of the twentieth century—especially those written by emerging young writers. The first issue at hand in this chapter is a contemporary overview of recent developments in the culture, politics, economics, and lifestyle of those who live in the Republic and Northern Ireland. The socioeconomic changes, for instance, in the North and the Republic have radically altered everyday life through media communication and greater mobility. The Republic's entry into a global economy has irrevocably changed Irish culture. The contested sites of gender and sexuality and the success of women's rights and gay/lesbian rights are amply manifested in the novels in the last decade of the twentieth century. These changes, along with the 1990s Northern Peace talks, are imperative to understanding the last decade of Irish novels. The second task in this chapter is to develop a working theoretical strategy to help us open up and understand the issues of gender, sexuality, the body, and the regulation and parameters of power. Because the contemporary Irish novel is formally sophisticated and often technically innovative, offering the reader new cultural, political, and economic contexts that are radical departures from earlier periods, we need a critical reading strategy equally contemporary and sophisticated.

Contemporary History, Culture and Economics

As recently as June1993, the Irish Senate passed a "bill into law abolishing all previous laws criminalizing homosexual acts between men, and replacing them with a new gender-neutral law with the common age of consent with heterosexuals and no special privacy restrictions."[1] The gay rights activist

Senator David Norris addressed the Irish Senate at the time of the passage of the Criminal Law Bill; in his address Norris outlined the history of laws concerning homosexual practices and sexual privacy, tracing the policing and regulation in relation to religion: "This is for me a happy day, for my fellow legislators have chosen as the law makers of a free and independent Republic to liberate the gay community from an oppressive, corrupt and deeply damaging law whose origins are shrouded in the mists of ancient religious prejudice."[2] Interestingly, in this address Norris cites an article in which a Judaic scholar traces the origin of abolition of homosexuality to the religion's need to mark itself off from the other religions and mentions that in all the other religions—in Greece, Rome, Canaan—homosexuality was a matter of personal preference. While the Vatican established religious mandates, Ireland after the Norman invasion was regulated by English law. It was not until Henry VIII, argues Norris, "seized the monasteries, and incidentally took control of the ecclesiastical courts, that this behavior made the transition from sin to crime for the first time in an Act of Henry VIII of 1533."[3]

There were actual convictions under this act, including those of the Reverend Nicholas Udall, author of *Ralph Roister Doister*, and Bishop John Atherton, who was executed. Capital punishment remained the penalty for the offence of sodomy until 1861 when the punishment was reduced from death by hanging to life imprisonment by the Offences Against the Person Act. Naturally, Norris wishes to implicate the British legal system for the inequality and intolerance of difference:

> By effectively wiping the lingering shame of British imperial statute from the record of Irish law our colleagues in the Dail have a done good day's work. . . . I have always said in defiance of comments from abroad that the Irish people were a generous, tolerant, compassionate and decent people and that this would one day be reflected even in that sensitive area of law governing human sexuality. . . . As the great apostle of Catholic emancipation Daniel O'Connell said in pleading his case at the bar of British public opinion, human dignity and freedom are not finite resources. . . . This is the kind of Irish solution to an Irish problem of which we as Irish men and women can feel justly proud.[4]

Despite the fact that Norris wishes to appropriate the Criminal Law Bill as an exclusively *Irish* example, Norris finally admits at the end of his address that discrimination and prejudice are deep-seated *Irish* heterosexual society problems. Alluding to a member of the Lower House objecting to the Criminal Law Bill because it would be the "thin edge of the wedge and he might have to witness the horrible spectre of two men holding hands at the bus queue," Norris lashes out: "From the cradle I have been brainwashed with heterosexuality."[5]

Finally giving voice to homosexuality, many contemporary Irish novels challenge the "brainwashed with heterosexuality" traditional Irish culture and attempt openly to explore topics of homosexual experience in an Irish context. As Ide O'Carroll points out in her Introduction to *Lesbian and Gay Visions of Ireland,* part of the gay community's mission is to find a homosexual paradigm in a heterosexual cultural matrix; O'Carroll argues that this "theme is the desire to reconcile being lesbian or gay with being part of a heterosexual family and a society dominated by heterosexuals, while still remaining true to what we know is our way of being in the world."[6] Even with the Criminal Law (Sexual Offences) Bill having passed in 1993, a homosexual's prohibition concerning "coming out" is still daunting: "The difficulties encountered by many contributors in the coming out process warn us of the need to continue to educate, so that the next generation of lesbians and gays do not suffer loss and exclusion."[7] And so reconciling—or negotiating— Irish identity with homosexual identity is one of the themes or subjects taken up by contemporary novelists. For novelist Emma Donoghue, this identity would be one that would allow a "woman who loves women to live as an Irish woman" and to live in a world which does not constantly refer to the heterosexual norm.

In terms of women's issues, Pat O'Connor in *Emerging Voices: Women in Contemporary Irish Society* (1998) looks at the position and status of women in contemporary Ireland. According to O'Connor, "the concept of patriarchy is a key element in understanding the experiences of women in Irish society."[8] O'Connor points out that women in Irish society are defined by patriarchy because the structures of state, church, cultural, and societal norms all privilege the male, as well as, O'Connor adds, the social and cultural construction of heterosexuality. O'Connor cites Connell's work on "crisis tendencies" in culture and society as useful in understanding the changing role of women in Irish society:

> implicit in this book is the idea that there are what are called "crisis tendencies" within Irish society at both a structural and cultural level. Within the Irish context the most obvious structural source of these crisis tendencies is the changing relationship between church and state. There are other tensions, e.g., those between the current social and cultural construction of hetero-sexuality, which stresses men's economic position as a key element in masculinity, and the economic opportunities for women generated by an increasingly service-oriented economic system where there is growing demand for "flexible" labour.[9]

The economic construction of gender brings us to an important factor, if not the most important factor: change in national identity in the Republic of Ireland in the 1990s is due to the prosperous economy. Economic growth since the 1960s has transformed the social, cultural, and political aspects of identity through a demand for consumer goods, urbanization, and mass media exposure.

After the founding of the Free State and during De Valera's era of leadership, Ireland pursued an isolationist and agrarian policy as an autonomously Irish ideal. From an economic standpoint, Ireland failed to join the modern world in terms of industry, trade and technology. From a national policy perspective, Ireland also failed to join the modern world in relation to cultural policy, individual rights and opportunities. According to David Hempton, Catholicism, however, fared well in this period, as "a traditional society dragged disproportionately quickly into the modern world on the coat-tails of an expanding British economy and a fearful subsistence crisis, Catholicism in Ireland offered important symbols of culture and identity to a population determined to preserve its ties with the past."[10] It is exactly the "anti-modernisation stance of the catholic church" that Maryann Valiulis argues in "Neither Feminist nor Flapper: The Ecclesiastical Construction of the Ideal Irish Woman" that helped to support the nationalist agenda in the subjugation of women in Irish culture, economics and society.[11] From church leaders to De Valera, the discourse on Irish womanhood was totalizing and self-affirming:

> The ideal Irish woman then—the self-sacrificing mother whose world was bound by the confines of her home, a woman who was pure, modest, who valued traditional culture, especially that of dress and dance, a woman who inculcated these virtues in her daughters and nationalist ideology in her sons, a woman who knew and accepted her place in society—served the purposes of the ruling Irish male elite. Political and ecclesiastical leaders sought to reestablish gender boundaries and hierarchy after the promise of equality and the experience of freedom in the revolutionary period.[12]

In many ways, the ideal Irish woman as depicted by the "ruling Irish male elite" is merely a fantasy or wishful thinking. During the Anglo-Irish war, the civil war and the early years of the Free State, women, especially educated middle class feminists, participated in roles outside of the narrowly defined domesticity of mother, wife and daughter. Roddy Doyle's *A Star Called Henry* (1999) fictionalizes the active participation by women in spheres outside of the home. However, De Valera worked diligently with ecclesiastical leaders in the 1930s, in particular, to limit women's sphere of influence, most notably, of course, in De Valera's 1937 constitution, which unequivocally relegated the woman to home and family. In the 1990s, "there are tensions too arising from the state's need for inclusiveness as a basis for its own legitimacy and the patriarchal nature of Irish public life," according to Pat O'Connor, "where the 'normal' situation is for men to represent women's interests."[13] Anne Mc-Clintock theorizes that women represent a "temporal anomaly within nationalism" which looks forward toward the future at the same time it wishes to freeze the "values" of the past: "Women are represented as the avatistic and authentic 'body' of national tradition (inert, backward-looking and natural) embodying nationalism's conservative principle of continuity. Men, by contrast, represent the progressive agent of national modernity (forward thrusting, potent and historic), embodying nationalism's progressive or revolutionary principle of discontinuity. Nationalism's anomalous relation to time is thus managed as a natural relation to gender."[14]

Other contemporary historians are equally unsympathetic with the ideology of the De Valera era and with "a population determined to preserve its ties with the past." For example, in *Rethinking Irish History: Nationalism, Identity and Ideology* Patrick O'Mahony and Gerard Delanty posit that the institutionalization of the Irish nationalist identity into the new nation-state established Ireland as backward-looking and conservative; they theorize: "historical responsibility of the dominant conservative strand of Irish nationalism for creating an institutional order that, inter alia, legitimated poor economic performance, inequality, low participation, the subjugation of women and the denial of civil rights to homosexuals, and that continues to impede the exploration of values for enhanced citizenship and greater cultural pluralism."[15] The Irish national identity implemented as a structuring feature of the new nation-state resulted, according to O'Mahony and Delanty, in a policy that solidified the status quo of the propertied class of the pre-independence era while masquerading as the "natural" evolution of Home Rule and self-determination. This view is again in line with Doyle's *A Star Called Henry* as well as Sebastian Barry's *The Whereabouts of Eneas Mc-Nulty* (1998) which graphically, even brutally present the middle class as users of the working class and poor. O'Mahony and Delanty believe that Ireland's foreign policy, constitutional order, individual rights, and collective identity were molded for decades after:

> The Irish national identity code that was institutionalised after the successful separatist movement, and which represented a particular synthesis of the different positions within the mobilisation phase of the movement, adopted a primordial relationship to the outside based on rejection of the culture of modernity; advocated a conventional relationship to cultural identification by subordinating the autonomy of citizens; ultimately produced a constitutional order that built in weak, liberal rights within a traditional-theocratic framework; and developed a conservative relationship to the social based on institutional de-differentiation and opposition to all forms of progressivism. This

identity code and its social programme was at one and the same time an ideology reflecting dominant propertied social interests but still supported by a majority, a cultural pattern that was functionally useful for the building of a conservative institutional order, and a restrictive determinant of capacities for agency and cognitive innovation within the society.[16]

In terms of economics, De Valera and the first generation of postcolonial Irish leaders could not keep the Gaelic myth and the economy going at the same time. The depression era, the 1930s economic war with Britain, neutrality during World War II, and heavy migration in the 1950s made it evident that Ireland needed more than nationalistic identity to make it a prosperous nation.

The 1990s socioeconomic prosperity can be traced back to the transformation that began with the switch from a subsistence economy to a market economy. In the late 1950s policies were implemented to end Ireland's economically depressed, isolated, agrarian, and rural culture. While the cultural price paid for economic prosperity can be lamented by outsiders or scholars, the people of the post-De Valera era wanted a higher standard of living, consumer goods, and economic opportunity coterminous with the rest of Europe. In the 1970s, when it joined the European Community, Ireland underwent a change that involved the foreclosure of farms that could not produce economically viable goods to compete in the European markets. Joining the European Community also signaled other changes; for example, less and less emphasis was placed on local culture and traditions, and people began to be more mobile. Because of the latter changes, Jim Mac Laughlin in "Ireland in the Global Economy: An End to a Distinct Nation?" believes that Ireland has become "literally a foreign country" in the last three decades: "I would argue that the sources of these changes, like the causes of many of our social problems, are due to the fact that Ireland has become a postmodern *society* before becoming a modern *nation*. The modernisation of Irish society in the Sixties and Seventies has now been followed by a process of postmoderisation since the Eighties, and not just at the level of Irish music, dance, cinema, identity politics and literature, the very country itself is being restructured and recreated."[17] In "The Bases of Regionalism," Kevin Whelan points out that these trends and Ireland's 1973 entry into the European Community has damaged traditional Ireland at the "townland" level. The townland level is the "neighborhood level" or the practical farmland community size, which in the past shared farm work, tools, and equipment. The disintegration and yet lasting fierce loyalty to this regional measurement is depicted by Whelan: "In recent years, mechanisation of farming, increasing individualism and mobility, and the huge growth in non-farming families in the countryside have all reduced social

contacts at the townland level, seriously diminishing its economic and social solidarity. Yet the townland itself is still a living social reality as is
demonstrated by the recent successful campaign in Northern Ireland
against their abolition in the interests of postal rationalisation."[18] Despite
this loyalty, Whelan wonders if the traditional stable and rigid regional
boundaries should be maintained now that Ireland is a part of the EC and
global economy: "does the traditional region, statically defined in local,
fixed and essentially rural terms have any continuing purchase in this di-
versified, mobile and dynamic world?" (12). Whelan points out that there
is also a downside to the "fixed" boundaries of region: "the very notions of
place, territory and identity embedded in the regional construct may well
disenfranchise those who have been displaced or alienated from it; it may
also have inbuilt gender and generational biases" (12). In contrast to Mac
Laughlin's reading of contemporary Ireland as "literally a foreign country,"
Whelan believes that Ireland is moving in the right direction: "Stable regions with fixed boundaries may create an arbitrary, artificial sense of identity which ignores differences and individuality. The construction of
regions must therefore involve their deconstruction" (12).

Perhaps the "deconstruction" of regions has come about quite predictably through modernization, which has led in turn to the urbanization
of Ireland. The last three decades of the twentieth century have turned Ireland into "a foreign country" because of the socioeconomic transfer of rural
and farming populations into urban and suburban areas. These changes, according to Timothy J. White, produced a new consumer class in Ireland:
"The reality of Irish socioeconomic development has meant flight from the
countryside and an abandonment of many of those values associated with
the traditional rural way of life. Capitalism has crept into the countryside
as new entrepreneurs, merchants, and shopkeepers have incorporated the
traditional farmers into the money economy."[19] White believes that this
process has led to a demoralized rural population who were forced to make
the transition from traditional farming to modern capitalism. Overall,
however, Ireland's population has followed the route of other Western industrialized societies by moving out of the country and into towns and
cities for work. One difference between England's late-eighteenth and
early-nineteenth century industrial revolution migration to cities, for example, and Ireland's 1960s post-industrial migration to cities is that contemporary Ireland has been simultaneously subjected to a media and
communications barrage that amounts to a form of cultural imperialism.
Similar to other postcolonial countries, Ireland absorbed Western capitalist
and media hegemony at the same time it was modernizing and urbaniz-
ing/suburbanizing. Again, White criticizes Western, capitalist forces that
have and continue to impinge on Ireland:

The dominant Western capitalist culture has no right to invade and conquer the cultures of other nations. Every nation has a right to preserve its own culture. Nevertheless, the Westernization of the world continues. In the case of Ireland, Western culture, especially that which emanates from the United States and Britain, has become increasingly evident in Irish society. . . . The principal mechanism of acculturation or cultural imperialism in the case of the inculcation of Western values in Ireland has been the mass media. . . . The result is "technetronic ethnocide" as the indigenous society loses its ethnic and cultural identity.[20]

What is evident is that "technetronic ethnocide" is the price paid for the end of isolationism, the development of new business investment and technology, and for the generation brought up in the 1950s and 1960s with the possibility of a higher standard of living.

In the last decade of the twentieth century there has been unprecedented growth in the Irish economy, earning the Republic the nickname of the "Celtic Tiger." According to Denis O'Hearn, the term "Celtic Tiger" entered popular usage on August 31, 1994, "when the investment bank Morgan Stanley compared the Southern Irish economy to the East Asian 'tiger' economies,"[21] comparing Ireland with Hong Kong, Taiwan, South Korea, and Singapore. But O'Hearn is quick to point out that "'rapid' is a relative concept," and that Ireland has not had the rapid growth of its Asian competitors: "What makes Ireland exceptional is not its similarity to East Asia, but the fact that it maintained *moderate* growth during a sluggish period for the rest of Europe."[22] Ireland was the only EU economy actually to improve in the 1990–1995 period, but only, O'Hearn adds, has 1993 been truly "exceptional for Ireland." O'Hearn worries, too, about the statistics that attribute Ireland's rapid growth to what he calls the "real cause" of the "rapid expansion of exports by transnational corporations, particularly a small number of US computer and pharmaceutical companies who use Ireland as a low-tax and low-cost staging point to get their goods onto continental European markets."[23] O'Hearn is concerned about Ireland's economy because expansion in this arena means that profits are not staying in Ireland and the closure or downsizing of a large corporation in Ireland would have a detrimental effect on the whole economy. The Celtic Tiger may be a paper tiger, as O'Hearn states: "It is difficult to say just how much of Irish economic activity actually really is a phantom of such corporate accounting."[24]

Nevertheless, the idea of the Celtic Tiger lunged forward when Dublin was established by *Fortune* as "Europe's Most Improved City for Business" in 1997. Not merely most improved, Dublin was named the top business city in 1997 above (in order) Amsterdam, Barcelona, and Prague, with Ireland's former colonial capital, London, coming in a lowly seventh place. Current conditions in Dublin, according to *Fortune,* indicate that, "Employment is up, emigrants are returning, and prosperous young Irish folk crowd a new downtown of bars, fancy restaurants, and theatres."[25] *Fortune* praises Dublin's ability to reinvent itself, especially in the areas of high tech and specialized financial services industry. In terms of investment Dublin has benefited from telecommunications, financial services, tourism, and Intel's decision to base its production of Pentium microproducers and other products in Leixlip (west Dublin), which employs four thousand people. With the influx of money comes the elements of the good life: luxury products and services, celebrities from football to film stars, and the industry that follows them. This aspect has greatly enhanced the image of Dublin. During the last summer of the decade and century Dublin found itself in a "feel good" mood as Victoria Adams (a.k.a. Posh Spice) and Manchester United's David Beckham tied the knot in rented Luttrellstown Castle, while filmmakers and stars, from John Travolta to Sean Connery, cooed over Dublin's new found jet-set status.

Yet, Dublin's jet-set status, one commentator, Liam Fay, argues, gives Dublin the image of a city that is irresponsible, "What Dublin has become, above all else, is a party town for the idle rich. With its myriad castles for hire, numerous golf courses the size of east European republics and, who could forget, a stellar range of celebrity chefs, the city makes the ideal playground for boozy footballers, shopaholic pop stars and Hollywood hell raisers with more money than taste."[26] The romantic idea that Dublin coincides with the cultural renaissance of fin-de-siècle Paris Fay also puts down; he argues that the conservative nature of contemporary Dublin "coincides with a widespread feeling of public self-satisfaction and private insecurity. It's a period of conformity, consensus and inertia. Those who have benefitted most from the economic boom admire their own estimation of their acumen and insight so much that it is impossible for them to admit that much of their wealth has been accumulated through distinctively uncreative means, such as property speculation, low-risk investment and sheer good fortune."[27] As Telecom Eireann shares went public and prices soared during the summer of 1999, others were trying to bring the country back to earth with figures that show that Ireland has the second highest level of poverty in the industrialized world for the second year in a row. Those who have not benefited from the economic boom are as bad off financially as ever, if not worse.

Women, especially single mothers, have not fared well from Dublin's prosperity; Intel's investment has no impact on their lives. While Dublin booms all around them, some residents feel as if they are starving at the feast; native Dubliner Cathy Sherwin, single mother of two teenagers, "tells how numerous apartment complexes have been built in the area, and how residents 'put up with filth and noise and dust for two years. We were told there would be a lovely hotel, with great facilities which we could avail of. Since that hotel opened, the residents around here have been refused entrance. There is constant discrimination, on the grounds of your address or your accent.'"[28] Without a doubt, the Celtic Tiger has not found its way into the homes of all the inhabitants in the Republic. A September 1999 broadcast on (American) National Public Radio featured the plight of the "have-nots" in Dublin during this phase of economic growth; Posh Spice notwithstanding, interviewer Rebecca Davis was told that the "common people" call the Celtic Tiger the "selfish tiger."[29] In terms of women, Pat O'Connor states that indeed the "Celtic Tiger" may not be so ferocious: "References to Ireland as a 'Celtic tiger' are misleading since 90 per cent of the increase of employment between 1971 and 1996 was in women's employment. Furthermore, these trends cannot be simply accounted for in terms of an increasing number registering as available for work since the actual numbers of women in (paid) work has risen steadily and consistently over the period."[30] What this statistic means is that women have moved in to fill up the service and low-paying jobs. Following EU trends, women in Ireland are concentrated in "areas such as domestic services, health, footwear and clothing, education and retail trade (Employment in Europe, 1996)."[31] Despite the fact that increasing numbers of women are more and better educated than ever before in Ireland, "women constitute 65 per cent of those in the professional services sector but only 24 per cent of those in administrative, executive and managerial occupations."[32] According to O'Connor, organizational structure, procedure and attitude at management and executive levels in Irish companies continue to resist women entering into the high-level decision- and policy-making ranks.[33]

Unlike the Republic, the measurement of progress has not been charted in terms of economics for Northern Ireland. In the last thirty years, progress in Northern Ireland has focused on human rights and the peace process. This was not always the case for Ulster. In the nineteenth century, Northern Ireland followed in the footsteps of northern England in terms of industrialization; for instance, Belfast had a world-class ship-building enterprise, most notably the ship builders Harland & Wolff (who built the Titanic). With coal and iron ore from northwest England and southwest Scotland only a short sea journey away, linen and other textile manufacturing prospered. With the capital for building provided by investors in Glasgow and Liverpool, Ulster's lines of trade were with Great Britain. As Ulster prospered, the larger cities in the south, Dublin and Cork, were kept out of this economic loop. Economic prosperity for Ulster was all about Great Britain and international trade, which partially explains the strong resistance to Home Rule in the nineteenth and early twentieth century.

The other major factors that contributed to anti-Home Rule sentiment that continues to divide Ulster to this day are religion and national affiliation. Because the long saga in the North is the proper subject of another book, or, more likely, several other books, I would attempt to summarize here only the key historical events of the twentieth century that bring us up to the 1990s. An appropriate place to begin is with the Government of Ireland Act (December 1920), which finally introduced Home Rule to the island of Ireland; however, the Act, brokered by military leader Michael Collins and other revolutionaries, divided Ireland into two separate states. This divide manifests the twentieth century's origin of conflict between Catholics and Protestants in Northern Ireland. The "new" Ulster was gerrymandered to serve Unionist ends; Unionists felt that they were particularly vulnerable as a minority in the whole of Ireland, and so they redrew the map of Ulster to insure a Protestant, Loyalist majority in the North. Historically, Ulster, one of "the four green fields of Ireland," was composed of nine counties: Donegal, Cavan, Monaghan, Antrim, Down, Tyrone, Armagh, Fermanagh, and (London) Derry. The new Ulster, however, is composed of the latter six counties; Donegal, Cavan, and Monaghan were lopped off because with them, the balance of power in Ulster would rest with the Catholics. The Act of Partition, which mandated the new Northern Ireland remain in the commonwealth, did foresee the two Irelands reuniting in the future, "as soon as may be after the appointed day" the two states would establish a so-called Council of Ireland. That day of reunion has never come.

The new Northern Irish government ruled with a mixture of self-preservation, fear, and jingoistic emotion. Threats from the twenty-six counties and especially from the IRA fueled distrust and prejudice against Catholics in the six counties. This feeling was not entirely without cause; in 1937 the Constitution of the Irish Republic claims Ulster to be under its jurisdiction:

> Art. 2 The national territory consists of the whole island of Ireland, its islands and territorial seas.
>
> Art. 3 Pending the re-integration of the national territory and without prejudice to the right of the Parliament and Government established by this Constitution to exercise jurisdiction over the whole of that territory, the laws enacted by that Parliament shall have the like area and extent of application as the laws of Saorstat Eireann and the like extra-territorial effect.[34]

The Republic's claim of *de jure* jurisdiction could only help to fuel the Loyalists' fears (real or politically manipulated) in the North. Apart from extremists or those living on the border in the Republic, the people of the Republic of Ireland quickly set about governing themselves and dealing with their own problems. The radical separation between the north and the south is manifested in the Republic's lack of concern and the lack of interest in the issues and disputes of the Troubles in Ulster beginning in the 1960s. Many of the novels in the last decade from the North, in fact, often sardonically refer to the ignorance and lack of interest of the people in the Republic regarding the problems facing the Irish in the North.

Indeed, the problems facing the Irish in the North were problems of the minority Catholic contingency because the Protestant majority did not consider itself Irish at all, despite the fact their ancestors may have been in the North for hundreds of years. The principally Scottish Presbyterian Northern Irish thought of themselves as British. Perhaps this is the first lesson to learn when considering who is who now and the present difficulties facing the peace process. "The Way Forward" is blocked by a fundamental unwillingness on the part of the Loyalists to break with Britain and to subject themselves to anything Irish. In "The Limits of Britishness," Jennifer Todd outlines the three key elements of the Unionist's British identity. The first element is that Ulster Unionists believe that they have a shared set of cultural characteristics that are British, not Celtic or Irish. Second, according to Todd, Unionists identify with British state institutions. And third, the Unionist identity is constituted by what it is *not:* Irish, Catholic, Nationalist.[35] The majority in the North is a good example of Anderson's "imagined community," which is made of up of a "limited" and "sovereign" group of people who are "imagined as a *community,* because, regardless of the actual

Figure 1.1—Northern Ireland house wall mural ("Cuchulainn—ancient defender of Ulster").

inequality and exploitation that may prevail in each, the nation is always conceived as a deep, horizontal comradeship. Ultimately, it is this fraternity that makes it possible, not so much to kill, as willingly to die for such limited imaginings."[36]

Imagined communities exist both for the majority and for the minority in the North; these communities are everywhere evidenced in the propaganda in the North. The propaganda is so fierce and thick on both sides of those who self-righteously claim Ulster that even ancient mythical heroes, such as Cuchulainn, are appropriated by each group. While W. B. Yeats may have romanticized Cuchulainn as hero of the ancient Celtic race, both Protestant Loyalists and Catholic Nationalists utilize Cuchulainn to propagate a historical, racial lineage. The battle of the painted murals in Derry and Belfast honor Cuchulainn as a symbol of present-day struggles both for the "Irish" and for the "British." One Loyalist mural featuring Cuchulainn connects him to "Ulster's present day defenders," and directly defines him as anti-Irish: "Cuchulainn, ancient defender of Ulster from Irish attacks over 2000 years ago" (Figure 1.1).[37] We can learn a great deal about the Loyalist mentality from the images used in this mural. The gray ghostly figure of Cuchulainn bound to a rock (island of Ireland?) in a swooning gesture, with the white dove of peace resting on his shoulder; meanwhile, the khaki-uniformed present day descendent of

Figure 1.2—Northern Ireland fence wall mural ("Irish out—the Ulster conflict is about nationality").

Cuchulainn, holding an armelite, stands on a carpet of the British Union Jack, with the red hand of Ulster flag next to him, while the caption states: "We will maintain our faith and our nationality." On the adjacent wall, the mural text states: "Our message to the Irish is simple/hands off Ulster/Irish out/The Ulster conflict is about nationality" (Figure 1.2). As we can see, "Ulster's present day defenders" are not *Irish,* they are British, even if they are in reality predominately of Scottish origin; for the Ulster Loyalists, *British* is infinitely superior to Irish even if these British subjects happen to be living on the island of Ireland.

From Gaelic literature, Cuchulainn, known for his strength, was educated by poets and warriors in the court of his uncle, King Chonchobor of Ulster. The reason Cuchulainn is available as a symbolic image for British appropriation is because the hero was defender of *Ulster* against warring parties in the South, which is precisely the position that Ulster finds itself in modern times. For example, one of Cuchulainn's most famous adventures occurs when he alone defends the army of Queen Medb of Connacht. Nevertheless, Ulster is in Ireland, and therefore Cuchulainn can also be appro-

Figure 1.3—Northern Ireland house wall mural ("I nDil Cuimne" St. James Rd., Belfast). Reprinted with permission.

priated by the Irish Nationalists. In a powerful warrior image of a dying Cuchulainn, Irish Nationalists have connected the hero to the present day struggles to free Ulster of its invaders (Figure 1.3).[38] The Gaelic text, "I nDil Cuimme" ("in loving memory"), refers to the names of the local Irish Republican Army who died "in action" inscribed on the plaque to the right of Cuchulainn's head. The draping effect of Cuchulainn on the letter "I" clearly resembles the image of Christ sacrificed on the cross; the principle distinction for the IRA, in particular, is that Cuchulainn, unlike Christ, dies with sword and shield in hand. Therefore, several ideas are packed into this rather simple image: Similar to their ancient heroic counterpart, the listed IRA members sacrificed their lives attempting to drive the enemy (British) out of Ulster and they, too, died heroically in battle.

Needless to say, the last thirty years of mural painting has been devoted to the strife originating from the civil rights movement of the 1960s, popularly called "the Troubles." After nearly fifty years of Unionist domination, the Northern Ireland Civil Rights Association began to record the laws and policies used to discriminate against Catholics in the North. Catholics faced unfair practices in employment, housing, and voting rights. For example, in order to vote one had to be a ratepayer or householder; succeeding Unionist governments kept Catholics from voting by denying them housing that would grant them voting status. With this kind of pigeonholing, the Unionist majority maintained its power. When these tactics failed to work, Unionists had the ability to redraw the voting districts; the gerrymandering that determined the Northern state could also determine a voting ward. Influenced by the civil rights movement in the United States, the civil rights movement in Northern Ireland drew international attention when one of the first marches in Derry on October 5, 1968, was banned by the Unionist government, which called upon the Royal Ulster Constabulary (RUC) to enforce the ban. Unfortunately for Stormont, television cameras captured images of the RUC beating the marchers; the Unionist's plan to stop the marchers forcefully served only to draw attention to and magnify the problems in Northern Ireland.

Serious violence erupted on New Year's Day 1969 when marchers on a four-day, seventy-five-mile route from Belfast to Derry were ambushed on the last leg of the walk. In *The Troubles,* Tim Pat Coogan describes how march organizer Michael Farrell attempted to divert the violence at Derry: "Farrell and his helpers managed to manhandle and marshal the marchers at the front of the procession to safety when the stoning began, but those at the rear, particularly young women, were singled out for especial attack. Apart from being stoned and beaten, sometimes with cudgels with nails driven into them, a number were driven into the freezing waters of the River Fahan."[39] Rioting followed in Derry for the next week. Considered a no-go area, the Bogside became "Free Derry" for a week when the Stormont government failed to control the area.

Later that year, violence escalated during the summer marching season. Jim Callaghan, Britain's Labour Home Secretary, sent troops to Derry on August 14 to quell the "Battle of the Bogside." Originally, British troops were supposed to reestablish law and order and then withdraw; British troops have now been in Northern Ireland for thirty years. In October of that year the Hunt Report was released, the contents of which caused Loyalists to riot on Shankill Road in Belfast; the Hunt Report called for the Royal Ulster Constabulary (RUC) to disarm and for the Protestant militia, the B-Specials, to disband. The first Northern Irish policeman died in these riots and signaled that the Troubles were now an intractable three-way situation: Nationalists, Loyalists, and the outsider British (government and troops) who often appear to Loyalists as Nationalist sympathizers. The latter component, an outside British element, helped to ignite the fire under extreme reactionaries such as the Reverend Ian Paisley who formed the Democratic Unionist Part in 1971 and who still (along with his son, Ian Paisley, Jr.) works to frustrate the peace talks in the year 2000.

From 1969 on the Troubles form a long chronology of incident after incident. One of the most well-known incidents occurred in Derry on January 30, 1972, when British troops shot and killed thirteen people in what is now infamously called "Bloody Sunday." On March 24 the British assumed direct rule over Northern Ireland. Revenge was achieved in the bloody, vicious cycle of violence on Friday, July 21, 1972, when nineteen Provisional IRA bombs exploded in Belfast; "Bloody Friday" killed nine and injured one hundred thirty people.

These incidents fueled the attack-and-counterattack cycle in the North that did little to strengthen popular support for any paramilitary group. Yet, in the early 1980s the H-Block hunger strike protests did arouse emotional and humanitarian support for the Nationalist cause. IRA prisoners considered themselves prisoners of war and held that status until 1976, when Britain changed its position; after this, terrorists were sentenced like all other common criminals. IRA prisoners refused to wear regular prison uniforms because they believed that they were prisoners of war. "On the blanket" became a common phrase for one who is incarcerated, because prisoners who refused to wear the prison uniforms were given nothing to wear at all, and so from 1980 to 1984, they wore only their bed blanket. After the prisoners refused to clean out their cells and smeared excrement on the cell walls (the Dirty Protest), prisoner leader Bobby Sands, started the H-Block hunger strike. Prisoners began their fasts on a rolling basis so that eventually a prisoner would die every week of starvation. A prisoner dying every week, Sands believed, would bring the tough Thatcher government to the bargaining table. Sands started the protest on March 1, 1984, and died on May 5. He became an instant martyr and an international heroic figure. Ten prisoners in all died over the 217 days the strike lasted. Even though the hunger strike did not achieve all its objectives in terms of Thatcher's government, it achieved much more in terms of public support. The drama and suffering of watching men die one by one whipped up support for Sinn Fein, making the party more mainstream and strengthening its position in subsequent negotiations. The drama and suffering also sparked more violence as some Nationalists turned to the IRA in order to avenge their anger at the senseless suffering and intractable situation in the North.

Women's issues and political involvement often took a backseat to the sectarian concerns, which were inevitably constructed in masculine, even hypermasculine terms. Recently, Irish critic and feminist Monica McWilliams has attempted to call attention to the use of military weapons in *domestic* violence creating the climate of the North, which is steeped in stereotypical masculine aggression. McWilliams's studies on domestic violence in the North support a growing body of evidence that shows that the "availability of guns in Northern Ireland meant that more dangerous forms of violence were used against women within the context of their own home."[40] In her materialist study, *Women in Northern Ireland,* Megan Sullivan discusses McWilliams's views: "McWilliams cogently argues that domestic violence and sexist sectarianism should be read for the ways they are encouraged by constructions of masculinity (rather than as instances of individual deviance), and she indicates that in Northern Ireland there is a peculiar problematic: the militaristic nature of the state means that weapons have been more available than in other sites, and that these weapons have often been used against women."[41] This masculinist domination runs through all efforts of self-determination in the North. The power grid is *not* sectarian; the manifestation of power is the entire grid. When women attempt to unite as a gendered political group, they face the situation that both sides of the political debate are equally invested in patriarchal status quo and, of course, this status quo has established a priori its political, religious, and racial allegiance. Differences are not easy to overcome; "the feminist movement in Northern Ireland had initially hoped to foster a unitary women's identity that could transcend the polarized ethnic divide between Catholics and Protestants, nationalists and loyalists."[42]

The conditions in the North were to get worse before they got better in the 1980s. The Anglo-Irish Agreement was signed by Prime Minister Thatcher and Irish Prime Minister Garret Fitzgerald on November 15, 1985. On the one hand, the agreement was protecting the Protestant majority: "The agreement was clearly aimed at the rise in Republican support. It provided in Article 1 that there could be no change in the status of the

North without the consent of the majority."[43] Yet, Unionists were so unhappy with the Anglo-Irish Agreement that there was a huge protest outside Belfast City Hall and fifteen Unionist MPs resigned in protest. The Unionists did not like the new role of the Irish government spelled out in Articles 5 to 7. According to these articles, the Republic would be involved with the Northern terms of proposals for minority population in the North and have a say in police authority and security forces. The fact that Thatcher, an ultra-conservative, and Tom King, Secretary of State for Northern Ireland, signed this document confounded the Unionists. As Coogan puts it: "Who now could Unionists trust in England?"[44]

The vicious cycle of violence was first challenged when the Social Democratic and Labor Party (SDLP) leader, John Hume, who assumed leadership in November 1979, repeatedly attempted to organize talks with Sinn Fein leader Gerry Adams in the 1980s. Despite the fact that violence continued through this period, John Hume and Gerry Adams jointly announced that they had a right to "national self-determination" and rejected an internal "settlement" in the North. Violence continued into the 1990s; devastating violence by the IRA and the Ulster Freedom Fighters (UFF) left a total of eighteen people dead in two incidents in October 1993. External negotiation culminated in the Downing Street Declaration released on December 15, 1993, by British Prime Minister John Major and Irish Prime Minister Albert Reynolds. The Downing Street Declaration calls for self-determination and for peace talks to include multiple parties, including Sinn Fein's and Loyalist paramilitaries' representatives, as well. Both Unionists and Sinn Fein decided to study the Declaration instead of offering any polemical statement right away; meanwhile, extremists (for example, Ian Paisley) were shooting the Declaration down as a sellout.

Peacemakers tried repeatedly to negotiate "The Way Forward" through the 1990s as paramilitary ceasefires on both sides came and went. After bombs and violence at Drumcree during the marching season for several years, there was a breakthrough in negotiations in April 1998 with the Good Friday Agreement. The Good Friday Agreement, a sixty-five-page document, called for decommissioning and power sharing. The agreement was sent out to every household in Northern Ireland to inform the people of the conditions of the agreement because the Good Friday Agreement would be put to a popular vote on May 22, 1998. The Irish Republic also had a referendum on the Agreement. The support was unprecedented: 71.2 percent of the North were in favor, while 94.2 percent of the Republic voted in favor of acceptance of the Agreement. In September an assembly was elected with Ulster Unionists taking twenty-eight seats, SDLP twenty-four, and Sinn Fein eighteen. Despite wide-spread support for the referendum, there were dissenters who wished to make themselves heard.

Dissenters did in fact make themselves heard during the summer of 1998 through violent means. There were two major incidents in the summer of 1998 that were heartbreaking for both sides of the sectarian battle. Marching season at Drumcree had been volatile the last few years, but when the new Independent Parades Commission announced that it would not allow the Drumcree march down the Garvaghy Road, the situation turned violent. On July 12, three Quinn brothers—Richard, eleven; Mark, ten; and Jason, nine—died when their home in Ballymoney was gasoline-bombed. Motivation for the attack seemed to stem from the fact that their mother, a Catholic, was living with a Protestant man, while the boys attended a Protestant school in the predominantly Loyalist neighborhood. Locals in Ballymoney were shocked: "I never thought anything as appalling as this would take place in Ballymoney. . . . The people who did this do not represent us." Another woman stated, "This is awful. To harm children is beyond belief. I don't know what those responsible were thinking about."[45] David Trimble and other officials, including the Orange Order Deputy Grand Chaplain, the Reverend William Bingham, called for the Orangemen to leave Drumcree, the latter stated, "a 15-minute walk down the Garvaghy Road by the Orange Order would be a very hollow victory, because it would be in the shadow of three coffins of little boys who wouldn't even know what the Orange Order is."[46] The second incident of the summer occurred in August 1998 when the Real IRA made itself heard with a bomb that ripped through the town of Omagh, killing twenty-nine people. It was the worst single attack in the history of the Troubles. President Robinson after visiting the scene reported that "she had met a Protestant man in the hospital with his young son. He said his Catholic neighbor had asked him yesterday morning 'gosh you must hate us'. 'He said "absolutely not," because that was what this was designed to do,' she said."[47]

Most of 1999 found the peace process participants treading a thin line between their constituencies and their traditional adversaries. Trimble risked alienating Unionists by appearing weak or backing down to the Nationalists, whereas, Gerry Adams gambled on peace at the risk of losing the support of his constituency and losing the confidence of the IRA. It was a game fraught with dire consequences: one's friends could suddenly become as dangerous as one's traditional enemies During the last summer of the decade, while Dublin enjoyed its first city status and the Celtic Tiger roared on, the Northern Ireland peace process appeared to be at an impasse. Despite the widespread popularity of the Good Friday Agreement, politicians found negotiations difficult. The summer of 1999 found the peace process at a crisis point. British Prime Minister Tony Blair set a Thursday, July 15, deadline for the negotiating parties involved to resolve the decommissioning stalemate and establish the new power-sharing executive. Basically an arbitrary

Figure 1.4—Riddell cartoon ("Peace Process—Let's park here—OK—Bad Thursday Agreement").
Reprinted with permission.

date, Blair's deadline came and went, prompting David Trimble to state to the Sunday *Telegraph:* "The problem is that when you reach the target date and you haven't got the matter solved, what should you do? Do you drive into the wall or do you put the brakes on?" This statement was picked up by the press. One political cartoon depicted the situation as the "The Bad Thursday Agreement" (Figure 1.4); the missed deadline and failure to reach an agreement on decommissioning and power-sharing allowed both sides in Northern Ireland to point the finger—for the moment—at Tony Blair.[48]

Former United States Senator George Mitchell, who had previously acted as a negotiator in the North, was once again called upon to help break the stalemate. At the end of November, David Trimble received 58 percent of the Ulster Unionist Party (UUP) vote for the successful launch of the executive in accord with the Good Friday Agreement. Hailed a hero by the supporters of peace, Trimble was labeled a traitor by staunch Unionists. Predictably, the Reverend Ian Paisley used Trimble's ability to persuade the UUP to go forward with the peace process as an opportunity to blast him: "every vote cast today in the Waterfront Hall for Mr. Trimble is a vote of shame. It is a vote of darkness, a vote that tramples on the graves of innocent victims and a vote that not only tramples on them but dances on their graves." Paisley continued dramatically, "Every hand raised for Trimble today and for his prophecy is a hand just as much the enemy of Ulster as a hand of the IRA."[49] Nevertheless, on December 2, 1999, British and Irish governments signed the Good Friday Agreement, which formally canceled the Republic of Ireland's constitutional claim on Northern Ireland and established a new Protestant-Catholic power-sharing government.

Gender, Bodies and Power

The idea of the body has not been adequately explored in criticism with regard to the Irish novel. In "The Erotics of Irishness," Cheryl Herr points out that "one feature that almost no one mentions is the relationship between the Irish mind and any kind of body."[50] Herr theorizes that the "identity-obsession" in Ireland "marks a social repression of the body on a grand scale."[51] I agree with Herr that the materiality of the body is lost in both the public and private sphere, and yet it is the body—or contestation of the body—that is at the heart of the Christian religion, important to societal regulation, and precisely the recipient of violence, punishment, and incarceration in Ireland. It is the body in the Irish consciousness that first and foremost needs to be interrogated.

There is a long history in the West of philosophical discourses on the body. For instance, Greek philosophy developed an idea of somatophobia. The Platonic dialogues repeatedly warn us that irrational needs and desires of the body (*soma*) put the rational mind or soul at risk; the body is likened to a cell or dungeon that imprisons the soul or the pure, incorporeal true being. This idea was assimilated into the Christian tradition, in which body as matter is treated as contaminating and dangerous and that sees, like the Greeks, the separation between the body and soul or spirit. In fact, if anything, the body of the Christian *should* suffer. Temptation is there for the body to overcome; indeed, a soul is rewarded if it can keep its corporeal body under control and not succumb to its passions and appetites. In addition, the body was traditionally read as a manifestation of a sinner's true acts of sin through diseases such as leprosy.

With Descartes the body is relegated to nature, and so the soul becomes separate and distinct from nature. The body is governed by the laws of nature, which are physical and causal; the mind or soul is incorporeal. Descartes established an irreconcilable dualism that has had not only philosophical ramifications but also cultural effects as this dualistic approach to the mind and body is reflected in the various branches of knowledge (disciplinary boundaries between arts and sciences) and medicine. Traditional cultural constructions include the stereotypical dualistic characteristic of the body as feminine and mind or intellect as masculine. Yet, the most damaging and obviously erroneous element in dualism is its inability to explain the fact that mind and body do communicate and do impact on each other. Twentieth century philosopher Gilbert Ryle dubbed Descartes's idea of the mind "the ghost in the machine," because Descartes could not adequately account for the mind in its corporeal "prison." For Ryle it is a mistake (what he called a "category mistake") to try to think of mind analogously with the body; if we think of the body as a material thing (substance), then we are tempted to think of the mind as an immaterial thing (substance). Thus, the human comes to be thought of as a thing inside another thing: an immaterial thing inside a material thing. If we think the body acts by mechanistic causality, then we try to think of the mind acting by a different sort of (mental) causality. Ryle's alternative is to think of the mind not as any sort of thing but as the activity of the body—the mind is what the body does. An intelligent person is not someone inside of whom ghostly mental activities are carried out, but someone who acts smartly, cleverly, responding quickly and imaginatively to whatever problems she faces. Other philosophers have tried to negotiate dualism from varying angles. For instance, Locke construed the body as a possession or as the property of the subject; the subject controls her "goods" by selecting what it is her body should do (such as work or motherhood). Another solution to Descartes's dualism depicts the body as an external conveyer of internal feelings and thoughts: the body can both give the mind information (that pan is hot) and express the mind's deepest recesses (expressive dance or movement).

Much earlier, Descartes's younger contemporary, Spinoza, argued for a substance prior to and more basic than both mental and physical characteristics. For Spinoza neither mind nor matter are things (substances) but attributes of the one mind-body-neutral substance, God or nature (in much the same way Ryle later argued, in effect, that mind was an attribute of matter). A contemporary reading of Spinoza might see that neither mind nor matter are ultimately real things but human constructions of some more neutral stuff of raw experience; in other words, parts of our experience we find convenient or useful to interpret as material objects classifiable into conceptual categories and causally regular or normal, while other parts of our experience we find it convenient to interpret as personal, more private thoughts, feelings, and desires. From this neutral base there could be constructed any number of schema of mental and physical characteristics. Accordingly, a person, for example, might be made of two, three, or more "souls," one of which remains behind at death—like a ghost—while others leave the body to join the ancestors, and still others disintegrate, and so on; or, that the outer, public world is constructed as various combinations of two, three, or more basic substances joined by forces of condensation and rarifaction, for example, or that entities in the outer, public world (e.g., trees, rocks, streams) are ensouled just as we are. From this, we can see that the possibilities are inexhaustible.

Inheriting the philosophical problem of the body, contemporary continental philosophers such as Gilles Deleuze and Michel Foucault reformulated the problem more in terms of Spinoza, Kierkegaard, and Nietzsche rather than in terms of Cartesian dualism. The most influential thinker concerning the body and power in the latter half of the twentieth century has been Michel Foucault. Foucault's work is concerned with the circulation and discourse of power with the body or "self" as a kind of cog in the larger societal machine. In the Irish context, Foucault is useful in terms of analyzing power not as a "top down" force or imposition; rather, his work helps us to understand that power exists at all levels of society. This approach is useful because it allows for a more accurate and precise account of the complex nature of any society, power, and the bodies in that society. A traditional idea of power, what Foucault calls "juridico-philosophical," indicates that the "sovereign" figure rules individuals and their bodies. The "juridico-philosophical" formulation of power is unilateral, and thus too simplistic: "Between every point of a social body, between a man and a woman, between the members of a family, between master and pupil, between every one who knows and every one who does not, there exist relations of power which are not purely and simply a projection of the sovereign's great power of the individual." Instead, according to Foucault, the multiple points of the social body are "the concrete, changing soil in which the sovereign's power is grounded, the conditions which make it possible for it to function."[52] Moreover, in "Corporeal Representation In/And the Body Politic," Moira Gatens points out that "the body politic" assumes a universalizing male voice that further obfuscates the actual workings of power and relations of bodies. From Gatens's feminist philosophical perspective, the sovereign, "the will of the people," or "the body politic" all produce false unity and in turn falsify the very terms with which power and bodies can be analyzed: "The unified body functions, in political theory, to achieve two important effects. First, the artificial man incorporates and so controls and regulates women's bodies in a manner which does not undermine his claim to autonomy, since her contributions are neither visible nor acknowledged. Second, insofar as he can maintain this apparent unity through incorporation, he is not required to acknowledge difference. The metaphor functions to restrict our political vocabulary to one voice only: a voice that can speak of only *one* body, *one* reason, and *one* ethic."[53] This passage speaks directly to the position of women in the post-partition Ireland. The 1937 constitution explicitly relegates woman to domesticity, rendering her "neither visible or acknowledged." And in the North, that attitude is and pretty much remains that "the artificial man incorporates and so controls and regulates women's bodies in a manner which does not undermine his claim to autonomy, since her contributions are neither visible nor acknowledged."

Foucault calls this "voice" ideology; ideology also ignores disenfranchised peoples as well as micro levels of power that govern our daily lives. He is "trouble[d]" "with these analyses which prioritise ideology" because "there is always presupposed a human subject on the lines of the model provided by classical philosophy, endowed with a consciousness which power is then thought to seize on" (*Power/Knowledge* 58). In other words, we need to analyze the relationships among power, bodies, and gender as complex entities that have a day-to-day effect on individuals and escape from nationalistic slogans that Foucault finds vacuous. In *The History of Sexuality* volumes, Foucault attempts to concentrate on the "techniques of the self," as he stated in *The London Review of Books* in 1981: "When I was studying asylums, prisons and so on I perhaps insisted too much on the techniques of domination . . . I would like, in the years to come, to study power relations starting from the techniques of the self."[54] With the focus on subjectivity comes the focus on sex, not as a practice but as a discourse that affects all aspects of our lives; along with discourse is power:

> What is at issue, briefly, is the over-all "discursive fact," the way in which sex is "put into discourse." Hence, too, my main concern will be to locate the forms of power, the channels it takes, and the discourses it permeates in order to reach the most tenuous and individual modes of behavior, the paths that

give it access to the rare or scarcely perceivable forms of desire, how it pene-trates and controls everyday pleasure—all these entailing effects that may be those of refusal, blockage, and invalidation, but also incitement and intensifi-cation: in short, the "polymorphous techniques of power."[55]

According to Foucault, subjectivity, sex, and gender identification are defi-nitely not a priori, nor are they simple mechanistic functions dictated to us by "nature" or the natural world. What are given to us as normalized behav-ior and identification patterns are regulated and controlled through a process that flows through society.

One of the main tenants that Foucault puts forth is that our traditional Western, Christian, seemingly "repressed" society is that it is not repressed at all. Foucault theorizes that we are not sexually "repressed" but that the very claim is an excuse—a ruse—to produce discourse about our terrible, fictional repression. "We 'Other Victorians'" desire nothing more than the opportunity to *tell* or *write* our desires: in the confessional, on the analyst's couch, in our memoirs, and now in tabloids and on talk shows. According to Foucault, our desire is imbricated in the discourse we produce: "the nearly infinite task of telling—telling oneself and another, as often as possible, everything that might concern the interplay of innumerable pleasures, sen-sations, and thoughts which, through the body and the soul, had some affin-ity with sex" (20). Foucault connects this "nearly infinite task of telling" to the medieval confession as a site of truth production. The constitution of the sacrament of the penance at the Lateran Council of 1215, the tribunals of the Inquisition, and the substitution of interrogation for ordeal were "poly-morphous techniques of power" that over time established the confessional as a place where the truth of actions would be rendered in discourse.

For our purposes, what is interesting in Foucault's hypothesis is that he lo-cates the confession of the sins of the body, in particular, to the individual's newfound necessity of having to *name* the body and its functions and actions; it was only later that sins that one does not actually commit, "insinuations of the flesh" (19), had to be detailed. With the command to confess also came a discourse to describe "the respective positions of the partners, the postures as-sumed, gestures, places touched, caresses, the precise moment of pleasure—an entire painstaking review of the sexual act in its very unfolding" (19). Foucault depicts confession as an evolving entity that attaches itself to the dualistic Christian construction of the body. The sins of the body in the middle ages were the actions of the body, but by the time of the Counter Reformation, the sins of the mind were to be enumerated: "a shadow in a daydream, an image too slowly dispelled, a badly exorcized complicity between the body's me-chanics and the mind's complacency: everything had to be told" (19). While Foucault would not appreciate a "developmental" theory of the confession, it would seem that there is a progression in terms of what is expected of the individual's mental ability to remember and depict the actions of the body during confession. "Discourse," according to Foucault, "therefore, had to trace the meeting line of the body and the soul, following its meanderings: beneath the surface of the sins, it would lay bare the unbroken nervure of the flesh" (20). It is at this point that the West develops the obligation to tell, describe, and re-create in discourse the pleasures and sensations of the body; it is also at this point that sex becomes securely positioned as the mediator of the body and the soul. In terms of philosophical dualism, this puts sex into a new position—one that has the ability to act as a liaison between the "ghost in the machine" and the corporeal self.

Perhaps, then, this privileging of discourse about sex is the reason the West becomes compelled to discover scientifically "the truth of sex." If sex is the most fundamental link between the soul/mind and the body, then we should explore this connection until truth unveils itself. From a Foucauldian point of view, of course, truth is what is contained in discourse, but the emerging scientific community of the nineteenth century in particular believed that truth could be empirically proven—that it was possible to have the truth of sex: "The essential point is that sex was not a matter of sensation and pleasure, of law and taboo, but also of truth and falsehood, that the truth of sex became something fundamental, useful, or dangerous, precious or formidable: in short, that sex was constituted as a problem of truth" (56). Foucault theorizes that in the nineteenth century the sexual confession is reformulated in scientific terms through a five-step process: first, the "clinical codification of the inducement to speak" (65); second, a "postulate of a general and diffuse causality" (65); third, "the principle of a latency intrinsic to sexuality" (66); fourth, "through the method of interpretation" (66); fifth, "through the medicalization of the effects of confession" (67). The first step changed the moral or religious confession into an examination in which the patient is inspected and put through a barrage of questions in order to "confess" her pathology. Because the nineteenth-century medical community believed that one's sexual behavior "was deemed capable of entailing the most varied consequences throughout one's existence," it was paramount to detail laboriously—scientifically—every nuance of a patient's deviations, excesses, maladies, or deficiencies. The "postulate of a general and diffuse causality," then, allowed no one (children, adults, old people) to escape from the accusation that some sort of deviant sexual behavior might be the cause of his or her illness or pathology. The third element, the "principle of a latency intrinsic to sexuality," made it possible for the medical practitioner to force the patient to confess to something that was "hidden." Scientific discourse could draw out the difficult and hidden sexual truth. The fourth step solidified the practitioner's position in the new confession-examination by functioning as a kind of midwife to the truth of sex and by being in a position to *interpret* the signs of the confession. Interpretation constituted scientific discourse, which could do more than forgive or absolve one of blame; it could also name the *truth* of sex. Scientific discourse, in the last step of the process, declared that the whole of the sexual domain was no longer to be considered in terms of morality or prudence, "but was placed under the rule of the normal and the pathological" (67).

Therefore, an entire domain of life altered when the eighteenth- and nineteenth-century medical and scientific authorities assumed the territory of the confessional and assigned pathological discourses to sexual behavior. Knowledge was constructed concerning sexual pathologies so that guidelines for deviants could be established; in turn, the policing of sexual behavior developed an elaborate and multifaceted apparatus. Similar to the need to confess and create discourse concerning our repression, the fact that an activity or behavior was prohibited and policed gave one the impetus to engage in that activity or behavior; pleasure was extracted in knowing that the act was a transgression. Likewise, those who exerted control over others' sexuality also found pleasure in the enforcement of sexual codes: "The pleasure comes of exercising a power that questions, monitors, watches, spies, searches out, palpates, brings to light; and on the other hand, the pleasure that kindles at having to evade this power, flee from it, fool it, or travesty it. The power that lets itself be invaded by the pleasure of showing off, scandalizing, or resisting. . . . These attractions, these evasions, these circular incitements have traced around bodies and sexes, not boundaries not to be crossed, but *perpetual spirals of power and pleasure*" (45). The new discourses of regulation, therefore, excite and stir, and, according to Foucault, *produce* sexuality. "Sexuality," Foucault cautions, "must not be thought of as a kind of natural given which power tries to hold in check, or as an obscure domain which knowledge tries gradually to uncover" (105); rather, sexuality "is the name that can be given to a historical construct . . . a great surface network in which the stimulation of bodies, the intensification of pleasures, the incitement to discourse, the formation of special knowledges, the strengthening of controls and resistances, are linked to one another, in accordance with a few major strategies of knowledge and power" (105–106). This argument, of course, is anti-Cartesian in that it does not see the body as part of nature; the body and sexuality are as constructed as the category of "nature" or the "natural." Foucault posits the idea that science created modern sexuality and conceptions of the body, which are conceptions that serve certain functions. The "truth of sex" then is bound to a "knowledge" of sexuality that is constructed by those in authoritative positions: physicians, scientific researchers, the police, and other law enforcers.

Power and knowledge come together in the nineteenth century in order to regulate bodies and sexuality. Foucault locates four specific domains of the power/knowledge alliance: women's bodies, children, procreation, and (the pathology of) perversity. The "hysterization of women's bodies" is linked to two other targets of regulation, the "pedagogization of children's sex" and the "socialization of procreative behavior," because it is the site of heterosexuality in terms of sexuality and fecundity and in terms of conjugal power or subjugation (104). The female body was thought to be "saturated with sexuality," which caused innumerable pathologies ("female troubles"). This construction of the female body allowed authorities to analyze and scrutinize it in order to placate and control it; no doubt, authorities were titillated by the process and power and in turn produced narratives (medical explanations and remedies) that titillated. While it was understood that the children "naturally" engage in sexual play, it was at the same time something that was to be prevented: "Parents, families, educators, doctors, and eventually psychologists would have to take charge, in a continuous way, of this precious and perilous, dangerous and endangered sexual potential" (104).

From these two domains we can see that those in positions of knowledge and power dictate the norms of the objectified bodies of women and children that persist to this day. The next domain involves the management of the heterosexual society, which Foucault believes was tied to a "deployment of alliance" that was "a system of marriage, of fixation and development of kinship ties, of transmission of names and possessions," but that since the eighteenth century in the West has been tied to a "deployment of sexuality" (106). According to Foucault, a "deployment of sexuality has its reason for being, not in reproducing itself, but in proliferating, innovating, annexing, creating, and penetrating bodies in an increasingly detailed way, and in controlling populations in an increasingly comprehensive way" (107). The fourth domain that the power/knowledge alliance assumed was the designation of normalization through the pathologization of sexual diversity (nonheterosexual activity leading to procreation) or "perversity." Foucault theorizes that "in the psychiatrization of perversions, sex was related to biological functions and to an anatomo-physiological machinery that gave it its 'meaning,' that is, its finality" (153).

In the end, Foucault's argument is that the construction of sexuality, the truth of sex, is made to seem "natural" through science's would-be transparent or empirical discourses. If through empirical and objective methods science produces data on sexual behavior(s), then it is indeed capable of producing the truth of sex. One contemporary theorist indebted to Foucault is Judith Butler, whose *Gender Trouble* reopens the question of the "truth of sexuality" and gender: "The notion that there might be a 'truth' of sex, as Foucault ironically terms it, is produced precisely through the regulatory practices that generate coherent identities through the matrix of coherent gender norms."[56] Gender, therefore, for Butler is as constructed, controlled, and regulated as sexuality is for Foucault. We like to think of ourselves as genderized bodies, marked sexually, and that these categories are fixed and stable: there are only two genders, male and female. Contrary to this common view, Butler believes that gender is performed and that it is not natural or innate. Gender is created through the cultural normative of "heterosexualization": "*gender* is not a noun, but neither is it a set of free-floating attributes, for we have seen that the substantive effect of gender is performatively produced and compelled by the regulatory practices of gender coherence. Hence, within the inherited discourse of the metaphysics of substance, gender proves to be performative—that is, constituting the identity it is purported to be" (24–25). Gender coherence is in place simply because it is impossible to think of a human person without a gender.

This is an ontological problem that runs "deeper" than the sexed body. The sexed body gives us genitals, but even the category of reproductive organs becomes blurred in cases of hermaphrodites or transsexuals. Borrowing from Monique Wittig's formulation, Butler suggests that individuals outside of the heterosexual cultural norm of identification find it difficult to be made intelligible. "Women, lesbians, and gay men," Butler states, "cannot assume the position of the speaking subject within the linguistic system of compulsory heterosexuality" (116). Power is maintained, gender is regulated, and of course, sexuality is performed in a "compulsory" manner. Butler utilizes the idea that heterosexuality in our culture is compulsory from Adrienne Rich, whose influential "Compulsory Heterosexuality and Lesbian Existence" was first published in *Signs: Journal of Women in Culture and Society* in 1980 and since reprinted.[57] Rich boldly challenges the status quo of feminism and the entire society, which tacitly supports the "invalidation" of lesbian existence. She begins:

> The bias of compulsory heterosexuality, through which lesbian experience is perceived on a scale ranging from deviant to abhorrent, or simply rendered invisible, could be illustrated from many other texts than the two just preceding. The assumption made by Rossi, that women are "innately sexually oriented" toward men, or by Lessing, that the lesbian choice is simply an acting-out of bitterness toward men, are by no means theirs alone; they are widely current in literature and in the social sciences.
>
> I am concerned with two matters as well: first, how and why women's choice of women as passionate comrades, life partners, co-workers, lovers, tribe, has been crushed, invalidated, forced into hiding and disguised; and second, the virtual or total neglect of lesbian existence in a wide range of writings, including feminist scholarship.[58]

Butler's concerns are quite similar to Rich's, though she uses tactics other than analytic strategies; in order to disrupt the privileged territory of compulsory heterosexuality, Butler suggests a "queering" of gender performatives through "a repetition of the law which is not its consolidation, but its displacement" (*Gender* 30). From a philosophical point of view, what is interesting about Butler in *Gender Trouble* is that she combines Foucault's cultural theory with Deleuze's philosophy of repetition and difference. The idea of "queering" gender norms through a repetition means that one repeats in order to create *difference*. Difference has the power to disrupt, dismantle, and compromise the system of compulsory heterosexuality. This action is potentially danger-ous because the movement is surreptitious—and because it is not initially de-tected, it is not fully recognized by the heterosexual matrix or other institutions of regulation until it is "too late": difference has already started unraveling the system's power.

From a Deleuzian perspective, if we can repeat the past from a point of *difference,* then something *new* will emerge; the only way we can repeat the past from a point of difference is to think from a different point of view from the start. Hence, there are two forms of repetition: repetition of the Same, which affirms the dogmatic image of thought, and repetition with differ-ence, which truly thinks—thinks outside the boundaries of prescribed thought. The danger of discussing repetition with difference is that philoso-phers often inscribe difference in Identity, but that is not repetition with *dif-ference;* rather, it is repetition of conceptual difference. Conceptual difference allows variation inside its boundaries of thought but does not want thought to leave the preordained perimeters of recognition. What we need is an understanding of repetition with difference: "To restore difference in thought is to untie this first knot which consists of representing difference through the identity of the concept and the thinking subject."[59]

According to Deleuze, untying the knot of conceptual difference requires that we venture outside the boundaries of traditional philosophical thought with the "nomads" of philosophy (i.e., Duns Scotus, Kierkegaard, Niet-zsche). For example, the Greeks had an idea of knowledge acquired through recollecting the essential Form or Idea. Plato, in the *Meno,* for instance, sets out to show that we have a dormant knowledge that, when aroused, awak-ens, even in the slave boy, Meno. For Plato, then, the forms are universals that are *a priori,* but the "recollection" of universal truths also participates at a more mundane level, at the level of laws, rules, and systems of thought not necessarily tied to absolutes: repetition of the Same. Repetition, a recollect-ing forward, however, does not re-collect anything, but only collects over and over again for the first time: repetition with difference. Let me offer a lucid example that depicts the motion of thought in relation to difference and repetition. Kierkegaard devoted an entire text to the concept of philo-sophical repetition, *Repetition* (1841). In the following passage the narrator of *Repetition,* Constantin, offers the reader two versions of repetition:

"When the queen had finished telling a story at a court function and all the court officials, including a deaf minister, laughed at it, the latter stood up, asked to be granted the favor of also being allowed to tell a story, and then told the same story. Question: What was his view of the meaning of repetition? When a school teacher says: For the second time I repeat that Jespersen is to sit quietly—and the same Jespersen gets a mark for repeated disturbance, then the meaning of repetition is the very opposite."[60] Despite the deaf minister's story being the "same" as the queen's story, the minister produces a repetition with difference. Jespersen's mark, though achieved through a repetition of "disturbance," is repetition of the Same. In the queen's story, the fact that the minister is not aware of the first telling of the story—for he laughs only because the others laugh and, depending upon the queen's disposition, it is a more efficient way to retain his head—makes the telling of his story independent from the first. Secondly, the minister's story opens up the possibility of an ironic reading of the queen's version. The effect of the minister's story produces difference in that he creates not a copy of the queen's story but a simulacrum of the queen's story. The minister is outside the system of repetition of the Same precisely because he does the forbidden: he retells a story that cannot be copied, and the enactment produces repetition with difference. On the other hand, Jespersen's behavior produces a "mark" that verifies the original act of "disturbance." Jespersen's actions are performed in time, but the meaning of them are rendered in a system that privileges the authority of the original—in this case, the original mark. Generally speaking, the second mark lends credibility to the first and to the authority of the system. It is not coincidental that Kierkegaard's example of repetition of the Same concerns the maintenance of a hierarchical system of power. Jespersen may cause a thousand disturbances, but they would all be the Same in a system that has already molded the action to fit the "mark" and thus to be absorbed by repetition of the Same.

According to Deleuze, repetition of the Same is much like representation, which "mediates everything, but mobilises and moves nothing" (*Difference* 55–56). Conversely, the key to repetition with difference is movement, because it is the space traversed that causes the difference. Butler's text proposes that repetition with difference of gender constructs difference and achieves a disruption of the category of stable gender: "The repetition of heterosexual constructs within sexual cultures both gay and straight may well be the inevitable site of the denaturalization and mobilization of gender categories. The replication of heterosexual constructs in non-heterosexual frames brings into relief the utterly constructed status of the so-called heterosexual original. Thus, gay is to straight *not* as copy is to original, but, rather, as copy is to copy. The parodic repetition of 'the original' . . . reveals the original to be nothing other than a parody of the *idea* of the natural and the original" (31).

Utilizing Deleuze's strategy of repetition with difference, a parody of the idea of the gender construct of female therefore could be enacted by a transvestite. The repetition of the clothes, hair and makeup, gestures, and language of a female demonstrates that all these things that create "femaleness" are superficial props or affectations that sustain the idea of "female." Also, the transvestite is sexed male, and therefore "he" shows us that he can perform the female gender as well as the sexed female; thus, "maleness" is a cultural construct, too. This idea is Deleuzean difference: the transvestite—not unlike the minister to the queen—enacts gender and produces difference by showing the difference between the "original" (idea of femaleness) and the copy (what Butler calls performative) of the "original."

The performative disturbs what is "natural" by showing that gender is not natural or innate but something that is performed or enacted. Perhaps what is most disturbing about the enactment of gender constructs is that the enactment continues through virtually every action any of us conducts on a mundane, day-to-day basis: from the type of clothes or shoes we wear, to the public toilet we habitually frequent, to the judgments we make concerning other people's gendered persons. The strongest feature of repetition with difference in terms of gender might be that the body is actually performing, as Butler would say, or moving and enacting gender through dress, gestures or language. Performance theorist Peggy Phelan discusses the "marked" character of homosexual bodies and acts. Phelan theorizes, for example, that gay males who cross-dress are attempting to evoke the heterosexual "real" in order not to be "marked" as homosexual: "Realness is determined by the ability to blend in, to not be noticed."[61] In a discussion of the film *Paris Is Burning,* Phelan notes that the idea of attempting to "blend in" by cross-dressing creates a "paradox of using visibility to highlight invisibility" (96). To put it another way, homosexuals cross-dress in order to lose their "mark" of difference, i.e., of "queerness" or "gayness," by employing the citations of unmarked heterosexual femininity: "But this very passing also highlights the 'normative' and unmarked nature of heterosexuality. It is easy to pass as heterosexual because heterosexuality is assumed. In other words, what is made visible is the unmarked nature of heterosexual identity. The one who passes then does not 'erase' the mark of difference, rather the passer highlights the invisibility of the mark of the Same" (96). Capitalizing the "Same," Phelan concurs with Deleuze's repetition of the Same and with Butler's position in *Gender Trouble* because "one who passes then does not 'erase' the mark of difference," but rather reaffirms heterosexual norms.

With *Bodies that Matter* Butler tries to account for the body; she proposes a "materialist" perspective: "What I would propose in place of these conceptions of construction is a return to the notion of matter, not as site or surface, but as *a process of materialization that stabilizes over time to produce the effect of boundary, fixity, and surface we call matter.*"[62] While it is true that the constructivist models fail because they always already are embedded in the cultural/society norms from which they arise (even, or especially, when they are the most transgressive), they fail to account for a bodily manifestation (material). Still, the site of the body can never give us a conclusive "sex," let alone a sexual identity. We are most concerned with the issue that is wedged between the site and agency. Of course, agency is never simple volition. If this were the case, then subjective agency could wipe out the residue of heterosexual regulatory law by sheer force or "will power." As Butler points out, individuals cannot "will" their gender or sexual identity. The female who wishes to be male—sexually, socially, culturally—cannot change the raw fact that materially speaking, her body is sexed female.

In her attempt to modify her theoretical overreliance on "construction" in *Gender Trouble,* Butler philosophizes the body back into her concept of the gendered body. The first sentence of *Bodies that Matter,* however, indicates that Butler's agenda is similar to the earlier text's: "Is there a way to link the question of the materiality of the body to the performativity of gender?" (1). In one question Butler links the problematic and unresolved history of metaphysics to her own theory of performativity of gender. She then asks the Foucauldian question: How does "sex" figure into the relationship concerning the body and performativity? Following Foucault, Butler locates the body in the society's regulatory practices and in the regulatory norm that produces power to control, demarcate, and circulate bodies. Sex, Butler adds, "is an ideal construct which is forcibly materialized through time" (1). One's sex is not self-evident; it is a product of reiteration and citation performed over a period of time which solidifies one's sexual identity. This performativity materializes the body and the body's sex that, according to Butler, works "to materialize sexual difference in the service of the consolidation of the heterosexual imperative" (2):

> In this sense, what constitutes the fixity of the body, its contours, its movements, will be fully material, but materiality will be rethought as the effect of power, as power's most productive effect. And there will be no way to understand "gender" as a cultural construct which is imposed upon the surface of matter, understood either as "the body" or its given sex. Rather, once "sex" itself is understood in its normativity, the materiality of the body will not be thinkable apart from the materialization of that regulatory norm. "Sex" is, thus, not simply what one has, or a static description of what one is: it will be one of the norms by which the "one" becomes viable at all, that which qualifies a body for life within the domain of cultural intelligibility. (2)

Butler feels that with this proclamation she challenges several traditional attitudes that we typically hold concerning the body. First, Butler sees that the refashioning of the materialization of bodies "as the effect of a dynamic of power, such that the matter of bodies will be indissociable from the regulatory norms that govern their materialization and the signification of those material effects" (2), which means that the body is not "there" before there is a concept of a body in which to embrace or enfold the body. Second, the body's performativity validates the power discourse always already in existence. Third, "sex" is a cultural norm, not a bodily "fact." Fourth, Butler thinks that we do not simply assume an "I" or a subjective self, but only through a process of acting out or performatively constituting the "I" do we become a sexed self. Lastly, "assuming" a sex insures that we have a place in the heterosexual matrix. Yet Butler is concerned about those who cannot fit so easily into the heterosexual imperative; those who cannot fit into the heterosexual imperative, Butler claims, live in uninhabitable zones and must be considered as "abject."

One way to think about *Bodies that Matter* is that many of Butler's points are simply rewritten ideas from the earlier book. For example, in *Gender Trouble,* those outside of compulsory heterosexuality are unintelligible (women, lesbians, and gay men). In *Bodies that Matter,* Butler claims that bodies that do not adhere to heterosexual regulatory norms of the body are "abject": "The abject designates here precisely those 'unlivable' and 'uninhabitable' zones of social life which are nevertheless densely populated by those who do not enjoy the status of the subject, but whose living under the sign of the 'unlivable' is required to circumscribe the domain of the subject." The idea of the abject is, of course, not new. Julia Kristeva's 1980 *Pouvoirs de l'horreur* was translated in 1982 bearing the subtitle, *An Essay on Abjection,* and her text is greatly indebted to Georges Bataille. Yet, what is interesting in Kristeva's formula is that the abject—the very ability to name the abject—requires that one has some position of outsideness, some position of otherness. As Kristeva puts it, "The abject has only one quality of the object—that of being opposed to *I.*"[63] In her description, humans abhor those things that threaten the ability to survive and so they push them away or avoid them—things like feces, blood, saliva, and other bodily secretions. This configuration would mean that those outside the heterosexual matrix are objectified and grouped with those things that threaten our survival (feces, blood, saliva). Butler theorizes that those abjected beings are indeed analogous to feces and saliva:

> Such attributions or interpellations contribute to that field of discourse and power that orchestrates, delimits, and sustains that which qualifies as "the human." We see this most clearly in the examples of those abjected beings who do not appear properly gendered; it is their very humanness that comes into question. Indeed, the construction of gender operates through *exclusionary*

means, such that the human is not only produced over and against the inhuman, but through a set of foreclosures, radical erasures, that are, strictly speaking, refused the possibility of cultural articulation. Hence, it is not enough to
claim that human subjects are constructed, for the construction of the human
is a differential operation that produces the more and the less "human," the inhuman, the humanly unthinkable. These excluded sites come to bound the
"human" as its constitutive outside, and to haunt those boundaries as the persistent possibility of their disruption and rearticulation. (8)

From a philosophical point of view, it is difficult to understand Butler's argument. How can one be absolutely in an uninhabitable space if that individual indeed has materiality? Abstractly speaking, one always already *is*
somewhere, even if that somewhere is outside of a compulsory heterosexualist norm: one is outside. Also, attempting to constitute what *is* human or
humanness is an enormous ontological problem, and so to label nonchalantly what is *in*human is a specious proposition on Butler's part. While
there certainly may be *exclusions* for all kinds of people (foreigners, people of
one race or another, the working class), we do not usually accept the label of
"inhuman" as a probable or viable designation; primarily, "inhuman" is unacceptable because it relies on what *is* human to be absolutely defined.

According to Butler, the hermaphrodite is an example of "those abjected
beings who do not appear properly gendered" or those beings who cannot
be adequately defined by the gender binary pertaining to the sexed body. For
Butler a hermaphrodite would be not only abject but also "inhuman." As
Foucault points out in *The History of Sexuality*, a hermaphrodite was considered an error in nature; the body of the hermaphrodite was seen to bear
the evidence of a sin or curse: "For a long time, hermaphrodites were criminals, or crime's offspring, since their anatomical disposition, their very
being, confounded the law that distinguished the sexes and prescribed their
union" (38). From this perspective, excluded from the natural laws of the
body, the hermaphrodite is also outside the boundaries of humanness. However, Butler points out that Foucault valorizes the abject or inhumanness
that the hermaphrodite embodies. In his introduction to *Herculine Barbin,
Being the Recently Discovered Journals of a Nineteenth-Century Hermaphrodite*
Foucault, Butler states, "imagines Herculine's experience as 'a world of pleasures in which grins hang about without the cat.'"[64] On the one hand, it is
Foucault who first suggests that sexual identity is "prior to any categorization of sexual difference, is itself constructed through a historically specific
mode of *sexuality*" (*Gender* 23); on the other hand, Butler is rightly suspect
when Foucault privileges Herculine's body as a pleasurable site: "Smiles,
happinesses, pleasures, and desires are figured here as qualities without an
abiding substance to which they are said to adhere" (24). It would seem that

the pleasures and desires of someone sexed both male and female would be understood in terms of the *gender* one chose to identify with and if it were possible to have a relationship in which one was not a "freak" or abject.

To effectively illustrate my point in contrast to Butler's argument, I will use an example from contemporary American literature (since I do not know of an analogous example in contemporary Irish literature). In Larry Mc-Murtry's novel *Buffalo Girls,* the narrator, Calamity Jane, writes letters, seemingly to her daughter, Janey, that re-create the experience of living through the heyday of the American Wild West. It is not until the very end of the text that we find out that Calamity Jane never had a daughter (and Janey may be an alter ego or idealized version of herself). She tells Janey, "I wanted you so much I made you up—it was not planned, I had no intent to deceive, the words just came. No sooner had I written them than I could see you. . . . You are the child I would have chose, Janey, had I been normal."[65] For an entire novel we identify with plain-speaking Calamity, seeing her as a good-spirited individual who crossed established gender boundaries and sometimes received scorn, but certainly not as abject or inhuman. In fact, it is precisely her "humanness" that we enjoy and identify with the most. Near the end of the text, however, Calamity feels the need to "confess" to Janey that she is "odd":

> I was born odd though, Janey—not that I was an idiot or didn't have enough toes or fingers—there are other ways of being odd. When I was young I looked more like a man than plenty of these little soft fellows—I think there are plenty of fellows who would have been happier being a woman—but of course they were not given the choice, no more was I. It's sad to be odd, Janey—I used to envy Dora, to think what a comfort just to be a woman as she was, even though at the time she might be crying her heart out because of some trick of Blue's. Dora wasn't always happy but at least she was never odd—stuck in between, as I was.[66]

The fact that Calamity is aware of gender roles—"I think there are plenty of fellows who would have been happier being a woman"—and that she sees herself "stuck in between" the sexed norms indicates that she knows society's score. Yet there is nothing about Calamity's confession or about the information in her confession that immediately makes her "inhuman" or even necessarily abject. Her life has obviously been different, she has been marginalized and excluded; not because of her sexed body, but because of her confused or mixed gender "citations" (no one *knows* she is hermaphroditic).

In this way, Calamity upsets the gender norms, but not necessarily because of her sexed body. Gendered female at birth ("Martha Jane"), Calamity Jane knows that she is "odd" and "stuck in between," yet she still subjectively identifies herself as gendered female, although her behavior and habits are characterized as "male." Butler theorizes that those on the other side of the boundary who are under erasure are abjected and at best "come[s] to bound the 'human' as its constitutive outside, and to haunt those boundaries as the persistent possibility of their disruption and rearticulation" (*Bodies* 8). In contrast to this totalizing discourse, for example, critic Biddy Martin even-handedly states in "Extraordinary Homosexuals and the Fear of Being Ordinary" that "we should remember that the internalization of gender and sexual norms, the shaping of bodily surfaces and boundaries as effects of social injunctions are not coterminous with the psyche or its tasks as a whole."[67] Martin of course recognizes the paramount role of gender in shaping our identity:

> Gender identity does often seem to organize or define the very processes through which it itself takes shape, thus, to constitute a ground. After all, the culture tends to arrange virtually every dimension of social and psychic life around sexual difference, as if our sex were the core and cause. To contest that construction of our sex as core and cause does not or should not negate the integration or coherence that a particular configuration of sexual difference, in its articulation with other aspects of social and psychic life, achieves and sustains individuals over the course of time. Interactions between organisms and environments produce articulations of which our relation to sexual difference is a crucial piece, but not exclusive cause.[68]

While Martin points out the necessity of gender identification, she also refuses to generalize or totalize these identities because the very particularities inherent in identity will produce difference among individuals. Calamity Jane works out an interaction "between organisms and environments" that allows her to survive above and beyond her "oddness." "Stuck in between," Calamity Jane's sexed body does not fit into the matrix of the heterosexual norm; nevertheless, Calamity is not inhuman or even abject. If we remember Kristeva's formula, the abject—the very ability to name the abject—requires that one has some position of outsideness, some position of otherness: "The abject has only one quality of the object—that of being opposed to *I*." Then we can see that although she has an awareness of her difference, her "heterogeneity," Calamity does not abhor her body or herself. Unlike Herculine, who committed suicide, Calamity does not loathe her body; in fact, she says, "You can't run off from what you are though—you have to make camp with what you are, every night, Janey."[69]

From Foucault we get the constructedness of sex, while Butler calls our attention to gender construction and the heterosexual matrix. Phelan, too, provides a way of thinking about the regulatory norm, and the fact that those operating within the boundaries of the norm are "invisible" because "unmarked." Yet it is my contention that intelligibility comes at a level other than the sharply demarcated sexual/gender binary traditionally expostulated by heterosexuality. To proclaim abjectness for those who are different from the binary is not theoretically helpful, because, first, it requires a position of self-objectivity that is not always available, useful, or even helpful; second, no matter how we attempt to turn a pejorative word like "queer" or "abject" into something positive, which is a contemporary strategy, we are still operating in the heterosexual paradigm that originally defined the words. In other words, Butler is still attached to the heterosexual construct because she theorizes *against* it, and thus she is trapped in its logic. For this reason, we need to look for other theoretical tools that do more than just play against the dominant matrix. Because Butler is too fixed, I would like to turn to Deleuze's theory of becoming, which is more flexible and adapts to what we have on the pages of the actual novels: radical shifts, diversity, deterritorialization, and repetition with difference.

Although Deleuze has been criticized by feminists for his term "becoming-woman," it is not difficult to see that the theory of becoming- or becoming-woman, is a way to overcome sexual bipolarization. There is no becoming-man because man is the regulatory norm, which means it is stable and in a position of authority; becoming-man would be Butler's compulsory heterosexuality. Anyone can pass through becoming-woman: "Majority implies a state of domination, not the reverse . . . it is perhaps the special situation of women in relation to the man-standard that accounts for the fact that becomings, being minoritarian, always pass through a becoming woman." Becoming unrolls movement as a series of events, freeze-framing the instances, focusing on the particularities of the body in motion against a plane or grid of power.

According to Deleuze, the plane of immanence or consistency reads a text for movement, speeds, "haecceities," and breakdowns and rejects typical "sense-making" strategies. Conversely, the plane of organization reads a text for stability, universalizing truths, and totality and rejects texts that are not predictable and easily categorized. Perhaps one of the more difficult points to understand about the plane of immanence or consistency is that it is not a "place" where we can conduct fixed measurements or categorize stable entities. The plane of immanence is motion, becoming, lines of flight crisscrossing, intersections, and multiplicities; rather than measurements for quantity, we must gauge speeds, velocities, intensities and affects. If we can momentarily harness or freeze-frame a reading that opens up a new perspective or a new way of thinking, then we can read for what is there: movement.

With the plane of immanence it also becomes evident that the cherished Western ideas of identity and subjectivity must be abandoned as the body, too, is a site of flows, intersections, and affects: the body without organs. The body is a machinic assemblage: "Nothing subjectifies, but haecceities form according to compositions of nonsubjectified powers or affects" (266). A haecceity is a "mode of individuation very different from that of a person, subject, thing or substance" (261); the word itself is taken from the medieval philosopher Duns Scotus by Deleuze to suggest a difference or individuation "distinct from that of a thing or a subject." The body and what we like to call "self," according to Deleuze and Guattari, is a mere threshold. The haecceity, then, is the gauging, charting and mapping the flow, alignments, and speeds of becoming in terms of thinking and language as well as in physical terms—in terms of the body. In their final text, *What Is Philosophy?* Deleuze and Guattari connect the haecceity to the event because an "event" is not a stabilized entity of meaning but a duration of time or a lapse that can be gauged only in terms of movement: "The concept speaks the event, not the essence or the thing—pure Event, a hecceity, an entity." The concept, in turn, relates to the plane of immanence: "Concepts are like multiple waves, rising and falling, but the plane of immanence is the single wave that rolls them up and unrolls them." The waves are strata: words, motion, situations, pictures, and texts of different sorts converging, crossing, aligning, and intersecting on the one plane of thought: the plane of consistency or immanence.

Our primary consideration is *thinking* about the body and how it functions as a gendered body and as a body that confirms to preestablished rules of power and behavior. Deleuze and Guattari remain emphatic concerning the correct status of thought, which helps us to push the boundaries of our thinking about the body: "Thought demands 'only' movement that can be carried to infinity. What thought claims by right, what it selects, is infinite movement or the movement of the infinite" (37). What is not thought is finite, static, and represented or representable; we can "know" it; is it stable. Becoming-imperceptible is thought in motion that accelerates to a point at which it becomes imperceptible: "Movement has an essential relation to the imperceptible; it is by nature imperceptible. Perception can grasp movement only as the displacement of a moving body or the development of a form. Movements, becomings, in other words, pure relations of speed and slowness, pure affects, are below and above the threshold of perception" (280–281). With this passage the several strands of thought concerning becoming, movement, and the body align on the plane of immanence. We can see that the radical push, the "boom" and the "bust," of becoming-imperceptible precipitates the breakdown of representation—liberating pure difference—and the collapse of subjective identity. The haecceity replaces representation in that we no longer can re-present some entity or some thing in terms of what we already know. In other words, we no longer re-present an idea; instead we present it as event, as discourse, as becoming or flow whose line we attempt to chart. On the plane of immanence, the body no longer corresponds or conforms to preexisting categories or transcendentals. Thought without category abandons sluggish thought and the crutch of what has already been thought, preferring instead to gauge only the haecceity: "eliminate everything that exceeds the moment, but put in everything that it includes—and the moment is not the instantaneous, it is the haecceity into which one slips and that slips into other haecceities by transparency" (280). "Transparency" is pure movement. Indeed, the movement necessary in becoming cannot be represented. No thing, no representation, can stand in for becoming: becoming is. As each chapter of this text progresses, we will see that the novelists have an increasingly difficult time capturing the transparency of the action. Prose cannot "clock" the movement.

In our discussion in chapter 2 concerning *The Woman Who Walked into Doors,* it is difficult to chart Paula's movement in the action of skillet-impacting-Charlo's-head. The decisive point in Paula's life—the raising of her arm, the torque of the skillet—escapes representation. And if we take the idea of becoming and open the space of the body and gender, then we see Paula's action as repetition playing outside of representation: repetition with difference. This action is decisive for Paula; it is singular and it changes her entire life. The prose that captures Paula's repetition is overall stable and does not slip off the page. In contrast, the novels we discuss in chapter 5, "Discourse and the Body: Velocity and Power," challenge our very ability to read and make conventional sense of them. In this way, *The Irish Novel at the End of the Twentieth Century* attempts to wrap thinking around what is actually presented in the contemporary Irish novel. Chapter by chapter, we spiral ever deeper into novels whose becoming and slippage off the page puts into question our ability to interpret. Contemporary Irish novelists produce meaning through form in their texts. As we know, language may or may not refer to the material world; all that we can be certain of is that language can tell us something about *itself.* Discourse comments on the world, but more importantly, discourse comments on discourse. Therefore we are interested in *how* discourse is produced in the novels as well as what is referentially posited. With each successive chapter, we become more engaged in this "meta" level of reading because the novels, themselves, begin to blur, begin to become imperceptible to our "normal" sense-making capabilities. The body of contemporary novels in Ireland tell us a great deal about the state of the novel as an artwork or as artistic form, which in turn tells us something about the state of discourse in contemporary Ireland. Discursive practices have changed along with all the cultural, economic, sexual, and political changes, and the novel presents, exposes, and parodies the shift.

Chapter Two 🔀

Irish Identity

Heterosexual Norms

> The lie of compulsory female heterosexuality today creates, specifically, a profound falseness, hypocrisy, and hysteria in the heterosexual dialogue, for every heterosexual relationship is lived in the queasy strobelight of that lie. However we choose to identify ourselves, however we find ourselves labeled, it flickers across and distorts our lives.
>
> —*Adrienne Rich,* Compulsory Heterosexuality

With this chapter we concentrate on novels that depict gender, sexual, and cultural norms in contemporary Ireland. We want to see how the body is typically presented and functions, how gender is typically established and regulated, and how these functions and regulations socially and culturally construct the "Irish Identity" in the 1990s novel. What will become apparent and is of keen interest to us is the way in which heterosexual boundaries are established then crossed. One of the major themes of the novels discussed in this chapter is female agency in a patriarchal, heterosexual society. An aspect that emerges in *The Woman Who Walked Into Doors* by Roddy Doyle and *Titanic Town* by Mary Costello is that female agency is limited, is circumscribed by the power structures in place, and is a historical reality. In both novels it is the female agency issue that most clearly demarcates the boundaries of sexuality and gender, the body and power.

In chapter 1 we discussed various theories of power, sexuality, and the body. From chapter 1, Foucault's third domain of the power/knowledge alliance, "deployment of sexuality," is an appropriate place to begin an investigation into how the Irish heterosexual society regulates itself. Foucault theorizes that the "deployment of sexuality" is "its reason for being, not in reproducing itself, but in proliferating, innovating, annexing, creating, and penetrating bodies in an increasingly detailed way, and in controlling populations in an increasingly comprehensive way" (*Power* 107). The ability to control and regulate is power, and power, Foucault theorizes in "The Subject and Power," is "a mode of action upon action."[1] Foucault believes that there is no "top down" power hierarchy, but that "power relations are rooted deep in the social nexus, not reconstituted 'above' society as supplementary structure whose radical effacement one could perhaps dream of."[2] In this, Foucault is critiquing a hierarchical Marxist theory of power as he emphasizes that all societies have power relations—however utopian conceived—and, in fact, "a society without power relations can only be abstraction."[3] In terms of heterosexual relationships and women, Marx said very little. Feminists have attempted to theorize the domestic space in terms of "domestic labor debate." However, women have benefited not from the negotiation of private work sphere (the home), but only in the public sphere (out-of-the-house paid labor). Therefore, we must think in terms of people relating to people in the power dynamic as well as people relating to or being dictated to by an "abstract" institution. Moreover, we are interested in how power in a heterosexist society is exercised and, more specifically in terms of gender relations, "What happens when individuals exert (as they say) power over others?"[4] In "Heterosexuality and Domestic Life" Jo VanEvery theorizes "that while heterosexuality has no essential character, it does have a hegemonic form in late twentieth-century Western societies."[5] The hegemonic form of heterosexuality is the institution of marriage. While VanEvery indicates that there is a lack of data on marriage as a form of hegemonic control, she names several studies that show that the effects of this cultural institution are hegemonic:

> Stevi Jackson points out that "the ideology of heterosexual romance tells us that falling in love is the prelude to a lasting, secure and stable conjugal union." Sue Lees reports that girls in North London see no alternative to marriage, despite recognising the inequality and subordination they can expect from it. There has been public anxiety (in the US and the UK), reflected in the pronouncements of political parties, churches, and others, about declining marriage rates and rising numbers of single parents. Government policies in most Western countries privilege marriage over other types of relationships (including heterosexual cohabitation) through tax relief and eligibility for various benefits.[6]

Sex and sexuality constitute an arena of power that is used to create and maintain male domination.[7] Heterosexuality is the cultural and legal norm.

The heterosexual structures in place at all levels of society promote a certain understanding of masculinity or what it means to be male, and femininity or what it means to be female. It is the "understanding" that needs scrutiny: "I am suggesting that heterosexuality, like motherhood needs to be recognized and studied as a *political institution*—even, or especially, by those individuals who feel they are, in their personal experience, the precursors of a new social relation between the sexes."[8]

The Irish psychologist Maureen Gaffney notes in her 1991 text, *Glass Slippers and Tough Bargains: Women, Men and Power,* that men and women have such different views of a relationship that "there are two marriages in every union."[9] Men, studies indicate, are happier in their marriage than their female partner, and when a man does express unhappiness in his marriage it "is more likely not to be reflecting discontent with his marriage, he is more likely to be reflecting discontent with his general life situation, mainly his job, than he is with his relationship with his partner. Yet, when the husband is unhappy, then the couple is unhappy."[10] The reason for this phenomena is that marriage is secondary to a man's self-esteem; "masculinity," or what it means to be a "man," is constructed differently than the woman's sense of self-esteem. Gaffney theorizes what she calls the "New Man," the new generation of men who could have potentially re-created what it means to be masculine. The "New Man" issue obscured the fundamental issue at hand: power. According to Adrienne Rich and Judith Butler, heterosexual society forces economically disadvantaged women and/or women of certain races or ethnic backgrounds to marry. The legal institution of marriage carries with it more than a partnership; it entails an entire heterosexist set of assumptions. Rich believes some women enter marriage for economic and physical protection, but women who marry for these reasons always enter the union as a sub-partner: "A woman seeking to escape such casual violations along with economic disadvantage may well turn to marriage as a form of hoped-for-protection, while bringing into marriage neither social or economic power, thus entering that institution also from a disadvantaged position."[11] Unfortunately, instances of motherhood and marriage in the novels we will be discussing in this chapter do not herald "the precursors of a new social relation between the sexes."

Indeed a prime example of a woman trapped in the heterosexual matrix is Paula Spencer in Roddy Doyle's 1996 novel, *The Woman Who Walked Into Doors.* Paula Spencer gives the reader a firsthand account of her working class Dublin life. Born into a large family in 1956, Paula O'Leary, "of 97, St. Francis Avenue," claims to have grown up in "a happy home," although her older sister, Carmel, disagrees with her on this point.[12] Paula admits that she is no longer sure what is memory, what is fiction, and what is a combination of the two. In *The Woman Who Walked Into Doors,* Doyle does a remarkable

job of giving a voice to Paula's tough-minded, ironic though often sentimental outlook on life. In fact, Paula is more convincing as a realistic character because of the seeming contradictions in her personality. The most
obvious contradiction is the fact that she continues to love her husband,
Charlo, up to the climatic point in the novel when she finally throws him
out of the house. Not only does she love him, she forgives him and often
blames herself for the beatings he has given her during their seventeen years
of marriage. In many ways, Paula is a "casebook" study of the "battered wife
syndrome," and it seems likely that Doyle is familiar with this condition because Paula corresponds at almost every level with the identifying characteristics of the syndrome. A definition of a "battered woman" is a "woman, 18
years of age or over, who is or has been in an intimate relationship with a
man who repeatedly subjects or subjected her to forceful physical and/or
psychological abuse."[13] Charlo, too, follows closely the "textbook" case of
the abuser or batterer: "a history of temper tantrums, insecurity, need to
keep the environment stable, easily threatened by minor upsets, jealousy,
possessiveness, and the ability to be charming, manipulative and seductive
to get what he wants, and hostile, nasty and mean when he doesn't suc-
ceed. . . . If alcohol abuse problems are included, the pattern becomes classic."[14] Charlo's abuse of Paula extends across the full spectrum of
punishments and abuses of domestic violence, or "battered wife syndrome."

    The syndrome, some criminologists, in particular, believe to be an unfor-
tunate nomenclature. In a recent article published from the proceedings of
the British Criminology Conference, Bronwyn F. Bartal situates the syndrome in the larger cultural and societal arena: "In some respects it might be
argued that the problems faced by battered women are a microcosm of the
wider problems of bias within the principles of the criminal law in general
and criminal defences in particular. An analysis of these principles reveals
other biases including those of gender, culture, race, economy, politics and
social structure."[15] With this statement Bartel suggests that the battered wife
syndrome, therefore, does not describe isolated incidents that are peculiar to
certain domestic situations. Rather, the syndrome corresponds to something
much larger—the entire political and societal structure. In *Theorizing Patriarchy*, Sylvia Walby discusses the ways that patriarchy brings about hegemonic
control; her chapter on violence very clearly points to the graphic and physical dominance that patriarchy maintains. Walby asserts that male violence
against women is often thought of as individual acts and would be "the last
place to which most people would look as a typical example of social pat-
terning of the relations between men and women."[16] Yet she argues "that
male violence against women has all the characteristics one would expect of
a social structure, and that it cannot be understood outside an analysis of patriarchal social structures."[17] Therefore, sexual violence in Western societies is

directly related to male domination and the exercise of power in the lopsided gendered matrix. Sexual violence is the logical outcome of women's inferiority that is evidenced in their political, economic, and legal status (witness the issue of abortion and a woman's right to choose in Ireland). If we then add in Foucault's prescription for power—a mode of action upon action—then one man's action on a woman is never singular. If it were singular, then the act would be punished accordingly. A man beating up a woman as an anomaly in the cultural and legal system would be justly punished because the community would be shocked and outraged by this uncharacteristic mode of behavior. However, the abuser's mode of action is not checked by another's mode of action (the police, other males in the family, or neighborhood) because it is so common and because the cultural and legal system sanction it. Therefore, the battered woman syndrome exists because at some level, society and culture support this kind of manifestation of power.

According to Pat O'Connor in *Emerging Voices: Women in Contemporary Irish Society,* late 1990s Irish heterosexual society still harbors the idea that women should serve the emotional, material, and sexual needs of men. Her study indicates that in Irish society in comparison to other EU countries women still perform "the bulk of household labour, including the care of children—despite the fact that they are increasingly participating in paid employment, largely on a full-time basis."[18] This cultural and societal setting provides sufficient evidence to suggest that women are still not equal to men, and that masculinity in the Irish context preserves its dominance. Power is not individualistic but tied to an elaborate system of privileges. O'Connor theorizes that images of masculinity ultimately legitimize physical dominance and violence:

> The idea that the ability and willingness to use force is a "normal" element in the definition of masculinity and hence an element in the social and cultural construction of heterosexuality offers a potentially fertile source of legitimisation for male violence whether in physical violence towards a spouse or indeed towards any woman, and also in pornography, rape, and sexual abuse. Evanson (1982) has suggested that the causes of marital violence were "the deeper assumptions of husbands that they have a right to dominate and the powerlessness of wives which make them legitimate outlets for aggression which cannot be vented on others." Typically, however, such issues and those relating to men's greater cultural value, and the legitimacy of their dominance, are ignored.[19]

The problem of lopsided gender equality in Ireland in the 1990s is a reality. This reality then spawns the "implicit colluding" of the state with domestic violence, with only one in five women, in a recent student on domestic violence, actually reporting violence to the Gardai. The women in the study reported that the men were rarely arrested.[20] In fact, O'Connor reports that based on the level of funding available to combat domestic violence, train social workers to recognize signs of abuse and help the abused, Ireland clearly perceives this violence as a "private problem."

In *The Woman Who Walked Into Doors* Doyle presents the reader with the inside version of this private problem indicating, at least implicitly, that this problem is not private but ravages the family and from there unfurls outward into society. In a recent interview Doyle states that the novel comes out of his experience of screenwriting for a BBC television series, "Family," in which the last episode is narrated from the wife's point of view. Pleased with the episode, Doyle believed that there was an entire novel to be written from this woman's perspective. As it turns out, Doyle was writing the book when the episode was broadcast: "when I started the novel, the episode was broadcast in Ireland, and then there were all sorts of denunciations. There's virtually nothing in the novel that is in the television series, which is very gritty, very hard hitting. And the denunciations came from all sorts of politicians, from priests, my old teachers union, virtually everybody queued up to condemn it in some way."[21] When Doyle is asked, "What was their problem with it?" he replies that he became the subject of sermons of everyone queuing up to condemn him for "undermining the sanctity of marriage. Which of course was exactly what I was doing."[22] In *The Woman Who Walked Into Doors,* both Paula and her sister Carmel "turn to marriage as a form of hoped-for-protection."

Paula's narrative begins with the young Guard who comes to the door to tell her about Charlo—although the reader is not told at that time about Charlo. Instead, Paula tells the reader how much she hates her doorbell and that the sound of it not only irritates her but brings bad news: "I still died a bit whenever someone rang it" (2). The second chapter begins with Paula's narrative of the night she met Charlo at a dance. Despite whatever we are eventually told about Charlo's brutality, Paula establishes the fact that she was immediately attracted to Charlo: "This wasn't a crush—this wasn't David Cassidy or David Essex over there—it was sex. I wanted to go over there and bite him" (3). As the Rubettes' song, "Sugar Baby Love," finishes and Paula remembers it—"Women always do" (4)—Charlo asks her to dance, and this dance seals her fate:

—D'you want to dance?
   I let him sweat for a bit.
   —Yeah.
   His timing was perfect. The Rubettes stopped and Frankie Valli started singing My Eyes Adored You. He must have planned it. His arms went through my arms just as Frankie went *My;* his fingers were knitted and on my

back by the time Frankie got to *Eyes*. He'd been drinking. I could smell it but it didn't matter. He wasn't drunk. His arms rested on my hips and he brought me round and round.

—But I never laid a hand on you—
My eyes adored you—
I put my head on his shoulder. He had me. (4)

This scene clearly establishes heterosexual dating rituals faithful to the era, the early 70s, as the male instigates the match and the woman responds affirmatively; more tellingly, this passage is a subtle foreshadowing of Paula and Charlo's life together. Similar to most wife batterers, Charlo is charming, and Paula even uses the word "elegant" to describe Charlo's mannerisms; this elegance may be evidenced in his timing in the above passage, which so impresses young Paula. Then, of course, the sad foreshadowing "But I never laid a hand on you" that is only slightly less macabre than "He had me." In addition to beating Paula, he also, like most wife abusers, makes her a prisoner in her own home.

Paula's narrative, however, is about herself and her own memory of her life. Skillfully, Doyle has given her a voice that is naive and rough but one with which we immediately empathize. Paula does not meditate on the philosophical aspects of her situation, nor is she eloquent in providing the details of her life, rather she is "real" and "speaks" with a working-class, plain-speaking brusqueness often awash in doubt. The doubt stems from her lack of formal education and her seeming awkwardness with the language. However, her self-doubt and lack of self-confidence are perhaps due more to her situation as a female who has been abused by her husband for the last seventeen years of her life rather than her lack of education. Studies have shown that abused women have an odd sense of self-esteem whereby they see themselves as having high self-esteem, perhaps because of their ability to survive such brutal conditions, and yet they clearly have low self-esteem because they stay in the abusive relationship.[23] With Paula we have a complex mixture of confidence and doubt, despair and hope. Doyle could have made Paula the ultimate victim by having Charlo kill her; instead, Charlo murders Mrs. Fleming during a bungled robbery attempt. It would seem that Charlo would have to kill a woman before his own death, and so in a way, Doyle trades Mrs. Fleming for Paula. Paula is fascinated and repulsed by Charlo's violent end, but she does not provide the reader with the details until near the end of the text. One thing is for certain, had Paula not finally acted—a clear act of agency—Charlo may have killed her and, more important to Paula, sexually and physically abused their teenage daughter, Nicola.

Indeed, the most significant point in Paula's life is her decision to end Charlo's reign of terror and throw him out of the house. Coming late in the novel, Paula's act of *difference* establishes the norm. Paula does wipe out the heterosexual regulatory law that had been abusing her: in her action and resolve to fight back, she pushes back the border that was established to contain her. Bodies change in their becoming. Paula has agency and acts on volition and this is becoming. Doyle makes Paula remarkable by granting her the power to become and to create *difference*. This can only be created, of course, after we realize how unremarkable Paula's life has been and that most of her decisions—her drinking, her loyalty to Charlo—have not been fortuitous.

In her narrative, Paula remembers her preteen and teen period to have been the time when her life started to go wrong. Her recollection, of course, is that those around her began to act queer and to treat her differently. After enjoying primary school ("St. Mary's"), she hates her secondary school ("the tech") because to survive she "had to act rough and think dirty" as the teachers and students tried to take advantage of her: "Waters and his wandering thumb and Dillon and his wandering snot made me feel filthy; there was something about me that drew them to me, that made them touch me. It was my tits that I was too young for; I'd no right to them. It was my hair. It was my legs and my arms and my neck. There were things about me that were wrong and dirty. I thought that then; I felt it. I didn't say it to anybody; I wouldn't have known how to and I wouldn't have wanted to. I was a dirty slut in some way that I didn't understand and couldn't control; I made men and boys do things" (35). Paula's teenage reaction is one of confusion—suddenly her body is very interesting to "men and boys." She wishes to be treated like a little girl at St. Mary's, yet she finds power in her looks and in the fact that she knows how to "strike" first. Paula "wanks off " Martin Kavanagh during Religion class and keeps Derek O'Leary at bay by grabbing his genitals. This action she states gave her power: "I had power, the only time in my life. I could make boys squirm. I tested it" (39). We can see that in Paula's teenage world the heterosexual "battle of the sexes" is literal and, for her, a battle for survival; she states emphatically, "I'd survived. I was someone" (41). Yet Paula is trapped in a patriarchal heterosexual society that means even when she is in control, when she has "power," the system controls her. Playing in the system to survive is the only alternative she has, but her hope of becoming a winner in this system is futile. Even Paula's twelve year-old brother wants to "feel" his fourteen-year-old sister, pleading "come on" and calling her a slut when she refuses. Apart from a few glorious instances of power over males, Paula quickly realized she was a loser in the heterosexual matrix no matter what she did or allowed: "It never stopped. Come on. You were a slut if you let fellas put their tongues in your mouth and you were a tight bitch if you didn't—but you could also be a slut if you didn't. One or the other, sometimes both. There was no escape; that was you" (47). Teenage girls have no power because the system has built an elaborate edifice; even if they survive by "wanking" boys in the back of the class, the action has always already been completely sanctioned and inscribed into the heterosexist matrix.

In addition, Paula is trapped by her working-class upbringing. Paula laments the fact that no one instructed her to take the exam in get into the Holy Rosary secondary school because had she, she feels she would have passed the exam and her whole life would have been different—no savage teachers or boys, no proving oneself through the physical manipulation of body parts, and no "thick" peers to impress. In this, the novel very clearly shows Paula's complete entrapment in her existence. It is her working-class background that fails to prepare her to take exams, even to be told to take exams, and in turn leads to the waste of her intellectual potential and to her forced survival in brutal school and social conditions. In terms of her family, Paula interestingly presents her mother as beaten down and her father as mean-spirited but not cruel to her. Her father, however, is cruel and abusive to Carmel, the oldest sister, and Paula very oddly states that she remembers the fights, "the screams and punches," though she now finds fault with Carmel because "she refuses to remember anything else, the good things about home and my father" (46). Paula's statement is especially odd because she goes on to give an account of her father's abusive behavior toward Carmel:

> It was hard for her, I know; she was the oldest and she had to fight all our fights. Fights—Jesus, they were wars. He tore clothes off her. He set fire to a blouse she'd bought with her first pay money. He dragged her up to the bathroom. He washed her face with a nailbrush. He locked her in our bedroom. He went after her when she got out. He took his belt to her in front of all her friends. He put me and Denise up on his knees and did horsey-horsey—it was embarrassing; I was much too old—while he stared at Carmel. He said that we were his girls, his great girls. He made Carmel go to the kitchen and make the tea; he told my mother to stay where she was. (46)

Paula's father is more than abusive, he is incestuously motivated toward his daughters—"horsey-horsey." He is also a misogynist because there is a deeper thread of hatred in his action than simple meanness or perversity; only a man who thoroughly hates women would be threatened by Carmel's maturation, her ability to earn her own money and her potential independence. Mr. O'Leary completely controls the household so that even his wife is frozen dumb while he abuses their daughters; it is likely that only a woman who had already had a taste of his anger would stand by so idly and let her husband abuse one daughter and fondle the other two. Mrs. O'Leary is forced to stand still and agree with her husband's insistence that it was for

Carmel's own good, "She nodded. She agreed with him even though she was shaking. I remember being terrified" (46). Astonishingly enough, the adult Paula still counters Carmel's view of her father with "He'd meant it for the best, being cruel to be kind" (47).

The above passage reveals that Paula's narrative is ironic in that she cannot see what she has hidden in her memory and now in her narrative. First, Paula's narrative does not account for the fact that her father was most likely abusive to her mother; if she knows, she cannot narrate it. What is also hidden is that Paula knows that after Carmel's departure she is next in line for her father's abuse. This situation in turn leads her—perhaps instinctively out of a sense of survival—to find a man who will take her away from her father. In a hetero-sexist society, as Rich notes, "bringing into marriage neither social or economic power, thus entering that institution also from a disadvantaged position," Carmel and then Paula, without education, trade, or hopes for a job in eco-nomically depressed Dublin, are forced to marry. Carmel states in the present, "—I'd have married anyone to get out of that house, she says.—I'd have mar-ried any invalid that asked" (47). Paula points out to the reader, however, that Carmel got pregnant, then got married. Paula, at least, manages to marry Charlo first, then get pregnant soon after; unfortunately, her husband is a "rep-etition of the Same," of her father. Still, the important aspect is that Paula does not see that she is in denial psychologically and narratively; her denial keeps her from seeing the similarities between Carmel's situation and her own, and she will not concede the fact that her father was abusive.

Much of Paula's narrative is driven by the simple need to assure herself that she came from a loving family, that Charlo did love her, and that her whole life has not been one big delusion. Arguing with Carmel concerning their father and their childhood, Paula cannot get her to concede that their family had been loving and her memories true. Denise, the younger sister, is put in the middle and manipulated by each sister. Paula believes that Denise always sides with Carmel because Denise is intimidated by the oldest sister. Paula is less interested in one-upping her sister than in validating her mem-ory of their father. Hesitantly, Denise admits, "—Yes, he was nice," which relieves Paula: "Jesus, I felt good. That proved it, what Denise had just said; I wasn't just making it all up. My stomach landed and took off. I felt secure. I felt sane. It's a valuable feeling. It's a long time since I took it for granted" (56). What Carmel does not see in her argument with her sister is that what is at stake for Paula is her entire sense of self. Pugnaciously determined to win this argument, Carmel does not let up on Paula:

—I know what you're up to, she said.
    —What?
    —I know.

—What?

—Rewriting history, she said.

—I don't know what you're talkin' about, I said.—I don't even know what you mean.

—I'm sure you have your reasons, said Carmel.

—Fuck off, Carmel, will yeh.

(I'm not. What Carmel says. Rewriting history. I'm doing the opposite. I want to know the truth, not make it up. She has her reasons, too.) (56–57)

Paula's need to rewrite history or, as she says, "know the truth," comes to the fore with Charlo's death. Paula tries to accept the circumstances of Charlo's death, but if she does accept them, then her life with Charlo will have been seventeen years of self-delusion.

The details of her own suffering are not interesting to Paula. What is interesting, if not crucial, for Paula is figuring out, rewriting, or writing over Charlo's last action. The reader has had a few instances of Charlo's treatment of Paula, but not a full account. Near the end of the novel Paula acknowledges the reader's perverse desire to know *exactly* what Charlo did to her, "Ask me. Ask me. Ask me." With a "Here goes," Paula provides the reader with a ghastly list of injuries she suffered at the "hands" of Charlo:

Broken nose. Loose teeth. Cracked ribs. Broken finger. Black eyes. I don't know how many. . . . A ruptured eardrum. Burns. Cigarettes on my arms and legs. . . . He dragged me around the house by my clothes and by my hair. He kicked me up and he kicked me down the stairs. Bruised me, scalded me, threatened me. For seventeen years. Hit me, thumped me, raped me. . . . He hurt me and hurt me and hurt me. He killed parts of me. He killed most of me. He killed all of me. Bruised, burnt and broken. . . . He never gave up. Months went by and nothing happened, but it was always there—the promise of it. (175–176)

Charlo is a fairly typical wife batterer who mixes physical abuse with emotional and psychological terror for the victim. Unlike batterers who must eventually face up to their crimes and so offer some sense of their reasons for abuse, we have no sense that Charlo has the typical excuses and justifications for his behavior that other abusers have. Interestingly, in parts of the narrative Paula presents Charlo's behavior as calculated and knowing, whereas most batterers feel that they have excuses for their behavior ("I lost control") or justifications ("she provoked me"). Many times after Charlo has hit or beaten Paula, he baits her and asks her how she got that black eye:

—Where'd you get that?

—What?

—The eye.

It was a test. I was thumping inside. He was playing with me. There was only one right answer.

—I walked into the door.

—Is that right?

—Yeah.

—Looks sore.

—It's not too bad.

—Good.

He was messing with me, playing. Like a cat with an injured bird. With his black armband, the fucker. Keeping me on my toes, keeping me in my place. Pretending he didn't remember. Pretending he'd never seen black and red around and in that eye before. Pretending he cared. (181)

In other parts of her narrative, Paula blames herself, which is typical of a woman in abusive situation, and yet she now sees the absurdity of her own culpability: "He hit me, he hit his children, he hit other people, he killed a woman—I kept blaming myself. For provoking him" (170).

One aspect that is certain, Charlo's behavior is sanctioned by the authorities and by Irish culture. When visiting a doctor about her injuries, she is asked if she had been drinking: *"Have you had a drink Mrs. Spencer?"*; friends and family members ask her what she said to him to provoke him: *"Did you say something to him Paula?"*; and finally, *"Why did you marry him then, Paula"* (171). In his study "Why Do Men Batter Their Wives?" James Ptacek states that the language that batterers use to describe their attacks on women indicates that the batterer is not in control of himself at the time of attack ("I went berserk" or "I just blew up").[24] At the same time, the men who say that they were out of control admit that their violence was purposeful ("to shut her up" or because she did not want to have sex). "This notion—that the batterer's will is somehow overpowered, that his violence lies outside the realm of choice, that battering occurs during brief irrational episodes—constructs a contemporary profile of the batterer as one who is not necessarily *sick,* but who is rather just *temporarily insane.* Seen from this perspective, the batterer is not abnormal enough to be considered a psychopath and not responsible enough to be considered a criminal."[25] Therefore, the same contradictions we see in Paula's presentation of Charlo are analogous to the contradictions in the self-presentation of the batterer. The important point, of course, is that the abuser is endemic of his culture, or "not abnormal enough to be considered a psychopath." Ptacek characterizes the excuses and justifications as "ideological constructs," noting, "At the individual level, they obscure the batterer's self-interest in acting violently; at the societal level, they mask the male domination underlying violence against women."[26]

Yet, the tortured years can be forgiven if Charlo's murder of Mrs. Fleming can somehow be justified or at least explained in such as way so not to puncture the hazy cloud of lies she has been telling herself for nearly twenty years. Attempting to deal with the police report and the news reports, Paula comes back to them several times in her narrative. The narrative presentation suggests that Paula cannot bear to think about the situation. Quoting the newspaper, "A post mortem by the State pathologist found that Mrs. Fleming had been struck twice across the face but there was no evidence of a sexual assault" (156), Paula is bothered by two things. First, she ponders why Charlo "struck" Mrs. Fleming when he was wearing an intimidating balaclava and he had a gun in his hand. Paula reasons that a sixty-year-old woman is not going to challenge a man with a mask and a gun, so why did he strike her? Why, too, she wonders, did he hit her hard enough for the official pathology report to confirm the blows, since there must have been marks? In this passage Paula confirms that Charlo hit her but only because he loved her and to keep Paula "in my place. He was so kind. He just lost his temper sometimes. He loved me. He bought me things. . . . He bought me clothes. Why didn't I wear them? Whack. But why did he whack poor Mrs. Fleming?" (157–158). Charlo's treatment of Mrs. Fleming troubles Paula more than his treatment of her, because at least his treatment of his wife was consistent and represented an emotional investment. Paula reasons that Charlo must have panicked when he saw the police, although she states that he never panicked before. The ramifications of Charlo's actions for Paula are huge not because she was still married to him, but because they belie Paula's version of herself, her marriage, and her love for Charlo. Paula asks herself, "What had happened?" (158), and she tries to suppress the answer because she knows what is at stake in the "truth": "I wanted none of the answers that started to breathe in me; I smothered them. They were all horrible. They were all just savage and brutal. Nasty and sick. They mocked my marriage, my love; they mocked my whole life" (158). What is interesting and tricky about Paula's narrative is that she has already been coping for the last year with the idea that her marriage and life have been sham. Her excavation into her past begins with Charlo's death—or so we are led to believe. Paula threw Charlo out of the house a year before he murders Mrs. Fleming and two years before the writing of her narrative. That Thursday morning Paula triumphantly throws Charlo out is the day she pushes against the confines of the order that was established to contain her. When she finally retaliates against Charlo, she cannot believe that the act could have been so easy—her years of being a victim had so duped her. The incident is a replay from Paula's past—repetition with difference from her own family's, her own mother's history—yet Paula does not consciously interpret it that way. That fateful Thursday morning both she and Charlo are hung over from the previous day's drinking. Paula notices Charlo looking at Nicola when he walks into the kitchen: "He looked back at her, up and down. Jesus—looking at it. Up and down. That was the thing in his face that killed me: the hate" (215). The hate in Charlo's face, we assume, manifests itself because his teenage daughter is working at a job, has a boyfriend, and, more importantly, sees her father for exactly what he is—something her mother cannot do. Paula believes that it was not sexual but rather pure hate: "But it was sheer hate. It was clear in his face. He wanted to ruin her, to kill her. His own daughter" (216). Paula does not realize—does not want to admit to the thought—that this is a repetition of Same of her father's treatment of Carmel some twenty-five years earlier. The difference between Carmel and Nicola is that Carmel had fewer options than Nicola: Carmel had to marry to escape. The difference between Carmel and Paula's mother, and Nicola and Paula, turns out to be defining. The episode I quoted above shows that Mrs. O'Leary fails to act to protect Carmel. Paula has failed to act of her own volition for seventeen years, but this Thursday morning she will act and in this action symbolically roll over the heterosexual norm and break down the very idea of a standard through a repetition with difference. We can interpret Paula's becoming-woman as a series of events—freeze-framing the instances, focusing on the particularities of the body in motion against a plane or grid of power: "I grabbed the frying pan. It was empty, just the fat. It wouldn't have mattered. He was looking straight at Nicola; he was going to make her get out of his way, rub against her. I could always tell when Charlo was about to move; his shoulders told you. They went before his legs. I hit him on the side of the head with the pan. Nothing stopped me. I didn't care about damage or noise; my arm let me. His legs went, he fell straight like he'd been hanged. He wasn't unconscious" (216–217). Paula hits him several times before she is able to push him out the door and coax him out the garden gate, and during these few moments, she must constantly reaffirm her initial becoming-woman; she must continue to *act* or he will retaliate: "There was no way I was going to give him the chance to talk to me, to even think. My mind was made up and he wasn't going to change it. I wasn't going to let him" (220). She knows his ability to turn the situation around; it is significant that she stays on her guard and does not let him attempt to plead with her.

In effect, Paula is a body moving against the heterosexual power dynamic; Charlo has the power structure on his side and seventeen years of success as a batterer. Paula's decision to strike Charlo with the frying pan to protect Nicola from an immediate attack and then her decision to throw him out for good demonstrate her agency: she moves against everything that she has known since her early teenage years. Everything she knows, including her own mother's behavior, points to her lack of agency. Indeed it is her repetition with difference over her mother's lack of agency that clearly emerges in the novel. This difference indicates that gender relations have changed to some degree, but obviously in Paula's case have not changed completely from her mother's era to her own in the 1990s. Paula's action also indicates that the traditional idea of the family is perhaps no longer completely dominated by a male patriarchal figure. Moving beyond patriarchy, there are alternatives for young women who do not wish to enter into, as Rich states, "marriage as a form of hoped-for-protection, while bringing into marriage neither social or economic power, thus entering that institution also from a disadvantaged position." Nicola could have been repetition number two, but Doyle points to a "new Ireland" in the 1990s. Not only is Paula able to act against Charlo and the heterosexual matrix that sanctions his violence, but Nicola is not forced into marriage as a way to escape Charlo's abuse.

Another form of repetition with difference occurs at the end of the text. After Paula throws Charlo out that fateful Thursday morning, Nicola, unsure of her mother's success, asks her what will happen now:

—What now? said Nicola.
—God knows, I said.—But one thing's for certain. He's not coming back in here again.
—Her face said it: she'd heard it before.
—He's not, I said.—I'll bet you a tenner.
—Okay, said Nicola.
—It was a great feeling for a while. I'd done something good. (225)

After another glimpse at the crime scene where Charlo was shot by the Guards, the very same conversation is presented in the text and concludes the novel. This repetition is interesting because the difference in terms of context and in terms of meaning changes for each conversant. In the first presentation, Paula has narrated the decisive Thursday morning events that end with Nicola half-believing Charlo will return and murder Paula, "He'll kill you now, she said" (217). In this first presentation Nicola believes that Charlo will return primarily, we are led to believe, because Paula is too weak to stop him. At the same time, Paula, somewhat dazed by her own actions, is indeed resolved not to let him come back. The second presentation, the repetition, could be Paula rhetorically representing the same conversation, or perhaps the same conversation did happen with the knowledge that Charlo is dead. What is most significant, however, is the fact that Paula wedges a visit—mentally or visually—to the crime in between the two. This confirms and validates the action she took on that Thursday morning and it indicates that she has come to accept the fact that seventeen years of her life were spent with an abusive and unloving husband. Her acceptance of what Charlo did to Mrs. Fleming is not, however, as lucid as the reader might wish; she states very matter-of-factly, "He saw the guards coming over the wall, he shot Missis Fleming and ran to get away in a car he couldn't drive"

(225), which does not take into account her earlier worries concerning his striking Mrs. Fleming and the possibility of sexual advances or abuse. Yet we have to recognize that this level of acceptance and acknowledgment of Charlo's deeds the day he was killed is all that Paula can manage at this point. Instead of a major catharsis, Paula reconciles what she is able to at this point in her life; perhaps this is more faithful to a "realistic" narrative of a woman who has been mentally, physically, and psychologically abused for nearly twenty years.

Novelist Mary Costello's 1992 *Titanic Town* is seemingly a tale of a girl coming of age in Belfast in the 1960s and 1970s. More subtly, and perhaps more powerfully, *Titanic Town* captures the politics and especially the gender politics during the violent late sixties and early seventies. A semi-autobiographical novel, Costello's mirror self, Annie McPhelimy, narrates her own coming of age, beginning with some of her first childhood memories, but increasingly the novel is dominated by her mother's involvement with the "Women for Peace" movement. Indeed most of the novel focuses on the narrator's mother, Bernadette "Bernie" McPhelimy. The novel brilliantly captures the gritty Belfast vernacular (Costello provides a "Glossary of Irish Terms" at the end of the book), which captures the bleak mood and resignation of high unemployment in Catholic communities. Costello also manages to portray quietly the impact of entrapment the legacy of the British Empire has on the everyday lives of Catholic Belfast. Even the streets that the Catholics live on are constant reminders of Britain's colonial presence: "The Troubles really got underway for me up the Kashmir Road one Saturday morning while I was attempting to buy a sirloin roast for the Sunday dinner. It was the morning after the Protestants had burned out Bombay Street. We went to see Aunt Minnie in Benares Street, which was just around the corner from the action."[27]

Former trophies of the British Empire, Kashmir, Bombay, and Benares cannot help creating a kind of collective unconsciousness in regard to identity and the politics of space in Catholic Belfast, because residents may never completely forget that Ireland was and now Northern Ireland is one of the last remaining trophies, however tarnished, of the former empire. The colonizer attempts to remake the colonized identity, David Lloyd has argued, because "it is the inauthenticity of the colonised culture, its falling short of the concept of human, that legitimates the colonial project."[28] What emerges, as Lloyd further suggests, is the hybridization of the colonial identity. In the Irish context, one is no longer fully Irish-speaking and nomadic, nor is one fully English-speaking and capitalistic; rather, the colonized becomes an imperfect hybridization. In Northern Ireland, according to Laura Pelaschiar, the masculine British, Protestant, or Presbyterian colonial couples with the feminine Irish Catholic native to create Belfast in all of its "ugliness": "The offspring of this sexual encounter is Belfast itself, and the ugliness of the fruit makes it clear that the intercourse was unnatural, an imposition rather than a sign of love, an act of violence closer to rape than to a normal sexual relationship: in other words an overt symbol of British colonization of Irish soil."[29] The image of Belfast as a bastard child, Robert McLiam Wilson's "Belfastards," is slowly being transformed by a 1990s generation of writers. Yet it should be noted that more positive views of Belfast tend to come from Protestant-centered narratives, such as Glenn Patterson's *Fat Lad* (1992) or McLiam Wilson's *Eureka Street* (1996). *Eureka Street* often portrays Belfast as a positively changing city, forgetful of its own violent past—forgetful sometimes even in the midst of crosstown explosions or other forms of sectarian violence.[30]

Early in *Titanic Town* the line between Protestants and Catholics is clearly demarcated. In the first pages of the novel Annie encounters her "first Protestant" (10) in the form of a little girl, about the same age as herself, while walking home from school one day near "what was to become, comically enough, the 'Peace Line' thrown up in the seventies to prevent impoverished Protestants and oppressed and impoverished Catholics from knocking the shite out of each other" (9). The Protestant little girl "marched up to me and took my medal in her dirty little Protestant paw. 'You're a Roman Catholic, aren't you?' she demanded—there was no use talking to Protestants, they have always insisted on calling us Roman Catholics" (10). This incident establishes several things early in the text. First, the Peace Line is a gray wall that, as Annie states, prevents the Protestants and Catholics from "knocking the shite out of each other" and has nothing really to do with a created and meaningful peace. Therefore, "peace" is a misnomer, and maybe not as "comic" as sadly ironic; the wall is merely a physical boundary, as Annie states, "a half-hearted and in places permeable Berlin Wall" (9), to keep the Falls Road-centered Catholics on their side and the Shankill-centered Protestants on theirs. Therefore, right away *Titanic Town* presents us with a unique sense of spatial and bodily distribution. Catholic and Protestant bodies should be kept apart.

Yet, the fundamental aspect of Annie's "first Protestant" account is the inevitability of Protestants and Catholics in Belfast encountering one another. The female grownup version of this encounter is Annie's mother, who is one of a handful of Catholics who work at the Fermanagh Warehouse and Linen Mills in the Village, a Protestant area. Because jobs are so scarce for Catholics, Bernie will not be intimidated out of job when the Troubles begin and the politics of identity becomes even more fierce than before. The point that Annie's encounter makes, however, is that even women with children will inevitably have to deal with others outside their respective neighborhoods, to say nothing of the male Catholics who almost always work for Protestant enterprises.

The third and most obvious aspect is the immediate distrust and biased misperception one little girl has of the other. These misperceptions do not come "naturally," of course; children on each side of the Peace Line learn from an early age whom to distrust and even whom to hate. Fourth, the fact that the Protestant feels she has the prerogative to touch Annie and even twist the religious icon on her school sweater "round and round on its loops of navy blue thread" indicates that the Protestant feels superior to the "Roman Catholic" (10). This assertion of power, however naive or innocuous, is analogous to the power situation overall in Northern Ireland at that time. Members of the RUC did not have any difficulty manhandling Catholics, and women, too, Bernie eventually discovers at Fermanagh Warehouse and Linen Mills, will attack other women when the power matrix and majority are firmly on their side.

Yet what is also evident in the explanation of "the 'Peace Line' thrown up in the seventies to prevent impoverished Protestants and oppressed and impoverished Catholics from knocking the shite out of each other" is that however impoverished the Protestants are, they are not impoverished *and oppressed*. As we discussed in chapter 1, Catholics in Northern Ireland were discriminated against on every rung of the social and economic ladder: jobs, housing, education, and voting rights. Our earlier Foucauldian formula for power, "a mode of action upon action," is appropriate for analysis of actions during the time period of this novel; yet it should be remembered that Catholic and Nationalist forces also exert "action upon action." Annie's father, Aidan, has been a lifelong believer in the Nationalist cause, although apparently he is not a member of the IRA; as a Catholic Aidan has suffered and continues to suffer discrimination—a bleeding stomach ulcer bears witness to his daily stress. Above all else, Aidan is the practical, realist member of the family who chides Bernie for her naiveté and idealism. Aidan often denounces Bernie's opinions and statements; the following example depicts Bernie's naiveté concerning economics and unemployment:

"I'll say one thing for the Protestants," Mother commented that night.
"What?" Father looked up over the *Belfast Telegraph*.
"They fairly know how to dress." Father rolled his eyes in good-humoured disgust. "No, but they do, Aidan," she continued. "They always look immaculate on parade. With their bowler hats and all. Not a speck on their white gloves, their very shoes gleaming. You have to hand it to them, they do know how to dress."
Father grunted non-committally behind the paper.
"Not like our boys," she went on, "they were pathetic at the Easter parade. Half of them hadn't even bothered to run a comb through their hair. No suits, no ties."
"No jobs," Father interrupted. And he didn't want to hear any more about it. (16)

One could argue that Bernie was merely making a statement on the Orange-men's clothes; she takes an interest in cloth and clothes because she is a seam-stress. In fact, when she finally resigns from Fermanagh Warehouse and Linen Mills because of threats and potential violence by Protestants, her comment is, "'It's heartbreaking that . . . was the loveliest material I ever worked with'" (89). Not to mention that having a job is no prerequisite to combing your hair.

However, the important point that this passage establishes is that Aidan (as a male) knows and understands more about the Troubles and the situation in Northern Ireland than Bernie does. This minor incident, too, similar to Annie's "first Protestant," is analogous to women's position in regard to the Troubles, society, and culture in Northern Ireland. Sarah Edge states in "Representing Gender and National Identity" that in "Northern Ireland Irish/Catholic women are situated as a double Other, both the Other to patriarchal male power and the Other to dominant British national identity."[31] The only role for a woman in this position of double Otherness is that of a mother. Indeed it is the "patriarchal male power" that first insures her obedience. Monica McWilliams points out in "The Church, the State and the Women's Movement in Northern Ireland" that the patriarchal web of church, state, school, and family trains girls to become obedient mothers: "The Church through the schools became providers of education while parents became providers of children who are faithful members of the Catholic Church. Not only were Catholic girls to model themselves on the image of the Virgin Mary by maintaining their chastity and purity, but equally they were called upon to adopt the mother's passive, unquestioning role."[32] While Edge's notion of the Catholic Northern Irish woman's double Otherness may be true, *all* women in Northern Ireland have been discriminated against, and in fact, in more recent decades Protestant patriarchy seems more determined, in the midst of its overall crumbling hegemony, to "keep women in their place." Recent statistics concerning women in roles of political representation show that Northern Ireland falls at the bottom of the list among its European neighbors:

in 1996, all Northern Ireland's members of the British and European parliaments were men. Men held 88 per cent of local council seats. Indeed, men rule all institutions of power—church, state, and quango. The old Unionist parties have no apparent interest in either women's votes or women's political energy. Women are there to make the sandwiches. The nationalists are little better. Sinn Fein has more women activists than the other parties, but on women's issues it needs continual prompting. The social issues women are normally deemed competent to deal with have no relevance for the parties. And in the political context of Northern Ireland, conflictual as it is, women are held to lack the toughness needed to fight and win.[33]

Needless to say, these statistics have benefited, as least marginally, from the effects of the woman's movement over the last thirty years in Northern Ireland. Evidence of the effect is found in women's community centers in Belfast started in the last decade of the century such as the Women's Support Network, the Belfast Women's Collective, the Belfast Women's Training Services, Women's Resource and Development Agency, and Women into Politics project.

When Bernie attempts to have the shooting stopped in the neighborhood during the day and joins with other women in the community, she is warned by Aidan that she will never get peace:

> "We're just going for talks, to find out what they want, what it takes to get peace in this place."
> "Whatever you do, you won't get peace."
> Mother turned on him, angered: "Why the hell shouldn't we get it? Peace to lead normal bloody lives for once, in this cursed country. That's what's wrong with this place: too many people think like you. You're defeated before you even get started, or you're pro-violence. It's time the rest of us spoke out."
> Father turned to us. "It's useless talking to your mother."
> Brendan giggled. Father gave him a dirty look. "Just don't agree to anything," he went on, "and don't get any more involved than you are now. Don't be making any promises. These boys are serious."
> "So are we." She sat down, rummaged in her bag and took out a cracked powder case. She quickly powdered her facial extremities: cheekbones, chin, nose and temples. She sprayed a shower of Blue Grass over her upper body, rearranged her handbag, stood up again. "And I'll tell you one thing, Aidan: I don't know about the IRA, but Deirdre and I are hellish determined."
> Father shook his head. "She hasn't a clue." (199)

The gender performances in this passage are stereotypically patriarchal. The essential feature is that Bernie is determined and committed to changing the political process so that people can "lead normal bloody lives for once," but the exchange with Aidan makes the political process appear beyond her comprehension. The gender performances with the powder case and the perfume further the idea that she is superficial and suggest she is preparing for a church social, not a meeting with the IRA. Also suggested in the passage are the gender solidarity performances—such as Brendan giggling at his father's criticism of his mother. Even though Aidan gives Brendan "a dirty look," the gender boundaries are well established; women are clueless when it comes to politics.

In fact, Aidan is correct; Bernie does not have "a clue" because she has no idea of the powerful patriarch machine controlling both sides of the power dynamic. If we get past the obvious political manifestations, then we can see that the heterosexual matrix has an established code which is much more pervasive and deeply rooted than either political faction. One basic idea that the British, the IRA, and the Protestants all agree upon is that women have no place in the political process: "Women are there to make the sandwiches." Factions one might think would be more egalitarian or impartial, the church and the media, also manipulate, use, and then disregard Bernie and Deirdre. The media is especially problematic for the two women because they lack the foresight to know that the media will skew their statements by cutting and making sound bites from the most sensational bits. The television station even identifies each woman with a group of which neither Bernie nor Deirdre had had any previous knowledge. The "Women for Peace" demonstration ends up a circus, and yet, if we look closely at this incident, we see that all the women are programmed to perform on cue for this circus: the estate Catholics and the posh Malone Road Catholics. Although the group let in by the media to storm the meeting causing a near riot may be led by the repulsive Mrs. French, the entire group is agitated by local IRA members and, of course, the media who set up the entire show. It is Mrs. French's group in the community who label Bernie a "tout" because she wants the shooting in the estate stopped during the day. It is this group, with Mrs. French in the lead, who constitute the Nationalist contingency unwilling to negotiate any solution except the absolute: Brits out of Northern Ireland.

The text clearly establishes the idea that Bernie and Deirdre are merely little cogs turning futilely while the actual wheels of power churn on. Power belongs to one gender and the women become a kind of media sideshow, whipping up frenzied debate but powerless actually to change anything. Both the British and the IRA patronize the women and their petition drive; the women are not able to effect a reduction of the violence. The idea that the women are clueless is illustrated when the IRA, supposedly the champions of the Catholic estate, gives a list of demands to Bernie and Deirdre to present to Mr. Brandywell, the English political ambassador. After fumbling in her handbag for the piece of paper with the list, and adjusting her glasses, Bernie begins: "One, a public declaration that the people of the thirty-two counties of Ireland should decide the future of the country. . . . Two, the withdrawl of all British troops from Irish soil by New Year's Day, nineteen seventy-five" (212–213). More than audacious, the IRA's list of demands begins with a call for the complete reversal of everything that the Protestants in Ulster stand for and the British were currently defending. It is not the IRA or Mr. Brandywell who suffer; it is Bernie and Deirdre who suffer as bearers of this ridiculous list of demands. For Bernie and Deirdre to innocuously read from this list of demands shows, as Aidan points out, they are indeed clueless. Patronizing but not completely unsympathetic to Bernie and Deirdre, Brandywell attempts to explain the situation to the childlike women:

> "Ladies, I'm afraid I'm going to have to be very frank with you. It is a difficult and delicate situation you find yourselves in, and I am most concerned that you should come to no harm."
>
> Deirdre's brown eyes expanded in her head, Bernie felt her throat go dry. Mr. Brandywell continued: "Equally, I am concerned that you should not be used by any group or individual. It is clear to me that you are honest, sincere women without thought of publicity or political ambition, who want to make a better life for your children and your community." He spoke nobly, as though addressing a public meeting. (214)

Surely ironic, Brandywell and company have already used Bernie and Deirdre for their own political spin, "negotiating" with the well-meaning Catholic estate women while the barbarous IRA continues its campaign of violence and causing harm to people on both sides of the "Peace Line."

Trained well by the heterosexual matrix, the women are seduced into more promotional work for the British, the church, and even the IRA (in an odd sort of way) when they undertake their petition drive. When the last photo opportunity is seized by the British, the women are discarded as no longer useful. Before being discarded, however, the women are played for fools one last time on live national television. Bernie and Deirdre present their signed petition to Mr. Brandywell on the steps of Stormont. In the process of collecting signatures and as she and Deirdre are about to present the petition, Bernie feels that she has made a contribution to the peace process—that she has actually made a difference in the system of control and power. But Brandywell's last photo opportunity with the women proves to Bernie that she is, indeed, without a clue.

> " . . . very well indeed." He was really hammering it home. "Well done. And how many signatures are on the petition, Mrs. McPhelimy?" he inquired. It sounded a bit rehearsed.
>
> "Just over sixty-three thousand, sir," said Mother with satisfaction.
>
> "All from Andersonstown?" called out one reporter.
>
> "Definitely," said Mother.
>
> The camera had moved out again to include all three as the photographers continued to flash and snap. Deirdre laughed down at them as they jostled one another out of the way. She turned again to the beaming politician.
>
> "Are you pleased with us, Mr. Brandywell?" she was heard to say over the hum.
>
> "Very pleased," Mr. Brandywell pronounced, a contented growl, "you've done very well indeed." (240–241)

Bernie realizes that she has been duped during the entire process: "She suddenly understood what they had done, how it would be seen how useless it all was. At that second her intuition told her that this would be the end, not the start of it. There would be no peace. There could be none" (241). This is the climatic point of the text in terms of the power situation. Bernie now knows that her inscription in the heterosexual matrix as a disenfranchised female in a sectarian war means that all parties will contain her and at best let her pursue futile political activities such as petition drives; for the British certainly know that sixty-three thousand Andersonstown signatures carry little or no real political value.

One is tempted to say that *Titanic Town* reinscribes the power matrix, not only depicting this era but in some covert manner sanctioning the gender politics and producing, in effect, a placid repetition of the Same. However, it could be argued that Costello's text does produce a kind of difference, a difference that is dependent on the fact that we can read through Bernie's sendup: the woman who parodies the role of man as peacemaker. Who could ever take her seriously? Her agency is analogous to a caged hamster: no matter how furiously he runs on his wheel, he will never get anywhere; so, too, Bernie can assert her agency in early '70s Belfast, but the limits of its effectiveness are always already proscribed and controlled. The power matrix does not take her agency seriously, and the only others who truly sympathize with her cause and take her seriously are also disenfranchised—women primarily but not necessarily. Her basically disenfranchised husband has only one last card to hang onto: his gender. To give over to her his patriarchal control would mean Aidan and others in a similar position would be at the absolute bottom rung of the ladder of society. Therefore, sectarian politics in *Titanic Town* fights on a united front in the gender war, colluding to keep women "in their place"—politically ineffective and bodily inscribed.

We can learn a great deal about gender politics from novels devoted to one gender or the other. Among contemporary novels that have this striking feature are *One by One in the Darkness* by Deirdre Madden, *Paddy Clarke Ha Ha Ha* by Roddy Doyle, and *The Salesman* by Joseph O'Connor. An interesting contemporary novel set mostly in rural Ireland, *One by One* presents a matriarchal universe. *One by One* provides a more conscious gendered narration, whereas *Paddy Clarke* and *The Salesman* present male-centered narratives, which, to put it bluntly, are like hundreds of other male-centered narratives. Reasons for male dominated narratives usually involve women's historical lack of agency—women were typically less interesting because of the social and cultural restraints placed on them. With *Paddy Clarke,* the 1993 winner of the Booker Prize, the narrative point of view is a ten-year-old boy growing up in the new Barrytown housing estate. While Doyle's novel is revealing, often comic as well as sad, the gender relations depict a skewed ten-year-old male perspective of racing, fighting, and male one-upmanship with Paddy's ill-understood mother the only featured female. Published in 1998, O'Connor's *The Salesman* is a savage, compelling, and suspenseful novel, but it presents a completely male-centered universe. In the epistolary novel, narrator Billy Sweeney writes to his daughter, Maeve, who is in a coma after being beaten by four thugs during a robbery. One of them, Donal Quinn, escapes during the trial; Quinn is the one who threatened her with a blood-filled syringe—a popular Dublin robbery method. Sweeney hunts down Quinn and the novel consists of Sweeney's memories with Maeve's mother, who is now conveniently dead, and his ever-changing situation with Quinn. In another context, *The Salesman* is a novel worthy of critical scrutiny, but in terms of gender relations it replays the male-centered novel and in terms of bodies and power it definitely replays typically Irish political and Irish working-class fictional scenarios.

However, with *One by One* we have a conscious and revealing record of Northern Irish Catholic females coming of age at the end of the twentieth century. When the novel opens, Cate is boarding a British Airways flight from London to Belfast. Middle sister Cate is the sophisticated and stylish sister who works for a woman's magazine in London. The oldest sister, Helen, is an attorney in Belfast; she defends politically motivated murder defendants. She is the smart, tough and outspoken sister. Sally, the youngest sister, is a schoolteacher at the same primary school all the sisters attended, and now she lives with her mother. Sally is portrayed as the "weak" sister, having suffered from nosebleeds as a child, and coddled by her parents. Each sister embodies a prototype: the one who got away, the smart loyal one, and the shy, homebound one. In this way, Madden makes her characters a little too wooden, a little too predictable. Nevertheless, the text provides insight into the contemporary female gendered world of Northern Ireland.

A recent critique by Michael Parker of *One by One* focuses on the larger political issues presented in the text and dwells on the father's and uncles' involvement with the civil rights marches in the late 1960s and early 1970s. These scenes are flashbacks that provide the reader with a picture of the sisters' childhood and set up the tragic death of their father. Parker states that the text "immediately draws the reader into Madden's preoccupation with issues of authority and agency; here, however, one finds a much more explicit engagement with the larger narrative of Northern Ireland and its impact on identity formation, alongside her recurring concern with the nature of family politics."[34] I agree with Parker's argument that the text is preoccupied "with issues of authority and agency," but I would argue that these issues are presented in the framework of female gendered agency in 1990s Northern Ireland. Parker's actual critique affirms the larger political scene through a discussion of the male characters. Yet the entire text, set in the present, is completely female centered. The father's murder, which hangs over the heads of the sisters and mother, occurs two years prior to the present narrative timeframe. The only major contemporaneous discussions with males are Helen's: one with her law colleague Owen and the other with her conveniently gay friend David.

In *One by One* the sisters are hybrids: Catholic family-oriented women interbred with a post-feminist career oriented independence. The smallness of the sisters' upbringing merges with their opportunity for education and professional careers. Their close-knit upbringing is presented in the text: "The scope of their lives was tiny but it was profound, and to them, it was immense. The physical bounds of their world were confined to little more than a few fields and houses, but they knew these places with a deep, unconscious knowledge that a bird or a fox might have for its habitat."[35] Yet, they knew, too, of the world outside that they were not a part of:

> They recognised this most acutely every July, when they were often taken to the Antrim coast for the day, and as they went through Ballymena and Broughshane, they would see all the Union Jacks flying at the houses, and the red, white and blue bunting across the streets. They thought that the Orange arches which spanned the roads in the towns were ugly, and creepy, too, with their strange symbols: a ladder, a set square and compass, a five-pointed star. They knew that they weren't supposed to be able to understand what these things meant; and they knew, too, without having to be told that the motto painted on the arches: "Welcome here, Brethren!" didn't include the Quinn family. (75)

In this way, the Quinn family is similar to the McPhilemy family: Catholic and in the minority in Northern Ireland. While we don't know what becomes of Annie in *Titanic Town*, we do know what happens to Helen, Cate, and Sally, for it is the present time of the novel. If we compare, for example, Bernie to Helen because both are committed to political justice, then we can see that Helen twenty-five years after Bernie is far more successful at working in and against the law, politics, and the judicial system. Also, we may see that in the 1990s Helen is the true offspring of women like Bernie. Here we may see the value of an earlier generation of women like Bernie McPhelimy. I would therefore reassess Bernie's lack of agency on this one point and argue that Bernie's true power lies incubating, finally emerging in the 1980s and 1990s with educated and professional Catholic women in Northern Ireland.

Helen and Cate represent for different reasons the new educated and liberated Catholic in Northern Ireland. Helen, single and in her thirties, finds that most of her peers are settled, having families and enclosed in their own worlds: "what she liked least about being in her thirties was how it becomes harder to make friends. Even without realising it, people's lives shut like flowers at dusk, became set in the cement of career, marriage, children, mortgage, pension funds and life insurance" (53). The heterosexual "social laws" (53) she discovers dictate that a woman in her thirties is basically an outsider if she is not married. Helen and David are close, in part, because they are both single people in their thirties. She and David also share the fact that both of their fathers were murdered in cases of mistaken identities; still, that fact alone would not draw them together in the closely formed bond that they have. One could imagine that such a friendship twenty or thirty years ago would end in a "marriage of convenience" that would allow David and Helen to seem "normal." In this, the novel does show that a thirty-something single heterosexual woman can remain unmarried and a thirty-something homosexual man does not have to be closeted in order to live in contemporary Belfast. The stigma of these two lifestyle choices is no longer unbearable.

The stigma, however, of a single woman in her thirties becoming pregnant and choosing to keep the child without the father's support is more apparent when Cate informs her family that she is pregnant. In London, Cate did not feel the pressure to conform, but coming home to Northern Ireland to deliver the news of her pregnancy makes her aware that it is odd, even in this era, to have a child without a father or a father's support: "Not that she'd needed to explain herself, up until yesterday, for in reality he had been kind to her, and had offered her all the help and support she wanted, which was none; she only intended to go on with her life without him, and she wondered afterwards why she had told him at all. . . . The only reason that she could dredge up was that it wouldn't have been either fair or decent to keep him ignorant of the situation" (90). Cate's mother, Emily, takes some time to come around the announcement:

> "What I know, Sally, is this," she said at last, "The next time Cate comes home from England for a holiday, she won't be on her own. She'll have a wee baby with her. And I can make the pair of them welcome, or I can always be reminding Cate, without saying anything directly to her, how bad a show it is for the child to have no father. And I could go on doing that until the child itself is old enough to know what is going on. But where would that get any of us? It's what your daddy was always saying, life's too short for that sort of thing. And a yet a bad show, Sally, what's happened. I won't be able to feel the way I ought to or indeed want to for a while yet. And you and Cate are going to have to bear with me on that. I know what is required of me, but it'll take time. Cate will have to be told that." (128)

From this passage we can see that Emily is divided in her reaction toward her daughter's pregnancy. Still, overall, "a bad show of it," is not too censorious a reaction considering that Cate's mother is a middle-aged Catholic woman. The changing role for females in Northern Ireland is also presented in the exchange between Helen and Helen's client, Oliver, who is charged with and guilty of a sectarian murder. Oliver wishes to deal with Owen because he is male, but because of her own self-confidence, this idea does not strike Helen until quite late: "She strongly suspected that he didn't like her either, that he would have preferred Owen to deal exclusively with his case. Maybe he thought that because she didn't come across as particularly sympathetic to him she wasn't going to make much of an effort on his behalf; or, even worse, he might even think that she wasn't up to the job simply because she was a woman" (171).

Lastly, a recurring image of Northern Ireland in popular thought is that of a fishbowl. The fishbowl of Northern Ireland, illustrated most explicitly in *Fat Lad* by the goldfish who continues to swim in circles, nearly touching nose to tail even after it is let out of the bowl and given freedom to move, is an image of the provincial attitude and behavior exhibited by both sides of the peace line in Northern Ireland. The stifling effect is all the worse by the media telescoping in on and magnifying every act of violence and every private tragedy in Ulster. Bernie certainly experiences the claustrophobic fishbowl effect that the media produces. The Quinn family, too, is exploited by the media after their father's murder. As in *Titanic Town,* the media is portrayed in *One by One* as rapacious, printing only what will be sensational enough to make good copy:

> There'd been the day after the funeral when she'd gone to McGovern's in Timinstown to buy some groceries, and there on the counter, on the front of one of the Northern Ireland newspapers, was a photograph of herself and Sally with their arms around each other weeping at the graveside. She'd felt sick, dizzy, furious all at once, she felt her face change colour. Mrs. McGovern, embarrassed on her behalf, leant over and folded the paper to hide the photo. "Wouldn't you think they'd know people had been through enough without doing things like that," she said, and Helen had stared at her, unable to speak. (47)

In such a small geographical area, any sectarian murder, even though carried out against the wrong person, receives huge press coverage; there is no such thing as private grief in Northern Ireland when politics is—or merely may be—involved. Also, one is guilty by association with any politically motivated violence. Helen's friend, David, whose father was also murdered in sectarian violence of which he was not the target, tells Helen that "in the press reports of the case, my father got tarred with the same brush as your man, they made no distinction between them. As far as the papers were concerned, they were two terrorists, they got what they deserved" (49).

The murder seizes control of the lives of the Quinn sisters in unexpected ways. When Cate returns to London after her father's funeral, his mistaken "terrorist" legacy also follows her. Shortly after her return to work, she notices that her English co-workers treat her differently. At first she thinks that there is a cultural difference between the English and the Irish in terms of processing death and grieving; then, she realizes that "[w]hat they were thinking only dawned on her slowly, and it was so horrible that she shrank away, afraid of having to confront it until she was forced to do so" (91). The media coverage in England of her father's murder registered only this: his culpability, and the stigma that she was another person from a family from Northern Ireland involved in the sectarian violence and, even more damaging, linked to the IRA. The matter comes to a climax when a freelance journalist whose work was commissioned in Cate's absence makes a remark that verifies her fears:

> As she looked through the initial work he'd brought along she remarked, "I'm sorry I wasn't in on this from the start, but I was in Ireland," and she didn't know why she added, "My father died."
> "Yes, I know," the man replied. "I read about it in the papers."
> Cate lifted her head from the material she had been glancing through and stared hard at the man, but he stared back coldly at her, and did not speak. "He thinks my father was a terrorist," she said to herself. "He thinks that he brought his fate upon himself; that he deserves the death he got." (91–92)

Afterward, Cate makes it known to a colleague at the magazine that this freelance journalist's work is deteriorating and that the magazine will not accept any more of his work. When her colleague seems surprised, Cate flashes anger and the colleague backs down. This scene is an interesting episode. The reader, sympathizing with Cate, feels that the journalist gets what is coming to him because of his prejudice and biases. Yet clearly Cate's verdict is hardly fair. One could even argue that it is as unfair, on a smaller scale, as the injustice against her father. Nevertheless, it is a rare though minor instance of a female gendered person having actual institutionalized power over a male gendered person in contemporary Irish fiction. Is this perhaps the source of the reader's sympathy?

Female agency in Northern Ireland in the 1990s is complex and owes a great deal to class distinctions. Although the Quinn sisters are daughters of a farmer, they all go to university and become professionals. Yet even with careers they quickly become victims of the larger male dominated institutionalized violence. It is interesting to ask in regard to the Quinn sisters if, as Edge states, "Northern Ireland Irish/Catholic women are situated as a double Other, both the Other to patriarchal male power and the Other to dominant British national identity"? Certainly Cate's experience in London with the male journalist points to a double Otherness. While most of the sisters' choices have little to do with politics, their lives continue to be overshadowed by their father's violent and wrongful death. It may be argued that it is the male dominated heterosexual society and its institutionalized violence that causes the Quinn sisters to draw further into a matriarchal world. With neither sister married, and one sister pregnant and choosing not to marry, it seems evident that *One by One in the Darkness* purposefully proposes an alternative to male domination and the heterosexual matrix that demands women marry men, especially pregnant women. With each of the three novels we have discussed in this chapter, it is clear that the legacy of patriarchal society and male dominated institutionalized power and violence remains a force in 1990s Ireland.

Chapter Three ▦

Bodies over the Boundary

I n this chapter we will interpret texts that present an unusual set of circumstances in the contemporary Irish novel. The novels in this chapter flagrantly disrupt the boundaries of gender and sexuality, which at first suggests that these texts are easily decipherable. Because of the evident and frequently ostentatious gender and sexual differences in such novels as Emma Donoghue's *Hood* or Tom Lennon's *Crazy Love*, we might assume that we are able to "see" and read the texts easily. But from the history of the Irish novel written in English, no precedent is available. In a recent collection, *Sex, Nation, and Dissent in Irish Writing* (1997), Eibhear Walshe brings together critics who focus on the intersection of homoeroticism, nationalism, and political radicalism. According to Walshe, the collection begins with "two moments in Irish history: the criminalisation of same-sex desire in Britain and Ireland by means of the Labouchere Amendment (1885), and the construction of the political and cultural project of the Celtic Revival with Yeats's first collection of poetry (1889)."[1] A concern for Walshe is the fact that "a lesbian and gay presence within any national literature troubles privileged formations of what traditionally constituted 'woman' and 'man.'"[2] In this chapter I am not concerned with the formation or manifestation of a national literature in relation to the contemporary Irish novel; yet, issues of an Irish homosexual identity are apparent in the recent novels.

Walshe believes that the decriminalization of same-sex relations helped homosexuals reclaim their identity. As we discussed in chapter 1, in June 1993 the Irish Senate passed a "bill into law abolishing all previous laws criminalizing homosexual acts between men, and replacing them with a new gender-neutral law with the common age of consent with heterosexuals and no special privacy restrictions."[3] One of the novels we will discuss in this chapter, Tom Lennon's *When Love Comes to Town*, was written and published before the bill was passed. Undoubtedly, identity has been a question for Irish authors for decades; yet it is not until the 1990s that we have blatantly "out" characters, or characters who desire to and eventually do come "out," in mainstream novels. We are reminded of Ide O'Carroll, who points out in her Introduction to *Lesbian and Gay Visions of Ireland* that part of the gay community's mission is to find a homosexual paradigm in a heterosexual cultural matrix; O'Carroll argues that a central "theme is the desire to reconcile being lesbian or gay with being part of a heterosexual family and a society dominated by heterosexuals, while still remaining true to what we know is our way of being in the world."[4] Even with the Criminal Law (Sexual Offences) Bill passed in 1993, a homosexual's prohibition concerning "coming out" is still daunting: "The difficulties encountered by many contributors in the coming out process warn us of the need to continue to educate, so that the next generation of lesbians and gays do not suffer loss and exclusion."[5] Despite the challenge, Walshe believes that the contemporary scene in Ireland is a positive time for "lesbian and gay culture."[6]

This chapter is divided into two sections: "Queering the Bildungsroman" and "Coming Out." "Queering the Bildungsroman" focuses on two coming-of-age and coming-out novels that struggle with reconciling their Irish identity with their homosexual identity—Emma Donoghue's *Stir-fry* and Tom Lennon's *When Love Comes to Town*. The section "Coming Out" interprets Donoghue's and Lennon's next novels, *Hood* and *Crazy Love* respectively, as post-coming-of-age novels that deal with homoerotic desire that is not fully "out" and looks at the problems and issues this raises for adults who engage in same-sex desire. Lastly, Colm Toibin's 1999 *The Blackwater Lightship* focuses somewhat obliquely on a family forced to come to terms with AIDS.

Queering the Bildungsroman

In an effort to produce an Irish homosexual identity, *Stir-fry* (1994) by Emma Donoghue and *When Love Comes to Town* (1993) by Tom Lennon, first novels for each writer, present a contemporary homosexual bildungsroman. There is something very 1990s about a homosexual bildungsroman. The bildungsroman is typically viewed as the recounting of the development of an individual from childhood to maturity. Maturity is reached and the novel ends when the individual realizes his or her place in the world after a series of life experiences that have over time a profoundly didactic impact. It is also thought of as an apprenticeship novel or novel of formation. Dickens's *Great Expectations* is a British example that follows from the original source of the genre, Goethe's *Wilhelm Meister's Apprenticeship*. The word itself, *bildungsroman,* was thought to have been coined by critic and philosopher Wilhelm Dilthey, who employs the term in reference to the work of Friedrich Schleiermacher.[7] It is interesting to put the contemporary homosexual "coming-of-age" novels in historical perspective because the 1990s coming-of-age novel also becomes the "coming-out" novel. Interesting, too, is Dilthey's hermeneutics, or "art of interpretation," which is committed to understanding and devoted to a *stable* reading of a text: "for the business of interpretation, there seems to me to be a further purpose behind such theorizing, indeed its *main* purpose," contends Dilthey, is "to preserve the general validity of interpretation against the inroads of romantic caprice and skeptical subjectivity, and to give a theoretical justification for such validity, upon which all the certainty of historical knowledge is founded."[8] In an age that interprets historical discourse without presence or empirical truth, "theoretical justification" based on the "validity" of "the certainty of historical knowledge" appears itself to be a fiction. Taking to task the bildungsroman genre's own "romantic caprice and skeptical subjectivity" and showing it to be historically sexual and gender biased may twist the genre in such as a way that we have new meaning or even a new genre that repeats the genre with difference. This form of the bildungsroman deterritorializes Dilthey and the genre.

In order to understand how these novels produce difference and deterritorialize the bildungsroman, we need to consider Dilthey's five essential elements of the genre. First, the *bildung,* or education, formation, cultivation, or shaping of the main character is essential to the genre—this young protagonist is traditionally gendered male. Second, the protagonist has a strong sense of uniqueness or individualism that in some way coincides or represents his culture, milieu, and era. Third, there is a biographical element; Dilthey believes that the author pours his experience into the text. Fourth, the psychological growth and maturation on the part of the protagonist positively affects the reader. Fifth, the individual comes into an idealized state of recognition of his human potential and directs his life toward that goal. In reference to each protagonist in *Wilhelm Meister's Apprenticeship* and *Hesperus,* Dilthey explains "how he enters life in a happy state of naiveté seeking kindred souls, finds friendship and love, how he comes into conflict with the hard realities of the world, how he grows to maturity through diverse life-experiences, finds himself, and attains certainty about his purpose in the world."[9] Dilthey acknowledges that "there had always been novels modeled on biography which followed the schooling of their heroes," and that "the most perfect example of such an account is Fielding's *Tom Jones.*"[10] But Dilthey qualifies: "the *Bildungsroman* is distinguished from all previous biographical compositions in that it intentionally and artistically depicts that which is universally human in such a life-course. The *Bildungsroman* is closely associated with the new developmental psychology established by Leibniz, with the idea of a natural education in conformity with the inner development of the psyche."[11]

One difficulty in translating the German *Bildung* into English is that the cultivation, formation, education, or coming of age are not exactly the same in contemporary Britain or Ireland (or even contemporary Germany) as they were (at least ideally) in a formal nineteenth-century German education. In the endnotes to her translation of Friedrich Ast's "Hermeneutics," Dora Van Vranken explains that Ast used *Bildung* in three ways: "forming" or "shaping," "development," and "education."[12] Van Vranken points out that "true to its concrete root-word, *Bild* (image picture), the *Bildung* still carried in Ast's time the centuries-old notion of "development" as "shaping the image of," a notion which the related word *Entwicklung* (development) does not contain." She concludes, "The meaning of the verb *bilden* parallels that of the noun. The adjective *bildlich* means 'graphic,' 'pictorial.'"[13] Historically we can see that the etymology of the word suffers a time lapse which is most glaringly seen perhaps in relation to a female bildungsroman. Historically, the English female cultivation novel supplanted the romance in late eighteenth-century England. According to Eve Tavor Bannet, "during the last decades of the eighteenth century in England, the language of *Bildung*—the language of instruction, of moral and sentimental education, and of self-cultivation—was applied, not to the lives of characters in novels, but to the desired effect of novels on the lives and characters of their largely female readership."[14] From a feminist point of view, the problem with this still popular genre (witness Jane Austen's renaissance in contemporary film versions of her novels) is that it is limited in its formula:

> Because the ideal heroine was designed as "a model" rather than a "warning" . . . and consequently allowed only one flaw—ignorance of the ways of the world—she was incapable of real moral or intellectual development. . . . This served to make her exceptional qualities seem vaguely more probable— she had had an exceptional education and upbringing, she was "unspoiled" by society. . . . The ideal heroine could be allowed to make the worldly errors it was hoped her example would help other young women to avoid, and she could be shown learning the prudence or judgement necessary to guard her in society; but since in other respects she was already all she ought to be, she could not otherwise develop.[15]

Interestingly, the first novels I will discuss in this chapter, *When Love Comes to Town* and *Stir-fry,* have aspects of the "lady novelist" formula because cultural and societal conditions regulate, although quite differently, the homosexual *bildung,* coming-out genre, as well as exploiting its didactic effect.

The queer bildungsroman also has the potential to further our understanding of the contemporary coming-of-age novel because, as queer and performance theorist Sue-Ellen Case has termed it, "the queer has been historically constituted as unnatural."[16] This argument, for example, will be used in the Lennon novel from a religious perspective by the protagonist's father. According to Case, the historical context frames homosexual desire as unnatural because it is not life-affirming—that is, non-reproductive and sterile—and is then circulated discursively at levels other than the sexual:

> Queer sexual practice, then, impels one out of the generational production of what has been called "life" and history, and ultimately out of the category of living. The equation of hetero = sex = life and homo = sex = unlife generated a queer discourse that reveled in proscribed desiring by imagining sexual objects and sexual practices within the realm of the other-than-natural, and the consequent other-than-living. In this discourse, new forms of being, or beings, are imagined through desire. And desire is that which wounds—a desire that breaks through the sheath of being as it has been imagined within a heterosexist society. Striking at its very core, queer desire punctures the life/death and generative/destructive bipolarities that enclose the heterosexist notion of being.[17]

In the novels discussed in this chapter, we will find repeated instances of the heterosexist society reacting to those who engage in homosexual desire as destructive, evil or unnatural. My original critique of Butler still stands: there is no "unnatural" or "abject" until "natural" or "human" can be fully and completely articulated. Case's statement, however, seems less invested in the ontological substance of "being"; instead, she is more concerned with the cultural and societal ethical or moral constructions of "natural" and "unnatural."

In *Stir-fry* Maria, a first-semester college student in Dublin, rents a room in a flat with two older women who just happen to be lesbian. Maria, naive and from the country, has no idea that Ruth and Jael are lesbian, which allows for a series of discoveries. Less polished perhaps is Tom Lennon's first novel, *When Love Comes to Town,* which features the coming-of-age and coming-out summer of Neil Byrne, soon-to-be UCD freshman. Perhaps a difference between these two novels and the classic bildungsroman is that the duration of the coming-of-age experience for each protagonist is presented in these contemporary novels in a few months instead of years; yet with Maria and especially with Neil there are memories from childhood that indicate the eventual direction of maturation. These scenes from childhood are key in the novel because they allow the reader to participate in a longer, ongoing process of self-discovery. For example, in *Stir-fry* Maria is discussing potential dates or boyfriends with the ultra-heterosexist Yvonne when Yvonne tells Maria, "Your problem is, your standards are too high."[18] Maria admits, "That's what my mother says," but then drifts into a memory from when she was nine: "that time she was allowed to sit up late to watch the Eurovision Song Contest, and had kept commenting how yucky the men were, with their big ears or furry chests. Mam remarked that Maria might end up an old maid, being too picky to be satisfied with any one man" (27). Similarly, in *When Love Comes to Town,* emotionally distressed Neil, dialing into RTE Marian Finucane's afternoon talk show whose topic is gays in Ireland, confesses: "'I just want to say, in reply to that last caller, that I've eh, that I've known my sexual orientation since I was ten or eleven.' Neil coughed to clear his throat. 'I didn't even know what being gay meant then, but I do know that I've always found boys more attractive than girls . . . So all his talk about evil propaganda is just rubbish . . . People like him will just have to accept that there are other human beings who are different. And I can assure him that it's not a glamorous lifestyle. In fact it's quite the opposite. It's a very lonely existence.'"[19] These passages and others in the texts show the reader that there is a progression that is consistent in the protagonist's behavior, attitudes, and emotional life.

Since Dilthey privileges the male protagonist, let us first take a closer look at *When Love Comes to Town.* Performance critic Peggy Phelan discusses the "marked" character of homosexual bodies and acts. Phelan theorizes that males cross-dress to evoke the heterosexual "real" in order not to be "marked" as homosexual: "Realness is determined by the ability to blend in, to not be noticed."[20] Even though Neil does not cross-dress he is paranoid about his behavior, manner, and speech: Does he act, gesture or talk queer? He goes to great lengths to appear to be "straight"—to be unmarked. In a discussion of the film *Paris Is Burning,* Phelan notes that the idea of attempting to "blend in" by cross-dressing creates a "paradox of using visibility to highlight invisibility" (96). Neil is popular and highlights his virility by being a star rugby player. The one glaring thing that marks him is that he does not have a steady girlfriend; this lack makes him stand out as he is constantly seen as the "spare prick" in relation to his friends, the "rhyming couplets": "Gary and Trish, Tom and Andrea, Joe and Mary, Paddy and Niamh . . . Tweedle dum, Tweedle dee, all the rhyming couplets were off to the beach—with Neil. We'll have to find you a girlfriend, Neil, one of the girls would say," and Neil, joking to hide the embarrassment, always has a comeback: "Only one?" (8). Standing out with his wit and humor in order to not stand out makes for a situation Neil detests: "he felt like he wanted to break down and tell them all about the real Neil. End all the pretence. Scream it out at the top of his voice for all the world to hear" (8).

In terms of the bildungsroman tradition, Neil also fulfills Dilthey's second characteristic of the genre by being a protagonist in a special or unique situation while at the same time reflecting the culture of his era. This occurs at two levels: the homosexual and the heterosexual level. Although Lennon's text is quite clearly, even didactically written so that we have sympathy and understanding for Neil, we are also provided a glimpse into the heterosexual matrix of Dublin in the late 1980s and early 1990s. It would have been easy to provide a monolithic portrait of the unsympathetic and prejudiced heterosexualist culture. Instead, Lennon provides degrees of acceptance of the homosexual on the part of individual heterosexuals. Neil's friend Becky and his sister Jackie and her boyfriend Liam are representatives of the "new Ireland": young, hip, and aware that homosexuality exists. All three accompany Neil to a gay bar at some point in the novel. Degrees of less acceptability are voiced by Father Donnelly and his mother, with his father, sister Kate, brother-in-law Dan, and potentially closeted old friend Gary, who reject Neil, at least initially, when it becomes known that he is homosexual. His father typically employs religion and the idea that homosexuality is "unnatural" to support his view of Neil's homosexuality: "'I told you I accept you as a homosexual, if that's what you think you are. But I don't accept *any* of your homosexual practices, it's flying in the face of God', his dad replied coldly" (151). This kind of "acceptance" is perhaps a middle-class liberal's try at acceptance, but obviously allows no room for Neil to *be* gay.

It would seem that if love is going to "come to town," then it will make its appearance in the gay bar that Neil first steps into early in the novel and subsequently visits on a regular basis. He sees the music video, "When Love Comes to Town," during his first visit to the bar and on a later visit. Song titles and popular culture are featured in many Irish novels from the 1990s. "When Love Comes to Town" is, of course, the title of a song by the Irish band U2 from their 1988 album *Rattle and Hum*. Lennon reprints some of the lyrics in his text as well as lyrics from a Sinead O'Connor song originally written by Prince and Annie Lennox's "Every Time We Say Goodbye." To be so captivated by a song that an author titles his first novel after it, that song must have some resonance in the novel, as well as indicating an impact on the author. And perhaps this aspect, however vague or slight, is the biographical element coming through the novel. Ostensibly a love song, "When Love Comes to Town," like other Bono-penned songs, has spiritual or religious meaning.[21] Similar to the speaker in the song, Neil is a lost soul or a person in need of being saved: "I was a sailor, I was lost at sea/ I was under the waves before love rescued me." This idea fits seamlessly into the *bildung* theme of the novel because "when love comes to town," Neil will find understanding and acceptance. "Love" will not "come to town" in the gay bar; the gay bar experiences will present a new world that will challenge Neil to grow as a person. Getting beaten up, meeting Shane, Daphne, Uncle Sugar, and the cross-dressers and eventually feeling at ease inside the homosexual community will all help Neil's progression to maturity.

The incident that has the most effect upon the reader is the scene outside the gay bar the night that Neil gets beaten up for being gay. The episode begins when Neil ducks out of the bar primarily to avoid the older homosexual Sugar's advances; Neil rushes out into the night to hear footsteps and then shouts of "*Faggot!*" and "*Fucking queer!*" and then the blows: "A thump in the ribs. A kick. Searing pain. Taste blood . . . On the ground. *Faggot! Queer!* Spewing hatred. Please stop. *Faggot! Fuckin' queer!*" (103). Sugar is the person who finds Neil and calls an ambulance, probably saving Neil's life. In this obvious turn of the story, Neil finds out exactly how much the hetero-sexual matrix esteems its "queers" and "faggots"; one is reminded of Butler's and other theorists' attempts to valorize by parodying words such as "queer" and "dyke" in order to produce different meanings of the words. Words ap-plied with kicks and blows seem unlikely in this context to take on a new valorized meaning: repetition of the Same is all that we come up with. "*Fag-got! Fuckin' queer!*" is not made into difference; rather, it reaffirms the power of the status quo of the heterosexual order.

A point that is not so obvious in this text, however, is the way that Sugar is subjected to the conditions established by the heterosexual matrix by Neil and other homosexuals. The older man preying upon the young Neil is so clichéd that it is amazing that Lennon used such a worn-out standard. Even his pet name is derogatory, but Sugar is never anything but helpful to Neil: initiating him into the bar scene, buying him drinks, driving him home, finding him beaten up in the alley, and "returning" his new watch. Yet Neil acts like a spoiled and coquettishly nubile girl with Sugar, which smacks of repetition of the heterosexual dating traditions and rituals—no difference. One form of power in the heterosexual matrix is derived from the sexually attractive; those who are desired for their sexual attributes have power over the less attractive. This game is played out every day, everywhere in the het-erosexual world as males desire more attractive females, and females desire more attractive males. Physically attractive people are a commodity or they help to sell a commodity through the commercialization and marketing of bodies. Neil is aware of his power over Sugar as the older man drives him home: "It dawned on him how much power he had over this middle-aged man, the poor fellow would have done anything for him. Ever willing to please, he wore his heart on his sleeve, awaiting the slightest whim from his new obsession. And Neil knew that he, of all people, should have been more sympathetic, but he also knew that any displays of sympathy were bound to be misconstrued by his lovelorn suitor. . . . It was flirtatious and cruel, he knew, but what else could he do?" (51–52). "Flirtatious and cruel," Neil's behavior is suggestive of the heterosexual matrix as he repeats the sexual power dynamic that he has been subjected to in the past. Neil is aware, as would be a young girl with an older man, that Sugar, driving a BMW and displaying a wad of cash at the bar, just might come in handy should Neil ever need to "sell" his youth and looks. These homosexual economics of sex are repetition of the Same—the heterosexist Same.

Economics indeed play a part in this novel. In *Novel and the Nation*, Gerry Smyth points out that Lennon's novel is very much a middle-class presentation of homosexuality in contemporary Dublin. Dying of AIDS, the working class "Daphne" is perhaps the novel's one realistic character portrait from the wider cross-section of gay Ireland. Neil's acquaintance with Daphne does in fact push forward his self-realization and adds to his maturation process. Yet, Smyth is critical of Lennon's class bias:

> The social and cultural milieu in which Neil circulates is obviously that of a reasonably well-off middle-class person, and this raises one of the perennial issues of queer theory—the extent to which homosexual existence is dependent upon a class discourse which it inevitably dismisses through appeals to a pre-class sexual essence. It could be argued that modern queer politics (indeed, the politics of all the new radical movements based on gender, race and sexuality) has become the constituency of social and educational elite which because of its background and training is better positioned to expose the contradictions of the *straightgeist*. By the same token, the privileged middle-class homosexual is as a rule more confident of his/her validity within the community as a whole.[22]

Academically speaking, Smyth may be correct; however, the one incident that puts Neil in the working-class milieu, visiting Daphne at his mom's apartment, makes him realize that his middle-class background is yet another kind of tourniquet cutting off his ability to be homosexual and in this way dismantles middle-class biases. Neil arrives by taxi with Shane to the lower-class area of Dublin where Daphne lives with his mother. Daphne's presence is announced by the graffiti scrawled on the wall: *"Eddie O'Reilly Is Bent"* (142). Despite the unfriendly neighborhood announcement, Neil is surprised by the openness and support shown to Daphne by his family and family friends. Strategically, Lennon places this scene near the end of Neil and Shane's visit:

> Daphne's sister went into the kitchen and her three friends stood in the hallway, doing their utmost to pretend that they weren't listening to Neil.
> "I'd like to book a taxi please . . ."
> Daphne's sister had rejoined her friends by the time Neil had finished his phonecall.
> "You're Neil, aren't yeh?" she smiled.
> "Yeah." Neil was taken aback.
> "Me bruds told me all 'bout yeh."
> "Did he?" Neil felt his face burning.
> "Don't worry, we don't give a fuck if yer gay," she said. "Do we girls?"
> Her three friends shook their heads, and Neil could see that they meant it.
> Then Daphne's sister stretched up onto her tippy toes and kissed Neil's cheek.
> "Thanks for visitin' him," she said.

> Neil just grinned at her. He couldn't think what to say. It wasn't everyday
> that he met four young girls with such liberal views. (147)

On the one hand, it is very easy to disparage this scene as token trip into Dublin's underside, not only lower-class digs, but also a visit with an HIV-infected patient in these lower-class digs. On the other hand, it is this experience that convinces Neil that he must tell his parents that he is homosexual: "in the backseat of that taxi, Neil made one of the biggest decisions of his life. Seeing Daphne the way he was had changed his life forever, he was going to tell his mum and dad" (148). In this passage, Neil makes a life-changing decision that is indicative of bildungsroman genre—the protagonist must make "a reasonably direct line from error to truth, from confusion to clarity, from uncertainty to certainty."[23]

Therefore, Neil's visit, however token and however middle-class a gesture, does function in this bildungsroman to push the "hero" into the confrontation that will lead him to greater truth, clarity, and certainty. The interesting feature of a "queer" *bildungs* is that the protagonist does not simply develop or realize his potential in a normative or traditional manner; rather, the homosexual protagonist achieves maturity in this novel by "coming out," which is a gesture of self-acceptance and self-realization. And yet, the entire reason for the coming of age and the coming out is that Neil in this instance must struggle against his familial, religious, cultural, and societal regulative practices. In order for "love to come to town," Neil needs to be accepted as "different," something that the end of the novel does *not* provide because his parents, his old friends to some extent, and his family accept him as a homosexual, but not as a practicing homosexual. They accept him as an asexual person:

> "Shane," his mum prompts.
>
> His dad nods. "Yes, Shane. She tells me that you weren't actually, you know . . ."
>
> Neil watches his dad contort his face in embarrassment, unable to bring himself to say those words. But now Neil understands the conditions. We'll love you, providing you hide your love away. . . . They always told him to tell the truth, but now it was clear to him that they didn't want to hear the truth. (174–175)

As a bildungsroman, *When Love Comes to Town* deterritorializes the genre by suggesting that a full realization of self and human potential is inextricably tied to coming *completely* out of the closet. While Neil's parents feel that he has completely come out about his homosexuality, Neil does not feel the same way. So do we have a botched bildungsroman (or is the homosexual version of the coming-of-age novel impossible because the heterosexual matrix will not let it come out) or more persuasively a deterritorialized bildungsroman?

Still, "Neil understands the conditions," and so we do have a developmental novel—perhaps even more so because Neil sees that maturity as a gay person in a heterosexual familial and cultural matrix means operating in the threshold of being and becoming. "Hiding his love away" literally means hiding the sexual body and its practices away from his parents and others who cannot bear to think about Neil's sexual life. As Sue-Ellen Case states, the "other-than-natural" desire "wounds—a desire that breaks through the sheath of being as it has been imagined within heterosexist society," and, I would add, traditional middle-class Irish Catholic society. The conditions for understanding for Neil dictate that his body is not to have any sexual movement so that homosexual-as-static entity is acceptable, but homosexual as a moving body is unacceptable. As I suggested earlier, *When Love Comes to Town* has something in common with the "lady-novelist" bildungsroman. Lennon's novel and the eighteenth-century female protagonist have agency only up to a certain point, as we recall Tavor Bannet's comment: "The ideal heroine could be allowed to make the worldly errors it was hoped her example would help other young women to avoid, and she could be shown learning the prudence or judgement necessary to guard her in society; but since in other respects she was already all she ought to be, she could not otherwise develop." In the same way, Neil is always already homosexual while his ability to be accepted by his family and friends is limited and his body restricted.

Neil has completed his "education" and maturation of self, but the self without movement is destined to be stymied. Neil has learned that his body is trapped in a heterosexual matrix that regulates his functions as a gendered and sexed body which must conform to preestablished rules of power and behavior. If we take the idea of becoming and open the space of the body and gender, then we will have no preestablished ideas of what we are *supposed* to think about the body and gender. Lennon's text, however, gives us the full range of the expected in terms of Neil's threat to the heterosexual order. One of the most telling scenes of heterosexual regulation and control is Neil's sister and brother-in-law's response to "Uncle Neil" interacting with their two kids. Lennon deliberately makes the scenes with Neil and his niece bookends in the novel. We meet Annie in the first few pages of the novel as she bursts into Uncle Neil's bedroom; this initial episode shows his popularity and trustworthiness as an uncle-figure. This situation changes after Neil comes out and his sister visits:

> Then the two gleeful children raced in the room. They made a bee-line for
> their Uncle Neil, but Dan stopped them in their tracks. Neil saw the flash of

blind panic in his brother-in-law's eyes as he held the two protesting children firmly in his grasp.

"Stop that screaming!" Kate snapped, slapping Danny on the bottom.
Unclean, unclean, ring my leper's bell. (165)

Lennon is playing out all the fears of the heterosexualist matrix with this scene: the prejudiced idea that "queers" are warped pederasts who will pervert and abuse children if given a chance. By the end of the novel, Kate and the brother-in-law plan to bring the kids over to see Uncle Neil, but Lennon's point has been made: the blind reaction is fear and repulsion. This scene serves to produce a desired effect on the reader that is the novel's second common aspect with the eighteenth-century women writers. The effect of this scene is different than the effect created when Neil gets beaten up outside the bar. The residual supposed sleaziness of the late-night gay bar scene is difficult to banish, and so even though one feels that Neil is victimized by homophobic hatred, he has put himself in a risky situation by going to the bar. The latter situation, however, when Neil has confessed his homosexuality and attempts to reconcile with his family, who reject him, does have an emotive effect, even perhaps a sentimentalized or melodramatized situation, in which Lennon nevertheless achieves his effect.

A similar reaction occurs in *Stir-fry* when seventeen-year-old UCD freshman Maria experiences repulsion when she first voyeuristically observes her two "roommates," Jael and Ruth, making love in front of the fireplace in the living room of their shared flat: "Furled up in the fetal position, the quilt over her head, Maria waited for calm. She thought perhaps she was going to throw up, but it was too far to the bathroom, so she swallowed it down" (98). Despite the fact that Maria had quite recently "copped on" (after living with Jael and Ruth a month) to the fact that her roommates are lesbian, naive Maria had never heard the guttural sounds that a woman having an orgasm makes. Conscious of her naiveté and her culchie (country Irish) standing in the big city, Dublin, Maria's bildungsroman movement from confusion to clarity and from uncertainty to certainty is self-conscious throughout the novel. Maria *knows* that she is in process. One might consider Maria a 1990s parody of Caithleen in Edna O'Brien's *The Country Girls;* Caithleen in O'Brien's novel also comes from the West and comes of age in Dublin. Gerry Smyth also recognizes the bildungsroman aspects of *Stir-fry* but does not recognize the irony and deterritorialization of a coming-out novel in the context of the tradition of the genre.[24] In the novel we have a female protagonist's formation or education and we have the idea that Maria is unique or individualistic. However, Maria's uniqueness is often simply portrayed as her inability to be a "normal" freshman and engage in the "normal" activities like dating, drinking, and dances. Maria's friend Yvonne is a strategic, almost "stock," character in the novel because she provides the essential contrast to Maria.

Obsessed with her looks, her on-again, off-again boyfriend Pete, and her general standing in the popularity charts, Yvonne is the voice of normality when Maria reveals her roommates' sexual orientation:

> "I just hope no one jumps to the wrong conclusions about you, Maria."
> "Sorry?"
> Yvonne had got her breath back. "Just because you live with them, I mean. Not that anyone would be likely to, since you've got hair down to your shoulders and you often wear skirts. Well, fairly often."
> Maria rested her forehead on the heel of her hand. "Look, they're both very nice. And they wear skirts sometimes, too."
> "Oh, I know," said Yvonne wisely, "but they'd have to, wouldn't they, as cover?" (76–77)

Indeed "wisely," Yvonne understands the need to be unmarked and that lesbians would not dress in drag to be unmarked, but would rather dress as straight heterosexual females "as cover" for their subversive sexual identities. Passing as a heterosexual is most important to Yvonne; in fact, for her it is socially and practically inconceivable to be anything but straight and normal. Passing, too, has become an act of survival for those who are different. According to Carole-Anne Tyler in "Passing: Narcissism, Identity, and Difference," we live in an "era of the passing of *passing* as a politically viable response to oppression. . . . For the mark of passing successfully is the lack of a mark of passing, of a signifier of some difference from what one seems to be."[25] Yvonne, then, would agree with Tyler that to pass successfully as a heterosexual when you know that you are a homosexual trying to pass or, according to Butler, perform heterosexual means that you "lack" the "mark of passing." Of course, Yvonne is attributing a kind of contrived agency on the part of Jael and Ruth, in this instance, that they may or may not have. In other words, is it possible to be lesbian and not bear bodily or material signs that the heterosexual community can read as a "mark" of passing? Neil worries about passing as a heterosexual in *When Love Comes to Town* and Yvonne worries about it for Maria because Maria claims not to see the "marks" of Ruth's and Jael's homosexuality.

The question of passing and bearing a mark or a sign of one's sexual identity is a curious aspect of Western culture. Ostensibly, the history of this mark is clearly to separate males from females for reasons of mating and for civic and domestic duties; yet a Foucauldian view of marking the body would point to the fact that marking the body is an excellent device for regulating society at several levels: sexuality, gender, class, region, religion, and race. Midway through the novel, Maria is on the threshold; she is becoming-homosocial and becoming-homosexual. The issue of passing unmarked has not yet manifested itself. There are, however, two actions, two becomings that will serve to "mark" Maria. The first occurrence happens early in the text when Maria and Yvonne are checking out the university social scene. Yvonne mentions that she has cramps, Maria offers aspirin, and when Yvonne declines, the text states: "It occurred to Maria to reach down and stroke the bent head, but she thought better of it" (28). Why this very nuanced gesture? Perhaps the answer lies in the second incident. The second becoming-passage is during the bus trip home with Ruth from a feminist meeting. Discussing the merits of an all women's group, Ruth gets irritated with Maria and states, "'I can tell I'm boring you; if it's not your scene, just forget it'" (58). What follows reiterates the first example: "Maria was considering whether, and then how, to say sorry, when the bus trundled round the corner. It jogged them home, cold and wordless. In her head, as ever, the words flowed easily: *I have no wish to hurt you,* and *teach me,* and *the room is warmer when you're in it.* Covertly, she watched the reflection of Ruth's dark curls bump against the window beside her. Once their eyes met in the glass, and they almost smiled" (58). This passage is a repetition of the first passage; it adds something as it deterritorializes heterosexual desire, and this works to supplement the meaning of the first instance. Because the first passage is so slight, the reader may have not noticed the first same-sex attraction displayed by Maria, but surely this incident cannot be misconstrued. Maria is at a liminal stage of her sexual-becoming. These scenes show that Maria's same-sex desire is slowing surfacing, slowly deterritorializing stable heterosexual normality.

From the above passage between Yvonne and Maria concerning clothes and hair, we see Yvonne begin her struggle to keep Maria on her side of the heterosexual-homosexual line, but, true to bildungsroman form, Maria will seek her individuality apart from Yvonne. Her quest for individuality is a sign of the times, especially for young women coming of age in the 1990s in Ireland, albeit Yvonne's 1950s attitudinal throwback. As a representative of her age, Maria's eventual coming out colludes with the novel's biographical element, the third aspect in Dilthey's formulation. Donoghue, who is well known in Ireland as a novelist, has also published scholarly work, *Passions Between Women: British Lesbian Culture 1668–1801* (1993) and has edited an anthology, *What Sappho Would Have Said: Four Centuries of Love Poems Between Women* (1997), as well as *Kissing the Witch* (1997), a collection of feminist fairy tales. In *Novel and the Nation* she is characterized as a leading public lesbian figure: "In recent years Emma Donoghue has become one of Ireland's most public lesbian figures. Scholar, playwright and novelist, Donoghue's work tapped into the wider libertarian movements overtaking the country and in its turn helped to raise the profile of homosexuality throughout Irish life."[26] Yet, in a recent interview with Stacia Bensyl, Donoghue acknowledges that coming out for Irish lesbians is still not a widespread practice:

> And in Ireland there's a general ethos of sort of making do with what you've got, as it were. I would say one particular aspect of the Irish lesbian and gay world rather than that world in any other country is that vast numbers are still in the closet. It's not as bad as it used to be, but still most people live with the closet in some form or another. I know a lot of people who are very out and proud when they're in Dublin, but back home down the country not a word to the family, and it might be the same about jobs, so there's a lot of living in two worlds. It's not that they're entirely in the closet, it's that there are things they speak about with their friends and there are things they speak about with their parents and that's two different kinds of conversation, so there's a real ethos of accommodation and working around conflict rather than facing it head on.[27]

The biographical aspects may be easy to interpret and use to identify Donoghue, but with the contemporary female coming-out and coming-of-age bildungsroman, I am skeptical that the author's life has much relevancy, beyond the incidental, to an interpretation of the text. The most compelling case for identification may reside with Donoghue's author-function—the textual narrative gains a kind of credibility.[28] In any case, we can say that Donoghue's fiction is heavily framed in the gay/lesbian context that contains a parallel in the life of the Irish gay community in the 1990s.

The fourth point of the psychological maturation of the protagonist in the bildungsroman form is certainly evident in the psychological maturation of Maria. Again, Maria is self-conscious of her lack of experience and says repeatedly to Jael and Ruth that she envies their maturity and experience, while they, of course, envy her youth. Jael turns thirty in the text and Ruth is twenty-three. Participating in heterosexual stereotypes to some extent, Jael plays the text's womanizer and Ruth the "battered wife" role, which leads Maria on more than one occasion to asks Ruth why she puts up with Jael's behavior. Donoghue has very clearly created Ruth and Jael as the quintessential butch-femme couple. Monique Wittig calls the butch-femme a "double-play" wherein sameness is coupled with difference, whereas Sue-Ellen Case's essay, "Toward a Butch-Femme Aesthetic," makes dressing up or dressing down stereotypically a site of difference.[29] According to Marilyn R. Farwell in *Heterosexual Plots and Lesbian Narratives,* lesbian narratives construct the butch-femme in order to show the heterogeneity of same-sex desire:

> As a parody of sex-gender alignment, the single subject of the butch-femme couple enacts the artificiality of gender difference through clothing and

personality. Clothing in particular becomes a trope for the artificiality of gender systems based on "natural" bodies. Both members of the lesbian couple cross-dress, not only one as masculine, but also the other as an exaggerated version of the feminine, with lipstick, high heels, and a short skirt. Ripe for metaphorical implications, the butch-femme couple is culture's version, its nightmare, of the female grotesque body, appropriating all sexuality to its sphere and control.[30]

Despite the fact Ruth does not wear lipstick or high heels, she is the feminine partner in the dyad; Jael, meanwhile, not only dresses for her butch role but more significantly enacts the stereotypical masculine role. I will come back to Ruth and Jael in my discussion of *Hood* because Donoghue has carryover from her first novel to the second, including the surreptitious move to insert Ruth into the last chapter.

What is important for our present reading is that the psychological games being played out between Jael and Ruth are too sophisticated for Maria, who expects everything to be black and white and people to say what they mean. In this, her youth, as well as her rural upbringing presents itself. And so, we have a twin psychological development unfolding in Maria: the dawning awareness that the game of erotics is hardly straightforward or predictable, and an urban sophistication and maturation that comes to bear on her own sexual orientation by the end of the novel and that she could not have obtained had she not come to the city. As these two forces unravel in the novel we are into the fifth aspect of the bildungsroman—full realization of the self's potential and the movement from error to truth, from confusion to clarity, from uncertainty to certainty.

Returning to the beginning of the text to the scene in which Yvonne accuses Maria of having an unreasonable standard when it comes to men ("Your problem is, your standards are too high" [27]), in addition to remembering that the men on the "Eurovision Song Contest" were "yucky" "with their big ears or furry chests," Maria also remembers that that night she went to bed and worried about the future. Every woman Maria knew at the age of nine is now a wife and mother except for a few teachers and "the young ones heading for the Uni . . . And of course Nelly the Nutter, who sat on the steps of the Town Hall, scratching her ankles" (27). At nine years old Maria "could not sleep for worrying what she would turn out to be" (27). Nelly the Nutter, oddly enough, is the one character who never appears in real time in the text, and yet Nelly haunts Maria's memories and stories throughout the text. At this point in the text, Nelly is presented as a female alternative: wife, mother, teacher, nutter. The possibility that Nelly was once like Maria seems to be a worrisome thought to Maria. What would make a female turn out like Nelly?

Later in the story, while vacuuming at her nighttime office-cleaning job, Maria thinks about a story her mother told her that week on the telephone concerning Nelly: "the town council had tried to house Nelly the Nutter in a cottage beside the chicken factory. One businessman fitted it up with basic furniture; another provided a second-hand vacuum-cleaner for her to keep the place nice. A visiting social worker found Nelly sitting on the floor beside the vacuum-cleaner, which had been on at full suction for five days. Nelly said she liked the sound. She wheeled the vacuum behind her when she went back to her rug under the bridge" (152). Donoghue offers the reader the full spectrum of womanhood in Ireland and suggests through the frequent mentions in the text of Nelly that women outside acceptable or normal modes of behavior end up on the other side of the boundary—under a bridge with a rug and silent vacuum-cleaner. Of all the stories to insert it would seem that Nelly functions as a perspective "role model" of the social deviant perhaps not unlike the way Ruth and Jael function as role models for a homosexual in a traditional heterosexual society. Our protagonist will not, of course, end up like Nelly, though she is perceptive enough to acknowledge the possibility, because she is a unique individual on her way to understanding and maturation. Worrying about "what she would turn out to be" is a characteristic of Maria, who is still preoccupied and introspective at seventeen years of age: "how much farther had she got with that question in eight years, she asked herself wryly" (27). This tendency is certainly in line with the genre of the bildungsroman, and Maria's memories provide the necessary period of maturation by showing a continuum of time.

For much of the novel Maria is engaged in two major pursuits: one, trying to find some way to "stand out" or to make herself distinct from others, and, two, trying to find a male partner or boyfriend. The first endeavor is perhaps most characteristically presented when she cuts her hair, assuming a "punk" style; her intention, so she says, is to look older and less like a culchie. Even Ruth and Jael are surprised, whereas Yvonne is shocked; the reader infers that she looks more "butch" than "punk." Interestingly, Maria's unrequited love-from-afar, Damian, begins to notice Maria after her radical shearing, which adds up only later when Jael informs Maria that Damian is bisexual. In effect, with her new haircut Maria has homosexually marked herself in a socially—even heterosexually—predictable way long before she knows that she desires women. Maria is "becoming-queer" but perhaps not at a conscious level. Yvonne, the voice of heterosexual reason, tries to convince Maria that she has should move out of the flat after she finds out about Jael and Ruth. Believing that her friend has been sucked into a bad, if not dangerous, situation, Yvonne tells Maria that "they got a month's rent out of you on false pretences" (80). When Maria denies Jael's and Ruth's culpability, she places herself in her flatmates' shoes: "They probably assumed I

knew" (80). Knowing that the standard in society is the heterosexual hegemony, Yvonne shoots back: "That's outrageous. I mean, it's not the first
thing that's going to spring into your head when you go househunting, is it?
I mean, you don't say to yourself, oh yes, must check whether my flatmates
are lesbian lovers, just in case!" (80). As a mark of distinction and difference,
Maria does not want to move out, even though she was shocked to discover
that Jael and Ruth are lesbian lovers, and so she stalls the conversation:

> "I appreciate your looking after me, I really do. Now, will you kindly lay off?
> I've been busy with my job; four evenings this week. I haven't had time to
> think whether I'll be moving out of not."
>   "What's to keep you there?"
>   "For one thing, I like them."
>   "I know you do, Maria, you're a very friendly person." Yvonne hugged her
> knees in exasperation. "But they're hardly your sort. I mean, don't you find
> them a bit, you know?"
>   "A bit what?"
>   She squirmed slightly. "Butch and ranty." (80–81)

Similar to the clothes and hair issue, lesbians are marked by a certain behavior. Hypermasculine, loud, rude, and raving are the marks that Jael and
Ruth supposedly bear. While Yvonne is a fairly innocuous individual, basically repeating what she's heard, picked up, or seen on television or in the
movies, she is not so innocent when we see her as representative of a much
larger cultural machine. Yvonne's small part in the proliferating of heterosexual values keeps the machine running smoothly. Her kind of name calling and labeling, not to mention misinformation, keeps order in the
heterosexual sphere; identified and marked, homosexual bodies are much
easier to segregate and regulate.

    Another female representative who is even more entrenched in the het-
erosexual matrix is Maria's mother, who is characterized as a devout Catholic
mother and homemaker from the west of Ireland. Maria goes home after an
awkward incident in Dublin that is a major turning point in the coming-out
and coming-of-age process. During Christmastime festivities, Jael, probably
having had too much whiskey, finds herself alone with Maria and, ever ag-
gressive, seizes the moment:

> "No mistletoe," said Jael briefly, and bent round to kiss her.
>   Later, trying to remember whether it was a short or a long kiss, an accept-
> able peck or a dangerous fusion. Maria had no idea. It was somehow balanced
> on the knife-edge between these definitions when Ruth's head came through
> the skylight. In the second her eyes took to get used to the dark, the others
> had lurched apart.

"Oh, sorry," said Ruth. The blank oval of her face disappeared down the hole. (188)

Jael very quickly "makes up" with Ruth, but unknown to Maria, Ruth has had a fear that Jael will want Maria over herself. This situation will play itself out at the very end of the text. Meanwhile, Maria has taken the train home, making the move backward on the road to progress, but this also can be part of the genre: "If the life of the world consists in the alternation of unfolding and enclosing, venturing out and returning to the self, then why is it not also to with the heart of man?"[31] In this case, Maria encloses and returns to her family and to what is familiar after several months of decisively unfamiliar surroundings, situations, and people. Yet, on her way home on the train, Maria remembers another early experience that once again connects the present Maria to the becoming-mature Maria. The memory involves a school friend, Nuala, with whom Maria skipped class, slipping "out into the back field to lie in the long grass and eat Kola Kubes" (194). The memory however fixes on the "odd time Nuala's eyes might catch hers in a lingering stare, and Maria would wait, but then the pale eyes would drop and the next remark always banal. That was all—no scandal" (194). The significance for Maria is that she now realizes that Nuala was the first person to excite her homoerotic feelings, and the "scandal," of course, is levied in the present as a value judgment.

Having already spent a disastrous weekend at home in the fall with Yvonne, Maria knows that "home" has changed for her, as she thinks, "What a boring little house" (194). Maria hears her mother on the telephone to Thelma, the aunt with whom Maria first lived in Dublin before taking the flat with Jael and Ruth, discussing a young unmarried pregnant girl who plans to keep her baby. The discussion alludes to Ireland's anti-abortion law that makes it necessary for those seeking an abortion to go to England: "'I suppose we should be grateful. Thousands of Irish girls going over on the night boat every year, they say. Terrible'" (195). The telephone conversation suddenly shifts in a direction that indicates that Maria's mother does not know about Maria's life in Dublin or her mental turmoil: "Her tone brightened. 'My own lassie? Came down early this morning. Oh, the hair, yes indeed.' And a cackle of laughter as she listened. 'No word yet, but maybe she's shy of mentioning names. Oh, I'm sure. The studies seem to be going all right, though she's not killing herself with work. Is that the truth? Aren't they all? Still, so long as she keeps well and passes her exams. The laddibucks can wait!' Her voice spiralled up into laughter again" (195). Overhearing her mother, Maria "wanted to walk into the hall, take the receiver from her mother's hand, and batter her across the forehead with it," (195) but she slipped outside instead. What is interesting, too, is that

Donoghue skillfully manages to insert on one page of text: unwed mothers-to-be, abortion, anti-abortion, her daughter's new "butch" appearance, her unmentioned but surely apparent "laddibucks," and Maria's anger and confusion at being wedged into that seemingly "abject" space, to borrow from Butler, of being neither heterosexual nor homosexual. Maria wants "Someone, anyone, to ring her up and ask her out and take these maddening questions out of her head" (153). Maria is teetering on the threshold, and her mother and her family at this point cannot begin to understand her homosexual becoming—which is made clear without a confrontation (unlike Neil's situation in Lennon's novel).

But Maria is not "abject," of course, she is rather becoming-women because she is now in an imperceptible space; she cannot make proper sense of her situation and feelings, though she tries, and the reader cannot completely enter into that space either. As we discussed in chapter 1, the theory of becoming- becoming-woman, is a way to overcome sexual bipolarization. There is no becoming-man because man is the regulatory norm, which means it is stable and in a position of authority; becoming-man would be Butler's compulsory heterosexuality. Although anyone can pass through becoming-woman, at this point in the text Maria is becoming-woman, *not* because she is potentially homosexual but because she is undecided and imperceptible. Yet, Deleuze and Guattari indicate that "the principle problem concerning this new threshold of deterritorialization of the voice is no longer that of a properly vocal becoming-woman or becoming-child, but that of a becoming-molecular."[32] Becoming-molecular is imperceptible deterritorializaton, a becoming that unrolls movement as a series of events, but one cannot stay interminably on the threshold. Neil, for example, is not allowed to fully become-imperceptible; his movement is arrested, his becoming-woman cut off.

True to the bildungsroman, the novel closes over this imperceptibility, crosses the threshold: how could you have a hero remain imperceptible when she or he must move from confusion to clarity and from uncertainty to certainty. Yet, as in *When Love Comes to Town*, queering the bildungsroman genre means that something "queer" indeed must happen to the protagonist. In Lennon's novel we have halfway measures; Neil is "out" and comes to an understanding. However, his understanding is that his family and the culture at large do not want him to be "out" sexually. And this situation has an uncanny likeness to the eighteenth-century lady-novelist phenomena: cultivate, yes, but only so much, and under very restricted cultural and societal circumstances. With *Stir-fry* we have an equally unsatisfactory conclusion. On the one hand, Maria cultivates an understanding of herself at the very end of the novel by leaving to find Ruth. On the other hand, because the novel terminates with the "what if" open-endedness of Maria simply standing before Ruth on Ruth's mother's doorstep, Maria does not deal with, let alone resolve, the larger cultural and societal challenges that go with the protagonist's realization of her full potential as a human being.

The realization of one's self must take place in the context of one's milieu and one's era. Not to do so is to violate the genre's form, and once again we have a queer version of the bildungsroman, which in this novel seems closer to Case's prescriptive, "Queer sexual practice, then, impels one out of the generational production of what has been called 'life' and history, and ultimately out of the category of living." Perhaps this is the case because *Stir-fry* reneges on its duty to "come out" actively along with the "coming of age" scenario. On the one hand, *Stir-fry* has a clean end; on the other hand, the novel simply ends, which invites the reader to imagine Maria replacing Jael in her butch role in the butch-femme dyad. Has Donoghue simply avoided the issue? We get a glimpse of the kind of reaction Maria would encounter if she were to "come out" to her family when Maria speculates on her mother's reaction to the confusion concerning those "maddening questions" in "her head": "In her [mother's] experience girls started out as ambitious as the lads, but by the age of twenty they were usually itching to settle down with someone nice and put up curtains. Maria had poured scorn on this argument. . . . She told her mother that this was just one more stereotype of female behavior which, given enough career guidance, newspaper articles and flat-heeled shoes, would evaporate. Mam said she would believe it when she saw it" (153). Because Donoghue has made Maria's mother so culchie and so traditional, it makes it impossible for her protagonist to confide in or come to her own mother. It is unlikely that "career guidance, newspaper articles and flat-heeled shoes" are going to be enough preparation for her mother to hear that her daughter does not fancy putting up curtains with a man but does fancy putting up curtains—and more—with a woman.

Returning to the effect that the novel may have on the reader, we have a curious situation. While effect is admittedly difficult to determine from reader to reader, *Stir-fry* could function as a self-help guide, not unlike *When Love Comes to Town,* to one on the threshold of homosexual-becoming. In this way, the contemporary convention's effect would not be sanctioned by an eighteenth-century sensibility or by contemporary heterosexual standards. In terms of the limit of the homosexual's sphere, Maria's ability to come out, Donoghue has limited her sphere of power and control, as do the lady novelists, by not making her come out pro-actively. In Lennon's novel, Neil at least comes out and then the parameters are set; Donoghue, however, has deliberately set her own limit by not allowing the reader to participate in the protagonist's actual coming out to know where the homosexual—Irish lesbian—coming-of-age boundary lies.

Coming Out

Donoghue's second novel, *Hood* (1994), connects to *Stir-fry* because it could be viewed in terms of a continuation of the first novel's story. In *Hood* we are presented with a lesbian couple, Pen O'Grady, the narrator, and her lover, Cara Wall, who have been together since they were about seventeen, and it is now some thirteen years later. Ostensibly, the novel is about loss and about grieving; the narrative covers Pen's week following her learning that Cara has been killed in a car accident. Many aspects of Ruth's and Jael's personalities appear in the characters of Pen and Cara; the most blatant similarity is that Ruth and Pen are the monogamous, sometimes suffering partners, whereas Jael and Cara each keep the long-term relationship going as they actively survey and play the field. Other aspects of Irish lesbian life appear in both novels. Because I was focusing on Maria's coming of age and coming out, I did not provide much discussion on Jael and Ruth's relationship. Indeed this relationship in *Stir-fry* deserves more consideration than I can reasonably provide in the present context.

A brief consideration of the butch-femme dynamic in *Stir-fry*, however, would be helpful in setting up a context with which to interpret *Hood*. As previously mentioned, Marilyn Farwell views the butch-femme couple as "a parody of sex-gender alignment, the single subject of the butch-femme couple enacts the artificiality of gender difference through clothing and personality. Clothing in particular becomes a trope for the artificiality of gender systems based on 'natural' bodies." Donoghue makes us very aware of the dress and mannerisms of all of her characters in both novels. Ruth's and Jael's gender artificialities function in equal distribution: Ruth has saved up from a civil servant job to go to college and is devoted to her studies, and she cooks, keeps house, wears feminine clothes, participates in feminist and gay and lesbian groups and is monogamous; Jael is independently wealthy, has traveled all over Europe, and repeatedly flunks out of college, and she wears black leather jackets, trousers, drinks whiskey, has a volatile temper, cruises the gay bar scene and is not monogamous.

Sue-Ellen Case believes that the origin of the butch-femme paradigm is to be found in Freudian psychoanalyst Joan Riviere's work and is published in Riviere's article, "Womanliness as a Masquerade."[33] According to Riviere, an intellectual or professional woman can perform in society or in her profession only if she shows that she has "'possession of her father's penis, having castrated him.'"[34] Case's reading of Riviere means that to "recompense for this castration, which resided in her intellectual proficiency, she donned the mask of womanliness."[35] The donning of the mask means that the woman performs a masquerade. The problem is that the heterosexual woman cannot "claim possession openly, but through reaction-formations;

whereas homosexual women openly display their possession of the penis and count on the males' recognition of defeat."[36] Case believes that this phenomena occurs in the butch-femme couple with the butch playing the role of proud possessor of daddy's penis and the femme masquerading as heterosexualist who cannot openly possess the penis. Case theorizes that these roles work together: "The femme . . . foregrounds her masquerade by playing to a butch, another woman in a role; likewise, the butch exhibits her penis to a woman who is playing the role of compensatory castration."[37] Jael's randy penis-bearing behavior is exhibited throughout the novel. Climbing the stairs to the flat one night, Maria hears a scream, silence, then "'Jael, get off me this instant, I mean it'" (108). Moreover, Jael flaunts the fact that former lovers keep in touch with her:

> Ruth's answer was cut off when Jael handed over her postcard. She looked down at the blue and white village scene, glowing under the sun. "What's this?"
> "Read it," said Jael brightly. "She's on Mykynos."
> Ruth handed it back. "No, thanks, it's yours." She turned away to finish the washing-up.
> Jael brushed past Maria at the door of the bathroom and murmured, "What do you bet she read the whole postcard coming up the stairs?" (97)

Significantly, Jael is proud of her past conquests and wants others to know about them, especially her current lover. Ruth is not only the spurned woman; she is also the masquerading heterosexual "wifey" washing up as her man/husband/butch/woman reclines on the sofa.

Donoghue updates her butch-femme couple in *Hood* by making them older and by blurring their edges a bit. Pen, like Ruth, finished college and then took a job at Immaculate Conception Convent where she teaches grammar to schoolage girls; she cooks, keeps house, wears feminine clothes, and is now overweight with, the reader infers, a rather voluptuous figure; Cara, like Jael, although she is not independently wealthy, has still traveled all over Europe, and has never worked a steady job, she wears "butch" clothes such as T-shirts that are tie-dyed or that bear various gay pride and lesbian mottos (e.g., "IF THE TRUTH COULD BE TOLD . . ."), cruises the Amazon Attic scene and is not monogamous. An interesting twist in this novel is the fact that we only have one person who presents the butch-femme couple. In *Hood,* Pen is the only half of the couple we have in the present; Pen without Cara or Pen lost in memory, reimagining Cara. Donoghue deterritorializes the butch-femme distinction at the end of the novel by the suggestion that Ruth will replace Cara; the femme-femme combination renders the heterosexual idea of opposites, male/female, as the "natural" formula obsolete. In fact, person-by-person and level-by-level, *Hood* pulls apart a normalized heterosexual reading strategy. *Hood* presents us with flowing and rolling boundaries of body, identity, and sexuality.

Still, the novel does not explicitly challenge the heterosexual matrix's boundaries, but perhaps more effectively throughout the text it is apparent that these lines are no longer applicable. To fight against or challenge the heterosexual norm is a passé game in this era. The novel presents the heterosexual status quo as inept and out of touch with what is going on in other spheres. A prime example of this phenomenon occurs at Pen's last confession:

> I was only halfway through my opening prayers when he muttered, "Good girl now. Tell me do you smoke?"
> "No, Father."
> "Do you drink?"
> "No, Father."
> "Do you give cheek to your mammy and daddy?"
> "No, Father."
> "Have you a boyfriend tell me now?"
> "No."
> "If you had a boyfriend, would you do bad stuff with him?"
> "No."
> "Aren't you the great girl. You have the conscience of a saint. Say a nice act of contrition now."
>
> While I was saying it he began the absolution, and he was finished before me. I sat on the window-sill outside, bewildered by the unearned compliments. It became clear to me at last that my story just didn't show up in their terms. I never much bothered after that.[38]

Rather comically, the Foucauldian analysis—savoring every detail of sin and bodily pleasure—is not available in 1970s Ireland because even the notion that a young woman could be homosexual was not or could not be thought. The priest's assumptions restate Moira Gatens's argument in "Corporeal Representation in/and the Body Politic"; Gatens points out that "the body politic" assumes a universalizing male voice that further obfuscates the actual workings of power and relations of bodies. From Gatens's feminist philosophical perspective, the sovereign, "the will of the people," or "the body politic" all produce false unity and in turn falsify the very terms with which power and bodies can be analyzed: "The unified body functions, in political theory, to achieve two important effects. First, the artificial man incorporates and so controls and regulates women's bodies in a manner which does not undermine his claim to autonomy, since her contributions are neither visible nor acknowledged."[39] The body politic in the form of the priest regulates Pen's body by setting the terms for her transgressions: smoking, drinking, disobedience to parents, heterosexual sexual activity. The priest does not acknowledge any other literally "unspeakable" sins because they do not or cannot exist: "Second, insofar as he can maintain this apparent unity through incorporation, he is not required to acknowledge difference. The metaphor functions to restrict our political vocabulary to one voice only: a voice that can speak of only *one* body, *one* reason, and *one* ethic."[40] Pen's body is over the boundary of this *one* body of heterosexual patriarchal order.

Perhaps the most disturbing aspect of Pen's confessional episode is that the patriarchal representative of the heterosexual order is not equipped to recognize that there could be sexual difference available to Pen; there seems to be no *language* available with which to state this kind of difference—or at least no language heterosexual order can comprehend. Language or discourse controls what we know and can know because we think and make distinctions in language; therefore, it is self-evident that control over discourse is power and this power in turn controls and regulates bodies and the body's movements. Language in the form of slogans or signs in *Hood* reflects popular culture (such as the above-mentioned T-shirt) and the availability of inexpensive semiotic gestures. Bumper stickers, badges, T-shirts, a Right to Choose banner, and pamphlets continually circulate throughout the text as a kind of subterranean acknowledgment that difference exists—on the margins, perhaps, but it is nevertheless there. One of the oddest and most arbitrary of these semiotic signs appears rather early in the text when Pen goes to a bookstore café for lunch:

> Out of the corner of my eye I have spotted her badge and am going light pink. It's not even one of those joined women symbols or a discreet labrys. It's a yellow badge with "BY THE WAY, I'M A DYKE" emblazoned across it.
>
> In order to dissociate myself from this lunatic I take a vast mouthful of pastry crust.
>
> She leans over and says, "That's quite a waistcoat." (92)

This incident is an interesting case of visibility and definitely a non-sanctioned heterosexual matrix form of communication. Badges and slogans may seem like a trite way to "take back" language and obtain the ability to speak and open up non-heterosexual discourses; still, we might think of it as guerrilla warfare. A surprise attack—BY THE WAY, I'M A DYKE—destabilizes language and forces us to confront this bold declaration. The woman who flirts or comes on to Pen may be wearing an overt badge of homosexual visibility, but apparently Pen is wearing a covert badge ("gaydar"?) that Pen questions: "But how did she spot me? It's a very flowery waistcoat I'm wearing, nothing Radclyffe Hall about it" (92). The problem of invisibility for homosexuals in

Irish society is undermined by the subterranean and the subtextual, which allows for a communication among those who can "read" the signs.

Yet Pen knows about the problem of "invisibility" in Irish society; ironically, the media has recently picked up on "invisibility," which should yield the invisible visible: "Nowadays 'invisibility' was supposed to be the big problem, but the way I saw it was, all that mattered was to be visible to yourself" (60). The media, however, has a blunt and predictable way of dealing with topics still not quite digestible by the heterosexual norm; rather than frighten the viewers into thinking that their neighbor or son or sister is gay by presenting the everyday prosaic sort of homosexual, the media focuses on spectacle, such as the outrageously costumed people who participate in a gay pride parade. Pen muses that she "didn't watch telly to see anyone remotely like me, anyway. Though it was fun to catch sight of the odd out-and-proud lipstick leather lesbian on a Channel 4 documentary" (60). The media wants show how different and "abject" a woman who desires woman actually is; the "lipstick leather lesbian" is supposedly not like anyone in your own family or even like anyone you know. Eibhear Walshe, borrowing from Jonathan Dollimore's theoretical position in *Sexual Dissidence,* turns difference around to say that there is not enough difference between the marked and unmarked, and it is the inability to distinguish the difference that causes heterosexual panic: "that the real threat in homoerotic desire is not difference but sameness. At the core of masculinist panic at the spectre of homosexual desire is the sense of reciprocity, the fear that, as Dollimore puts it, 'civilisation actually depends upon that which it is usually thought to be incompatible with.'"[41] Indeed, as Pen points out concerning lesbians, "most of the real ones I'd ever come across were quietly rebellious products of the suburbs, wearing waistcoats over ladylike shirts at dinner-parties" (60).

The most important word in this subterranean homosexual guerilla warfare of language is, of course, *hood.* The metaphor of the hood in *Hood* opens up a way in which to pull back the layers of the novel in order to see how it operates and deterritorializes the heterosexual matrix's expectations. In a tantalizing manner, the text offers the reader several "hoods." The first hood that we encounter is the red school uniform hood that Cara detests, as Pen remembers: "If I shut my eyes I could see Cara in uniform still, though I had watched her rip it up with relish on the day of the sixth-year party. The red hood she hated in particular; once, bored at the bus stop, she buttoned it on the wrong way round, over her face, and tried to get me to lead her on to the bus, with her repeating, 'I am noth a monsther. I am the elephanth woman'" (39). As the novel goes on, the reader is struck by the hood's redness and the fact that unable or unwilling to wear the hood properly, Cara is a kind of monster or freak. While the above quotation is in jest and the product of a bored teenager, the notion that Cara never wore clothes properly or looked right in clothes, never really "fit" into any particular niche (professional or otherwise) is brought up frequently in the text. Pen rhetorically asks Jo, "Cara looked most herself when she was naked, right?" Nervously, Jo answers, "Did she?" Unnoticed, Pen states, "I mean when she didn't have to decide what to wear, when she could sit on the grass all cross-legged and unself-conscious, reading the paper. . . . Whereas Kate . . . I can't imagine her naked" (239). In this interesting conversation, Jo does not know Pen's original attraction was not to Cara but to her sister Kate, and Pen does not know that it is Jo, not Sherry, who has been Cara's most recent paramour. Yet, the conversation is actually about who can pass as straight because part of the hood metaphor contains Pen's closetedness:

> "When I ring my mother she asks after my job first of all, as if that's Who I Am."
>   "That makes Who I Am a part-time market research analyst," complained Jo.
>   "You're not, are you? I assumed you were a full-time Amazon."
>   "Afraid not," she said, burying her nose in Grace's marmalade fur. "Hence the drag."
>   "I wasn't going to mention it," I said.
>   Jo met my grin, then asked, "So have you talked to your mother yet?" (240)

Pen, "a cradle dyke," has not "come out" to her mother, or to Cara's dad, or to Sister Dominic, her boss at Immaculate Conception school for girls. This "hoodedness" covers over the fact that Pen and Cara were lovers and partners in life which conceals, too, the level of emotional grief that Pen feels about Cara's death. Pen reads in the self-help book for grief that Robbie gave her, "'Homosexuals mourning their partners often carry a burden exacerbated by invisibility and prejudice,'" and she thinks to herself, "Somehow, what galled me most was that if it had been a husband, Sister Dominic would have given me two weeks off" (248). Yet, being hooded has its advantages, too, Pen thinks, in that at least she can grieve privately. We have seen, on the one hand, as Dollimore argues, that the inability to read the signs of sexuality is most threatening to the heterosexual order. Yet, on the other hand, Adrienne Rich theorizes that the lesbian woman is forced into closet in order to keep her employment and that this charade succeeds only when she performs the role of heterosexual *woman:* "A lesbian, closeted on her job because of heterosexual prejudice, is not simply forced into denying the truth of her outside relationships or private life; her job depends on her pretending to be not merely heterosexual but a heterosexual *woman,* in terms of dressing and playing the feminine, deferential role required of 'real' women."[42] Pen's job, for example, as a teacher at a Catholic school depends on her dressing the role of the "femme" and remaining closeted.

Donoghue also examines hood as a suffix that denotes a state, condition, character, or a body of people.[43] Thinking about Kate and Cara as sisters, Pen muses, "Only the odd gesture gave an unnerving reminder of their sisterhood" (113): "Funny word, that; why did 'hood' added to nouns make them into states of being? Perhaps sisterhood was a hood that sisters had to wear, or rather, two hoods. . . . Then what about maidenhood? Definitely the hoods off our old Immac uniforms, stiff red gabardine to shade us from rain and male glances. They were detachable, too. I remembered, and the bad girls used to unbutton theirs and lose them in the first week: how very suitable! And under the maidenhood was the maidenhead, and girls lost their heads just as easily" (113). While Pen has remained a maiden, Cara has not, another example of Cara's Jael-like behavior. Pen's musings on the maiden's head and the maiden's hood again suggests another layer to tear away, another hood to pull back, to reach the core meaning of *hood* in the novel. The hood that conceals, the hood that protects, the hood that teases one's desire, as in Pen's dream in which Kate—mysteriously unhooded—scorns Pen, all lead to the most erotic and most concealed hood of all:

> When I shut my eyes now, I was hovering over Cara, an inch from her cherry-red clitoris.
>
> The hood of the clitoris was not a hood to take off, only to push back. In fact the whole thing was a series of folds and layers, a magical Pass the Parcel in which the gift was not inside the wrappings, but was the wrappings. If you touched the glans directly it would be too sharp, like a blow. It was touching it indirectly, through and with the hood, that felt so astonishing. Like an endearment in a mundane sentence, or a cherry on a rockbun, the combination was all. It was not the bald revelation that thrilled me, but the moment of the revealing; not the veil or the bare body, but the movement of unveiling. (257)

The movement of the unveiling is the becoming-woman, but does not give us an essentialized meaning of woman, instead a becoming-woman. The act of pulling back the genital hood does not reveal anything except that it is necessary to pull back the hood; it is the enactment that is important. Not unlike language, one continues to unfold the hood as one unfolds meaning. If the hood is drawn back too far, there is no pleasure; and, if language is drawn back, either withheld or too explicit, there is no pleasure. The pleasure and the becoming are all in the movement. The female body's pleasure is in the fold and in the folding: the boundary is not visible and "meaning" never certain. *Hood* is giving voice to the idea that rigid boundaries are the things that hurt; the most obvious and seemingly intractable set of boundaries are those of the heterosexual matrix. Donoghue's text attempts to roll over these boundaries, create new possibilities, and (begin to) render the heterosexual norm useless and meaningless.

Tom Lennon's 1999 novel, *Crazy Love,* is an in-depth view of closeted Paul Cullen's world as a successful businessman in the economically vibrant Celtic Tiger Dublin of the 1990s. Married, living in "legoland," with one daughter and another child on the way, Cullen has successfully closeted his long-term same-sex desire, yet it has not gone away. *Crazy Love* is more than a coming-out novel; it is an often frenetic account of a thirty-year-old man who indeed "passes" as a successful heterosexual whose masquerade is more false the more he succeeds, and it is an account of the social, economic, and cultural value system in Dublin at the end of the twentieth century. The more economically successful Paul is, the deeper he goes into the heterosexual world; the more economically successful Dublin and Ireland are, the deeper they go into "technetronic ethnocide" with all its trappings of tacky material wealth. Both in the novel are to be rendered as false selves: Paul is split off from his true desire, and Dublin in all of its urban sprawl is cut off from valuing human life and the natural resources of Ireland. While Lennon is not nostalgic for a "lost Ireland," he is critical of the direction "new Ireland" is taking.

In fact, if anything, Lennon is propagating a need for a new Ireland in terms of accepting differences in lifestyle and values, social responsibility, and eliminating the crass one-upmanship of masculine business culture. These issues are established early in the text. An incident concerning differences occurs the night Paul goes out to dinner at a Chinese restaurant with his wife Anne and another couple, longtime friends Bob and Karen. At the restaurant, the four notice that two young men are obviously a couple as they hold hands and attempt to have a private and peaceful dinner together. Their peace and that of the entire restaurant are interrupted by three drunk homophobic and racist men who taunt and bait the gays as well as the Chinese restaurant workers. The tension is compounded by the fact that Paul also, but for not for any overt reason, feels uncomfortable and threatened. One of the drunks, the one whose "ugly leer contorting his face leaves the two lads in doubt that they don't exactly fit into his vision of Ireland," begins a verbal debate with the more vocal of the gay couple:

"Well, you know what they say," the gay guy replies, smiling benignly, "it takes one to know one."

You sense a silent cheer from your fellow-diners.

"He's married." The one with the tattoo is pointing at his blade-one friend.

"So?" The gay guy loops his eyebrows.

"Married with kids."

"My sincerest commiserations, but surely you realise that being married is no longer a guarantee."

Anne, Bob and Karen snigger, but you're experiencing a sickly sensation in your stomach.[44]

Paul is continually anxious that his heterosexual "cover" that allows him to function in a straight role will be blown, his guilty secret discovered. He is afraid of appearing marked in a society that permits drunken threats and buffoonery on the part of heterosexual males because presumably they are *un*marked. Tattoos, wife, and kids fail to mark the man who can play by the heterosexual matrix's rules. Paul thinks to himself that *demarcation* in contemporary society is simply not worth the effort. After the drunks have been kicked out of the restaurant and peace is restored, Paul notices that "everyone is watching the two lads at the corner table and pretending that they're not. The entire episode makes you feel justified in hiding away. Who would want to face such hassle on a simple visit to a restaurant?" (53). Being different marks a person and makes you open to society's gaze; a marked person is controlled in the power dynamic because he or she is *different*. This episode depicts bodies coming to near blows with bodies because of a slightly higher-pitched voice or clothes or mannerisms.

What is it that makes unmarked bodies want to humiliate or hurt marked bodies? We have seen these ideas in contemporary Irish society expressed repeatedly in the novel: Yvonne says lesbians are "butch and ranty," hence marked; Neil comes out of a gay bar, hence is marked and beaten for being marked; two young men cannot quietly enjoy dinner in a restaurant without being attacked as being "a bit funny," hence marked. As previously mentioned, in *Sexual Dissidence* Dollimore reverses the effect of difference, stating that there is not enough difference between the marked and unmarked and it is the inability to distinguish the difference that causes heterosexual panic and aggression: "the real threat in homoerotic desire is not difference but sameness. At the core of masculinist panic at the spectre of homosexual desire is the sense of reciprocity, the fear that the boundary will become erased, the threshold no longer perceptible."

Although he sets his novel in a middle-class environment, Lennon is aware that difference occurs at the level of sexuality and lifestyle but also at the level of economics and privilege. Despite Paul's own privileges of education, upbringing, and a good job in a booming economy, he is aware of Dublin's growing marginalized population. Paul is a part of, according to *Fortune,* the "prosperous young Irish folk" who "crowd" the "new downtown bars, fancy restaurants, and theatres." As we recall, *Fortune* praises Dublin's ability to reinvent itself, especially in the areas of high tech and specialized financial services industry. What Paul calls the H people, "Homeless and Hungry," have not benefited from telecommunications, financial services, tourism, and Intel's decision to base its production of Pentium microchip producers in a Dublin suburb: "'Homeless and Hungry', that's what their placards say, so what else can they expect you to call them. You don't like to admit it, but you've grown immune to their presence. However, outside Brown Thomas you see an undernourished and ragged-looking teenage boy, sitting behind a cardboard box, rocking continuously backward and forward in a demented manner. His hollow eyes stare out at the passing parade of Boomtown: Gucci and Armani, Celtic Tiger, the nightclub capital of Europe, the world's cultural capital, the city with money to burn" (65). In addition to the homeless, there are the working-class people who are also economically marginalized; in chapter 1 we noted that while Dublin booms all around them, some residents feel as if they are starving at the feast: "In her 35 years in Dublin, Cathy Sherwin, single mother of two teenagers, 'has never stood in Brown Thomas or purchased an item in Marks and Spencer.'"[45]

Related to the issue of the economic boom is Paul's uneasiness in the macho corporate one-upmanship world. Paul endures this kind of competition on a regular basis inside the company he works for, Carney Textiles, but he more poignantly suffers this masculine muscle-flexing with old college mates he occasionally sees. The person who annoys Paul the most is Wax Hennessy, an obnoxious corporate climber who wants to speak to Paul only in order to gloat over his latest promotion, new car, or even his virility, evidenced by how many kids he now has: "Two girls and an heir to the throne" (205). Paul thinks to himself that surely people like Wax do not "really" exist: "Apparently they do, because you are talking to one right now. He has a drip-dry face, and his emotions are more than likely controlled by the stock market, house prices, his bank balance" (204). The character Wax embodies the new corporate Dublin mentality that *The Irish Times* columnist Liam Fay characterized as "consensus and inertia." Wax's attitude is typical of "those who have benefitted most from the economic boom [and who] admire their own estimation of their acumen and insight so much that it is impossible for them to admit that much of their wealth has been accumulated through distinctively uncreative means, such as property speculation, low-risk investment and sheer good fortune." Paul makes the mistake of attempting to embarrass Wax in front of his "Number Two," a trainee under Wax:

> You halt his progress by drawing Number Two's attention to Wax's college days. "So, did he fill you in on his glory days in the candle factory?"
> Number Two stares at you as if you've just told him that his entire family had been washed away in a flash flood.
> "That's where he got his nickname 'the Wax.'"

> The Wax's face changes colour. Since college, he has worked tirelessly to lose his nickname, but the more fuss he creates, the more people persist with it.
>
> But he has vengeance on his mind. Two can play that game. . . . A slimy, condescending look has formed on his drip-dry mug. "Hey, what's this I hear about you being a leading light in the gay community," he says. . . . Number Two's demeanour has altered dramatically. It's become almost defensive, like he suspects you're going to try and wrap your arms around his neck at any moment. (206)

In Wax's world, the ultimate masculine put down is to be accused of or even suspected of homosexual tendencies; to find oneself in the company of homosexuals is guilt by association; Paul is implicated in Wax's system because he attempts to embarrass Wax using Wax's own logic.

By this point in the novel, Paul is on the verge of coming out—not by choice but because his wife Anne finds him masturbating while watching a pornographic male homosexual video. This nadir in Paul's life has to do with only one thing: his "crazy love" for Johnny Lyons.[46] Borrowing another song title, Paul's "crazy love" at first is a little difficult to fathom: Johnny is hired by Paul as his assistant for his blond and blue-eyed looks, but Johnny is completely incompetent and acts childishly. Paul, however, has a "*crazy*" love and desire for Johnny, a desire that, as with Neil in Lennon's first novel, did not suddenly materialize; Paul, too, has always known he was homosexual. After Paul's breakdown, he tells the psychiatrist that he listened to a DJ on a pirate radio station as a teenager because he was openly gay: "How his exuberant voice had you thrilled skinny, simply because you knew that he was gay. It was like he was sending signals out to you. He was the only one who made sense" (168). Paul does not tell the doctor that he turned the radio down or off whenever anyone was around because of his embarrassment and guilt. Still, at the beginning of the novel Paul is happily sitting in his car in backed-up rush-hour traffic because he has a view of a good-looking and muscular male cyclist; we know we have a precedent. A discussion of all the ridiculous situations Paul gets himself into for Johnny's sake would take an entire chapter; therefore, I would like to focus my discussion on the significance of the lines or boundaries drawn in the novel not only between gay and straight but lines of heterosexist behavior that clearly establish these boundaries though Lennon, too, would like to erase them.

Strident lines of heterosexuality block off and out certain kinds of territories throughout the novel. At the beginning of the novel, Johnny, too, poses as a heterosexual. Paul and Johnny go to lunch, where "the girl serving your table is pretty and once she's out of earshot, Johnny whispers, 'Wouldn't mind giving her a slap of the wet lad'" (58). Paul immediately recognizes this behavior as the kind he has employed in the past and yet is stung by the suggestion that Johnny might actually be heterosexual. Johnny sleeps with his friend Sara on the Wexford weekend trip so as to keep up the pretense to his friends that he is heterosexual. Still, Paul feels so intensely attracted to Johnny that he continues to pursue him. On top of an old railway bridge, of all places, Paul's first homosexual encounter occurs with Johnny. It begins with a characteristic quip, "Is that a telescope in your pocket or are you just glad to see me?"

> His hands circle your waist. Your life seems to skip out of a groove. The old ticker definitely skips a beat. He fits into your arms in a way no one has ever fitted before.
> "I sort of knew the first time we met," he says.
> "So did I."
> Did you really say that?
> "But I never thought it would come to this."
> "But what about Sara?"
> He utters a low, gurgling laugh, "What about her?"
> "Cover?"
> He nods. "Have to give my friends the right impression, don't I, and besides, I was just trying to make you jealous."
> The weekend in Wexford dissolves in your head and all the various parts reassembled in a new pattern.
> "When that sister of yours said she was your wife, I nearly puked, and because of that I got really pissed and then I did puke."
> You touch his hair, trace the outline of his face, run your fingertip across his lips. It's like meeting him for the first time. You're so happy and excited, you're afraid you'll forget to breathe. This is a once in a lifetime, of that you have no doubt. (109–110)

Johnny seduces Paul thinking that Paul is single, but Paul's lie inevitably catches up to him. Johnny is uncharacteristically sensitive to Paul's situation: "'It has nothing to do with you lying. Believe me, I understand why you did. But . . . it's just. . . . Listen, you have a young child, and a wife you're obviously fond of, you'd be mad to throw all of that away. Absolutely bonkers'" (157–158). In this, we see that the heterosexual matrix dominates Johnny's way of thinking, as he adds, "'whatever you are, you're not as gay as I am, and if you want to know the truth I'd love to be straight. Life would be so much easier. Like, I'd love to have kids and that, and not have to put up with all the pretence'" (158). Johnny clearly points out the boundary: gay or straight, and even if Paul appears to swing both ways, he can *pass* as a heterosexual, and that is what is important in a society in which heterosexuality is the norm.

Rather abruptly at the end of the novel, Lennon's text offers the reader a potentially boundariless society: Carney comes out about his son, Cliff, who is gay, and Johnny now lives in town with Paul and is adored by Paul's kids (though Anne still does not want Johnny around the children). From Lennon's first two novels we know that the author attempts to give us new ways of conceiving one's self as homosexual in Irish society; yet, we also know that he does not or feels he cannot deliver a completely happy ending. With *When Love Comes to Town* the conditions for understanding for Neil dictate that his body is not to have any sexual movement so that the homosexual-as-static entity is acceptable, but homosexual as a moving body is unacceptable; Neil is always already homosexual while his ability to be accepted by his family and friends is limited and his body restricted. Lennon gives Paul and Johnny a little more room to maneuver:

> The day you collected him from the airport still ranks as the day you finally shed your closet skin. The two of you snogged in front of everyone. Hugging and kissing usually goes unnoticed in airport arrival terminals, however, two men kissing mouth-to-mouth did attract a certain amount of attention. This was no pop video. This was real life. But no one said a word, and in fact, if anything, they seemed to silently approve of this spontaneous open display of affection. They seemed to like being reminded that this was a modern Ireland they were living in. That kiss broke all the rules you grew up with. It was a defining moment, the moment of release from the shackles of the past. (239)

Lennon goes all out to proclaim that there is in fact a new Ireland and that people like to be reminded of this phenomenon. Lennon certainly is more optimistic in his portrayal of homosexual relations and the lessening of heterosexual constraints in 1999 than in 1993. The tone of the ending is such that all people—certainly those who are homosexual—are better when society is able to drop the heterosexual norm boundaries and let everyone become whoever it is he or she wants to become: "You treat people better than you used to. . . . Your energy is no longer sapped up and wasted by the effort involved in leading that double-life. Now you know that you are finally moving on to wherever it is you are going" (240). Significantly, Paul is *moving* and becoming the person—sexually, socially, and morally—he wishes to become because the heterosexist restraints are relaxing or beginning to relax in the final year of the twentieth century.

Another novel also published in the final year of the twentieth century that deals specifically with the complexities of Irish male homosexuality is Colm Toibin's *The Blackwater Lightship*. *The Blackwater Lightship* was nominated for the 1999 British Booker Prize award, though J. M. Coetzee's *Disgrace* won. Toibin's novel, however, was voted best novel by the 1999 First People's Booker Prize with *Disgrace* taking second place in this competition.[47] The novel is popularly reviewed as a novel about three generations of

Irish women; Dora Devereux, her daughter Lily, and her granddaughter
Helen. When early in the novel Helen is confronted by Paul, a friend of
Helen's brother Declan, and told that Declan is sick, in fact dying of AIDS,
the reader begins to see the direction that this story will take. Yet *The Blackwater Lightship* does not directly confront AIDS or homosexuality in Ireland; rather, it takes a roundabout approach by ostensibly focusing on the
overall dysfunctionality of the Devereux clan. One could even view the
novel—and the jacket copy encourages this reading—as a novelistic *The Big
Chill:* friends and family come together in the country for short period of
time to face a crisis that provides the opportunity to expose and process past
emotional traumas in order to heal and move on in life. While I do not wish
to deny that this reading is viable, I would like to focus on the novel's *raison
d'être* which is Declan's AIDS, and in turn his homosexual friends who care
for him—and who have been caring for him without the knowledge of his
family—for years. There may be very good reasons why Toibin chose a
roundabout approach to the topic of AIDS in Ireland and decided the best
way to broach to the subject would be indirectly.

Findings from an end of 1997 survey indicates that cases of AIDS in Ireland are relatively low compared with the rest of Europe. Approximately 18
out of 100,000 cases are reported in Ireland compared to, for example, 130
out 100,000 in Spain or 85 out of 100,000 in France.[48] The cases of AIDS
infection are 593 with 308 deaths resulting from the disease. According to
the Irish Department of Health findings, 82 percent of reported cases are
male with 18 percent female and intravenous drug use being the leading
cause of the development of the epidemic (43 percent). However, RTE reported 209 new cases of HIV in 1999, an increase of 73 over the previous
year.[49] In the same report, Cairde, the non-government support organization for AIDS and HIV patients, stated that government strategies to prevent transmission of the disease have failed despite the effort to raise
awareness about HIV and AIDS. Awareness has increased at the end of the
1990s with mass media campaigns targeting youth, and providing school ed-
ucational programs and free testing. Evidence that this "awareness" has occurred in Ireland is provided in the novel when Helen tells her grandmother
the news about Declan: "There was something which she had forgotten: in
the corner of the kitchen sat a huge television; her grandmother had access
to all the English channels as well as the Irish ones. She watched documen-
taries and late-night films and prided herself on being well informed on
modern subjects. She knew about AIDS and the search for a cure and the
long illnesses. 'There's nothing can be done, Helen, so.'"[50] However, Mrs.
Devereux is not only informed but unusually open-minded; Mrs. Devereux
throughout the text is sympathetic to and supportive of Declan and his
friends Paul and Larry. The Irish Department of Health report states that

discriminatory attitudes may be changing because "cultural traditions and religion" are less influential.[51] Yet, another way to look at this open-mind-edness brought about by the media might be with irony because of the media's "technetronic ethnocide" of Ireland's culture. The Catholic Church's declining influence in Irish culture and society is evident, according to the Department of Health report, "in people's behavior, e.g., the decline in the marriage rates and increases in the number of couples living together. It is also evident in legislation in 1993 relevant to HIV/Aids prevention with the decriminalisation of sexual activity between men and the introduction of a common age of consent. Also in that year, condoms were made more widely available."[52]

The Catholic Church is interwoven into *The Blackwater Lightship*, most notably with Paul's same-sex marriage to Francois by a Catholic priest in Brussels, but also at the more mundane level of the everyday disregard of its tenets. The Irish Catholic Church's attitude toward HIV and AIDS is fraught with contradictions. According to Patrick Hannon in "AIDS: Moral Issues," the church cannot sanction the use of condoms because it contra-dicts the "Catholic tradition's sexual ethic."[53] While it is universally under-stood that condoms are the sexually active individual's best protection against sexually transmitted diseases, Hannon takes the high ground and begs the question:

> In view of the Catholic tradition's sexual ethic generally, and in particular, its proscription of the use of artificial contraceptives, it is not surprising that these issues have given rise to difficulty. The statements of episcopal confer-ences are especially concerned to insist upon the classical ethical values of ab-stinence and fidelity, and they are at pains too to point out that the use of condoms is not in any case absolutely effective. Neither of these positions should surprise us; the bishops would be less than true to their own tradition were they to ignore the first of these points, and no sane person could ignore the second.[54]

Declan apparently valued neither abstinence nor fidelity, and the reader is made to assume through Paul's narrative that Declan's reckless behavior in Brussels led him to contract the AIDS virus. Declan's behavior we will come to momentarily; first, however, the issue is the Irish Catholic attitude toward sexuality. Quoting the French Bishops' Conference Permanent Council's statement on AIDS, Hannon supports the view that abstinence and denial are the best remedies: "The current epidemic is an occasion for all to exam-ine their behaviour. Our society has too easily accepted and even encouraged superficial encounters and the exercise of sexuality dissociated from any con-jugal and parental commitment."[55] The warning is lucid: no sexual activity except by married heterosexuals, use no contraceptive. From this perspective, the Church seems simply unable to discuss the problem; as with Pen's confession to the priest in *Hood,* there is no language to engage with what the heterosexual matrix will not sanction. In this instance, borrowing again from Gatens, "the body politic" assumes a universalizing male and *heterosexual* voice that further obfuscates the actual workings of power and relations of bodies. The priest in *Hood* does not acknowledge any other literally "unspeakable" sins because they do not and cannot exist.

An interesting current attempt to "recognize" difference occurred in the mid-1990s when a priest used the pulpit to sanctify a misogynistic heterosexuality. In September 1995 Father Michael Kennedy of St. Mary's Catholic Church, Dungarvan, County Waterford, delivered a "shocking sermon" which set off the "the AIDS-avenger scare" in southern Ireland.[56] According to Kennedy, there was a young HIV-infected woman "avenging" the male gender, "a burning sense of grievance against the male sex," by having sex with as many men in southern Ireland as possible. The count, Kennedy stated, was up to "80 young men" and Kennedy had "personally traced about 25 of the men and that five had tested positive for HIV."[57] The fact that this story was not true hardly needs to be stated: statistics show that men are between two and twenty times more likely to infect women with HIV than women are likely to infect men. However, the behavior and actions of Kennedy do need some elaboration. Instead of recognizing difference through compassion or understanding, or making an attempt to reach out to the victim or victims, Kennedy's "sin and damnation" sermon echoes the standard Catholic heterosexual line of thought; moreover, Kennedy obfuscates the truly damaging issues concerning the AIDS virus. Exploiting his power to speak out from the pulpit, Kennedy covers over two points of Catholic Church culpability in regard to the virus.

First, Kennedy brazenly overlooks the fact that the Church has actually advanced the spread of the disease through its unwillingness to initiate sex education in church-run schools, and lack of protection through ignorance spreads the disease. Second, the priests' pedophilic behavior and homosexuality have contributed to the number of individuals who have or contracted the disease. Incidents that caused a media explosion less than a year before the Kennedy episode included the "November 1994 crisis over the extradition to Northern Ireland of a paedophile priest," which was "generally seen in Ireland as marking 'a watershed in the political life of the state.'"[58] The other incident that sparked media attention involved "An elderly Catholic priest," who "sadly died of a heart attack in a gay club in Dublin, in the company of two friends, also priests. The headline of the front-page article in *The Irish Catholic* newspaper read: 'Church Must Not Bury its Head Now.' Hundreds of people, including his parishioners and the Archbishop of

Dublin, turned out for the funeral."[59] In the United States, statistics show that Roman Catholic priests are dying from AIDS-related illnesses at a rate that is four times higher than that of the general population.[60] There are no statistics available for the Irish priesthood, but continual reports concerning priests who sexually abuse young boys suggest that homosexual and pe-dophilic behavior continues, and therefore we can assume that the AIDS virus has similarly and disproportionately infected the Irish priesthood.[61] Despite the lack of statistics, it would seem that there is a hypocrisy of si-lence in Patrick Hannon's take on the "moral issues" of AIDS. In fiction, too, we have pedophilic behavior recorded; in *Crazy Love* Johnny is sexually as-saulted by a priest while still at school. Lennon's presentation of Johnny's ho-mosexuality is not damaging to the priestly order because of Johnny's seeming lack of innocence and the idea that Johnny's sexual identity has al-ways been—since childhood—homosexual.

The issue of AIDS in Ireland, as we have seen in this chapter, is drama-tized in both *When Love Comes to Town*, with Daphne, and less prominently in *Crazy Love*, when Anne accuses Paul of potentially infecting her with AIDS the night she finds him watching homosexual pornography videos. Since ho-mosexual men are more likely to transmit the disease, Donoghue's work is less affected by AIDS; still, in *Stir-fry*, Maria flirts with a bisexual man, Damian, which draws our attention to the potential risk; in *Hood*, Pen discusses the potential danger of imbibing Cara's blood—especially when Pen knows that Cara is not monogamous. In *The Blackwater Lightship*, Declan's failing health due to the advancement of the virus is central to the text and the symptoms and different medications used to combat the illness are depicted. What is unusual about the novel is that the reader is never privy to Declan's own nar-rative—we never have access to Declan in the first person, only everyone else's story of Declan. This distancing, I would argue, keeps the novel from being "only" about a homosexual AIDS victim; rather, the distancing leads us to be less concerned for Declan's welfare than, say, his grandmother's or Helen's welfare. In fact, it would seem that Toibin has distanced Declan *too* much. Using an earlier analogy, the novel is a *Big Chill* without the centrality of death. Even though Declan is dying, and we expect the novel to end with his death, it becomes peripheral to the development of the novel—so much so that the novel ends with Lily visiting Helen's house in Dublin for the first time (while Declan is being re-admitted to the hospital).

I recognize that the strategy of the novel is to draw the reader into the seaside haven of a normal if somewhat dysfunctional but totally likable Irish Catholic family in order to make the case that "normal" families have mem-bers who contract AIDS and from this viewpoint we are subtly drawn into a sympathy for Declan we might not otherwise have. Without a lover, De-clan is cared for by his friends Paul and Larry who, we learn early in the novel, have been taking care of him for years without the knowledge of his family. Declan's sister, Helen, knows that he is homosexual, but his mother does not. The fact that Declan did not wish his illness to be known to his family becomes an issue of "coming out." Indeed, even though Helen knows that her brother is homosexual, he obviously does not share his life experience, friends, or relationships with her until Paul contacts her to tell her Declan is sick; therefore, from Declan's perspective he is "coming out" to his entire family. Lily, Declan's mother, does not show the open-minded attitude toward homosexuals with AIDS that Mrs. Devereux displays. The outing of Declan for Lily occurs at the hospital the day she finds out he is sick. The family dynamics are such that Helen does not straightforwardly tell her mother the truth:

> As Helen opened the door, her mother turned to the consultant. "Could I speak to you alone for a minute, please?"
> Helen waited outside and then walked down the corridor and stood looking out of the window. She knew what her mother was asking: the question she had refrained from asking Helen in the car. She had always wondered if her mother knew about Declan being gay, and was not sure now whether the consultant would tell her or not. But as she watched her mother walking out of the consultant's office and coming with her down the corridor, she knew that she had received a reply. Her mother's shoulders were hunched and she kept her eyes on the ground. It was years since Helen had seen her look defeated like this. (100–101)

A few pages later Lily confronts Helen for not telling her about Declan's homosexuality, and this opens up the bitter topic of Declan's closetedness to his family, which hangs over the entire novel. Interestingly, the novel plays out Emma Donoghue's recent assessment of the homosexual lifestyle in Ireland. According to Donoghue's very real experience, homosexuals live in two worlds: "I would say one particular aspect of the Irish lesbian and gay world rather than that world in any other country is that vast numbers are still in the closet. . . . I know a lot of people who are very out and proud when they're in Dublin, but back home down the country not a word to the family, and it might be the same about jobs, so there's a lot of living in two worlds. It's not that they're entirely in the closet, it's that there are things they speak about with their friends and there are things they speak about with their parents and that's two different kinds of conversation."[62] What we find out about Declan's "Dublin" behavior was that he, unlike Larry and Paul, was involved in many relationships, which suggests he contracted the HIV virus because he was sexually active with many partners.

The novel sets itself up, perhaps unwittingly, as judge and jury concerning Declan's past behavior by virtue of the presentation of Larry's and Paul's monogamy. To put it simply, Declan's polygamous sexual behavior gave him AIDS, but Larry, who is with an unnamed youngest son of a large family, and Paul, who is with Francois, do not have AIDS. Therefore, despite whatever sympathy we might feel for Declan's suffering, in the back of our minds, we cannot dispel the idea that his indiscriminate behavior led to his illness. In effect, Declan's body must suffer for his moral indiscretion. The "plagued" body is once again seized, surveyed, and punished for indiscretion that must be confessed but that in this novel never is. Declan never speaks; he is spoken for. Paul narrates Declan's story to Helen so that there can be no misunderstanding the fact that the body becoming-homosexual, Declan's body, engaged in "risque" behavior in Brussels:

> He would come for long weekends and he'd make us hang out in bars and clubs with him, and he'd usually abandon us at a certain time and then come back home in the early hours like a half-drowned dog. . . . He checked out all our friends from the Catholic gay organization and a few of them really fell for him—everyone fell for him—and he would bounce up and down with them for maybe two weekends, and then he'd arrive again and we'd know by something he did or said that he hadn't been returning So-and-so's calls, so we learned never to tell anyone he was coming. And then the whole routine would start again; he'd laugh about it himself. (174–175)

Paul tells Helen that Declan was mystified because neither he nor Francois "had it off with anyone else" (175) or wanted to have it off with anyone else. Declan's promiscuous behavior provides an origin, for those readers who need it, for the illness: polygamy and unsafe sex lead to becoming-HIV-positive, becoming-AIDS, becoming-dead. We have seen this moral played out previously in this chapter: Declan's wild behavior is like Neil's going to the gay bar, where Neil gets beaten up; Johnny and Paul can be happy only when they conform to monogamy; even polygamous Cara and Jael are the moral "losers" in Donoghue's novels. The ethical virtues of monogamy may operate for both homosexuals and heterosexuals, but the fact is that *The Blackwater Lightship* sets up a kind of moral punishment for Declan's multiple-partner sex life that is particularly damaging in a time and place in which the illness is still not fully understood. Declan's culpability reinforces the heterosexual matrix's notion: "Queer sexual practice, then, impels one out of the generational production of what has been called 'life' and history, and ultimately out of the category of living"; quite literally, Case's formula links with the homosexuals' contraction of AIDS because queer "sexual practices" are located "within the realm of the other-than-natural, and the consequent other-than-living. . . . Striking at its very core, queer desire punctures the life/death and generative/destructive bipolarities that enclose the heterosexist notion of being."[63]

In the end, Declan will be drawn back into his family circle and "forgiven," if you like, but the stigma of reckless and immoral behavior on his part blankets our entire reading of the text.

This stigma is also part of the larger issue of the homosexual body over the boundary of accepted heterosexual norms. Despite the fact that Declan never speaks for himself, Declan's body glides over the boundary of normality: because it is not *normal* to have AIDS, and bodies that are infected must have crossed the boundary from the norm to transgression. As discussed above, even the "AIDS-avenger," although heterosexual, must transgress and cross the moral and bodily line. Throughout this chapter, I have discussed the different way that the heterosexual and especially the homosexual body is marked, yet it would seem that one of the most powerful—and most feared—markers in contemporary culture is the mark of an AIDS victim. Hannon notes Mother Teresa's verdict: "AIDS is the leprosy of our times." Historically, we know what was done with and to lepers, and this knowledge is not very comforting or humane in the twenty-first century. The body severely marked by AIDS is also a body becoming at such great speed that it is imperceptible. Imperceptible, indeed, is Declan. We cannot *see* him in *The Blackwater Lightship.* In this novel Declan is imperceptible because Toibin does not allow Declan his own sexuality and his becoming; yet, this is not the fault of the author. Rather, Declan is unpresentable because socially, culturally, and sexually the reader is not prepared to see him. It is difficult to "represent" the unseen and the unexplored in our society and culture. Therefore, Declan does not so much slide off the page—he never even gets on the page. We do not chart his movement because he is not there to chart: the words are there, but they do not represent the body. The body has simply been excluded. The novels in the next chapter, challenge our ability to chart the movement of bodies because the bodies are definitely there, only always already becoming, but our difficulty lies primarily in the prose itself. The prose of "Immeasurable Distance" meets with its representation in that the bodies are slippages recorded on the page.

Chapter Four 🔹

Immeasurable Distance

Discourse, Bodies, and Power

"Immeasurable distance" refers to one's ability to "measure" the distance between, say, point A and point B. If however A and B cannot be clearly distinguished, demarcated, or identified, then there is no way to measure the distance between the one point and the other. The novels discussed in this chapter have a unique ability to slip off the page, to impair our ability to construct clear lines of thought. The novels in this chapter slip off the scale of representation, and so we must attempt to follow Deleuze's prescription to "grasp movement only as the displacement of a moving body or the development of a form. Movements, becomings, in other words, pure relations of speed and slowness, pure affects, are below and above the threshold of perception." Less concretely placed in a material and representational world, the novels discussed in this chapter are about words—and the power of words to destroy and to produce bodies. Moreover, the ability to give meaning to the past and to fix one's identity in the present involves processes of interpretation; these processes of interpretation, however, dictate power, position, and the ability to live a meaningful life. Politically speaking, this form of power may be the most potent; what we know—discourses on the world—*is* our world and our ability to be and become.

This chapter focuses on novels that try to measure the distance between a lack of sense or knowledge and sense or knowledge in order to render meaning. In Seamus Deane's *Reading in the Dark* (1996) the unknown past affects a boy's childhood and family; in Mary Morrissy's *Mother of Pearl*, Mary is haunted by suppressed memories of her early childhood as Pearl; Roddy Doyle's *A Star Called Henry* presents the indefatigable protagonist whose first difficulties in life include starvation and disease but whose biggest problem is belatedness—he is the second Henry born to his parents, the first one more powerful than a ghost, a star in the sky; lastly, Robert McLiam Wilson's *Ripley Bogle* is Beckettesque in its presentation of father/son legitimacy. Each character and his or her situation is missing the foundation that would concretely secure him or her to a knowable past, and thus, a secure present with hope for a meaningful life.

The novel *Reading in the Dark* carries in its title an analogy to immeasurable distance in that in the dark there is no way to measure the distance between point A and point B because you cannot *see* points A and B. In the dark one cannot be sure of objects and often imagines objects that are not really there. This analogy carries into the narrator's activity throughout the book: he is reading his family's history—its secrets—in the dark; therefore, he is never sure of truth or tangible objects, nor is he certain that the apparitions exist. Indeed, the text is filled with ghosts, phantoms, and apparitions, from the ghost his mother feels on the stair landing, to the she-devil who tempts Larry, to the field of the disappeared near his father's family farm—all are difficult to decipher and even more difficult to believe true. In "Belfastards and Derriers," Eamonn Hughes suggests that these are family-bound apparitions linked to the fact that Deane is writing a "Derry novel": "It is also, fittingly for a Derry novel, a stiflingly enclosed world and the action never strays beyond the confines of the family; indeed, the places of the novel are held together not by the streetplan of the city nor by the topography of the north-west but by a web of family relations."[1]

Liam Harte in "History Lessons: Postcolonialism and Seamus Deane's *Reading in the Dark*" argues that Deane's novel is a byproduct of Deane's critical work, especially the Derry-based Field Day project. According to Harte, the novel could be interpreted "from a postcolonial perspective, the novel could be described as an exploration of the problematic process of identity formation in a colonial context. As a member of the Catholic nationalist minority community in a Protestant unionist state, Deane's nameless protagonist's social and political status is that of the colonized."[2] Harte points out that the Field Day project ceased operations in 1993, but despite the fact that the "artistic and critical collective" no longer existed, "the political and cultural concerns that sustained it continue to preoccupy its leading proponents, not least Deane himself."[3] These concerns, Harte maintains, inform *Reading in the Dark*: "Pre-eminent among them are the disfiguring effects of both colonialism and postcolonial nationalism alluded to above, the crisis of self-representation produced by colonialist discourse, and the dynamics of power and resistance, history and memory, language and identity within colonial relations."[4] A Catholic growing up in Derry in the 1940s and '50s is analogous to a black growing up in the American south in the 1940s and '50s; and yet, as Hughes points out, Deane's novel is supremely personal and familial. The reading in the dark that takes place is due to the overarching political and historical circumstances inherited, how-ever unwillingly, by the narrator. Still, the space opened by the novel is not primarily political; rather, it is intimate, and indeed, as Harte states, involves "the problematic process of identity formation."

One aspect of Harte's postcolonial interpretation pertinent to my reading is the narrator's historical situation of being the first generation to benefit from the Butler Education Act of 1947, which situates the narrator "at a cru-cial conjunction of social and historical change, as the oral folk culture of his native community is about to be finally and irrevocably overlaid by the dom-inant state-sponsored culture of literacy."[5] The Education Act gives rise to the first generation of an educated, Catholic middle class.[6] In the novel this division is keenly demonstrated through, on the one hand, the boy's Aunt Katie and the mentally unstable Joe, and on the other hand by the priests at school and the lecture on the dangers of communism from the British priest working for the Ministry of Education. The former characters weave folk-lore and fable into stories that the boy attempts to interpret, but reading in the dark, he is unable to decipher them. The latter characters supposedly deal concretely with real world situations, presenting factual knowledge of recorded events, but these stories, too, are skewed and purposefully con-structed to tell a certain kind of story; the narrator thinks he can read these stories more easily and more clearly, but as it turns out, these stories are as cryptic and encoded as Katie's and Joe's stories.

What is in the dark past holds power over the narrator in the present. What are "only" stories in effect rule the boy's life. The segment titled "Pis-tol," occurring in January 1949, is the first incident recounted by the narra-tor in which a simple, in this case stupid, action is blown open into a full-fledged serious incident. The pistol had been a gift to the narrator's fa-ther from a German soldier detained in Derry after the war. Wishing to im-press his friends, the boy shows the gun to them, but the scene is witnessed by a police informer, Fogey McKeever. Knowing the implications of a Catholic having a gun and "since we had cousins in gaol for being in the IRA, we were a marked family and had to be careful," the narrator buries the gun in a field later that day.[7]

This superficial account is not the whole story because that night two po-lice cars show up at the house and begin to tear the place apart looking for the gun: "The linoleum was being ripped off, the floorboards crowbarred up the wardrobe was lying face down in the middle of the floor and the slashed wallpaper hanging down in ribbons . . . One policeman opened a tin of Aus-tralian peaches and poured the yellow scimitar slices and sugar-logged syrup all over the floor" (29), while another went to the shed and split open bags of cement and walked the dry cement through the house. Yet, this scene is only the beginning of the nightmarish night for the narrator, his older brother, Liam, and his father. The three are taken to the police station and interrogated. Having not found the gun in the house, the police use violence in order to obtain its whereabouts:

> Where was the gun? I had had it, I had been seen with it, where was it? Policemen with huge faces bent down to ask me, quietly at first, then more and more loudly. They made my father sit at a table and then lean over it, with his arms outspread. Then they beat him on the neck and shoulders with rubber truncheons, short and gorged-red in colour. He told them, but they didn't believe him. So they beat us too, Liam and me, across the table from him. I remember the sweat and rage on his face as he looked. When they pushed my chin down on the table for a moment, I was looking up at him. Did he wink at me? Or were there tears in his eyes? Then my head bounced so hard on the table with the blows that I bit hard on my tongue. (30)

The reader and the narrator do not find out until Part II that this incident is precipitated by Eddie, the narrator's paternal uncle. Although whispers and the odd half story had presented themselves to the narrator, all that he knows is that Eddie disappeared. His father will not talk about his brother because it is rumored that Eddie was an informer and that he fled to Chicago. The events involving Eddie happened in the 1920s after partition, and so, they hover, ghostlike, in the past. Yet the past affects the narrator in the form of violence.

The reason for the harsh treatment in the "Pistol" episode is made lucid in the "Sergeant Burke" episode, dated May 1952. Surrounded by a gang of bullies led by Willie Barr, the narrator and Rory Griffin are about to get beaten up. In a panic, the narrator throws a stone at the passing police car to get the attention of the officers inside and break up the eminent bludgeoning. This action proves to be worse for the narrator than the certain beating because it links him with police and, in particular, to Sergeant Burke. When Burke orders the narrator into the car, Barr interjects, "Fuckin' stooly. Just like your uncle, like the whole lot o'ye" (100). After a humiliating tour of the neighbor in which everyone sees that the narrator is in the police car, a fate itself worse than a beating, Burke addresses the narrator:

> "This is your second time in a police car, isn't that right?"
>   I nodded. Burke had been in charge the night they had searched the house for the pistol and interrogated us in the barracks.
>   "Well, now, weren't we the easygoing men to let your daddy go the last time? A gun in the house and him with the brother he had? His big brother, Eddie. Did you ever wonder about that, or ask him why? Ever ask yourself why? For some others must have wondered, if you didn't." (100–101)

Burke, of course, knows about the family's past, but one wonders why he teases the narrator into questioning the past in light of his troubles in the present. In other words, it seems strange that Burke would wish to reopen the past, a past in which Burke himself, as it turns out, participated. Yet Burke does not let the topic go; he further piques the narrator's curiosity, as the passage continues:

> I said nothing.
> "Now Barr, that big slag, he thinks he knows why. I'll do you one favour. I'll tell you this—Barr's got it wrong. I'd say your daddy has it wrong too. Maybe you should ask your mother, now her daddy's got sick—none too soon either. Still, there you are. Once an informer, always an informer. That's what they'll say. And we'll see what comes out in the wash, eh? Off you go."
> He pushed me out before him and waved me away. I walked across the Lone Moor towards home. I could see no way out. No one would believe me; or if they could see what had really happened, they'd still be doubtful. Because of Eddie. Wasn't that what Burke was saying? Yes. But also no. For Barr had got it wrong, he had said. But how could my father be wrong about his own brother and policeman be right? And what did my mother know that was different? (101)

Burke purposefully wishes to keep the appearance of Eddie-as-informer alive because of his own part to play in the post-partition drama of betrayal, and thus the "Pistol" episode raid and interrogation. Yet, oddly enough, Burke gives the narrator clues to the past—admittedly dull, rough clues that once again lead him to read in the dark. Not only is the narrator facing darkness in terms of finding out information from his family, but he knows that it is considered shameful to believe a policeman. This passage is also very important to the narrator's ability to piece together the past, and yet it comes at a great price. While the narrator has clues to the past, he is now bodily removed from societal and familial bonds. He attempts to run away from home, yet never gets very far.

After one attempt his father asks him why he did not take the punches; the narrator does not see the sense of getting "battered" (104) and says that that is stupid. In the heat of the father/son argument, the narrator finally blurts out that it is not his fault but the fault of the family's past:

> First, the gun. Now this. Was there something amiss with me? No, I told him, there's something amiss with the family. The police were on top of us long before I was born. If he wanted to blame someone, let him blame Eddie, not me.
> He hit me so fast, I saw nothing. My shoulder felt hot and broken. (104)

This incident with his father begins the narrator's subjection to ongoing violence, humiliation, and physical separation from others. His school friends do not want him playing football with them, and even his mother ostracizes the narrator both emotionally and physically. The mother emotionally distances her son because she knows that he is beginning to put together the past. Her part in the past is suspected by virtually no one—except detective Burke and crazy Joe. The mother and the father physically distance their son when he is sent to live with Katie, supposedly to help take care of his dying grandfather. Banished, he learns more from his sick grandfather and is beginning to be able to read more and better into the darkness of the past.

The narrator's determination to measure the distance between events in the past and make them mean something in the present gives him power; yet he finds that power useless because he cannot divulge to anyone else what he knows. And so the knowledge of the past actually pulls him farther away from the love and understanding he desires from his parents. While the narrator's father continues to believe that his brother Eddie was an informer, the narrator discovers not only that Eddie was not an informer but that his mother has always known that he was not an informer. The mother never tells the father because of her own secrets; these secrets, the narrator understands as he gets older, must be protected. The mother's secrets make the distance between herself and her son completely immeasurable: "It wasn't just that she was trapped by what had happened. She was trapped by my knowing it. It must be shame, I decided. She's paralysed by shame. She was ashamed of what she had done to my father" (234). The narrator silently tells his mother he will not speak of the subject, at the same time he needs to know more about her part in the incident:

> But I couldn't understand, not without knowing more. I wanted to ask her if she had loved McIlhenny at any time, really loved him. But I was afraid she might say she still loved him, or even that she loved him for the years in between, when she first went out with him, through his leaving her and marrying Katie, through her figuring him, with Joe's help, as the informer, through her tipping him off and seeing him flee and vanish to Chicago . . . finally through her meeting my father four years later and realising what Eddie meant to him and his family. . . . What, finally, did she not know when she stood with my father at the alter-rail to be married? That her father had ordered Eddie's execution? (234–235)

It becomes evident through reading in the dark that this situation is at once a political intrigue brought about by partition and the continuing colonial presence in the North, and at the same time a deeply personal and painful situation for the nameless narrator. His parents' marriage, his mother's relationship with Katie, and their entire family history is embroiled and trapped by the past that will not go away. Ironically, of course, everyone believes the "wrong" past: the actual past is much more damaging to the family and to the parents' marriage than the past that is commonly believed.

Knowledge gained by reading in the dark does not liberate the narrator, but further binds him to the ghosts: Eddie, McIlhenny, Larry, his grandfather, and, increasingly, his mother's loss of sanity. The narrator's identity is eventually released from the tight Derry hold when he goes to university in Belfast. Still, the mess of his family's past remains as an impenetrable barrier between him and his father, and certainly him and his mother. The narrator expresses a kind of pity for his father's innocence in believing, in utter shame, all these years that Eddie was an informer. His mother, too, he pities, but still in his mind he questions the depth of her knowledge. He cannot ask anything, but tantalizingly the distances yet to be measured could be met if only he knew what she knew:

> Of course, Joe did not go to the IRA with information about McIlhenny. He would not have known where to go. He went to my mother. I knew this without any doubt. It was as if she told me outright. It was she who brought Joe to my grandfather and had Joe tell what she saw that night of the eighth of July 1926 when he saw McIlhenny get of Burke's police car in the small hours of the morning. That's when Grandfather realised for sure the mistake he had made with Eddie. But even then, mother didn't know the full story of Eddie's death—just that he had been executed in error. But not on her father's orders. . . . What she knew was bad enough. McIlhenny, her sister's husband, the man she had once loved—maybe still loved—and who had ditched her, was an informer. Now she was informing on him. But rather than sentencing him to death, perhaps she was the one who then went and told him his cover was blown, that he better get out. And then she married my father, closing herself in forever, haunted forever. (241–242)

Those in the past were not any better able to read in the dark. We often think of "distance" in relation to time as duration, of time that has passed; yet the distance to the events in the present is as difficult to measure as the distance to events in the past. For example, the grandfather misreads information concerning a possible informer and executes the wrong man. The narrator's mother's love for McIlhenny is a kind of misreading, too. She and Katie certainly misread what kind of man he was, both being gullible to his charm, not to mention the grandfather's misreading of him. And so, while the novel is about post-partition in Derry and affords a postcolonial reading of the text, it also can be read as a very personal search for truth that does more to harm the identity of the searcher than bring him into enlightenment. Lastly, it is a novel that shows us that all reading is a kind of reading in the dark: all measuring of distances are interpretations performed in time, susceptible to the individual's ability to know and understand events. The people participating in the past—in their own present—are as fallible as the narrator twenty-five years later.

In *Mother of Pearl* the indecipherable past causes Pearl/Mary to destroy her own life and the life of her unborn child. The text presents characters whose primary feature is their sad, broken lives, the only exception being sister Stella, whose first action as a young adult is to emigrate; thus, what is left in Ireland are sad, broken individuals who cannot connect emotionally, spiritually or physically. *Mother of Pearl*, like *Reading in the Dark*, also presents the immeasurable distance between situations and events; the text repeatedly presents characters who create their own misery in their attempts to "measure the distance," to account for and to explain. It is not surprising that every reading is erroneous and every action resulting from these readings leads the character farther away from the truth of the situation. The text presents doublings and repetitions that take odd forms; for example, mothers and their offspring—biological or "adopted"—repeat and enact the same kind of mistakes. Nothing is learned, no knowledge passed on; in this way, one is reminded of Deane's novel in which one generation's silence and mistakes are repeated by the next generation's silence and mistakes.

In "Uncanny Families: Neo-Gothic Motifs and the Theme of Social Change in Contemporary Irish Women's Fiction," Anne Fogarty suggests that *Mother of Pearl* presents an allegory of motherhood and the feminine in present-day Ireland. Fogarty employs "neo-gothic themes and motifs" to show that these themes and motifs "provide a shared symbolic matrix for these very distinctive literary creations."[8] Her reading of the double mothering is a form of repetition that implicates the changing role of women in Ireland: "*Mother of Pearl* creates a story of double mothering, I would argue, in order to question the current divided and contradictory constructions of the mother in Irish society. In particular, it opens to investigation the notion that maternal love is a natural and instinctive aspect of the female psychic economy. In the complex story that Morrissy sets up, it is only the non-biological mother who is capable of experiencing a positive connection with the daughter that she has forcefully to create for herself. Her love, however, is portrayed as furtive, perverse, criminal, and tragically doomed to failure."[9] Yet, the biological mother, Rita Golden, is the mother who feels guilty; she muses: "But no matter how far back Rita went, she could not gainsay the terrible truth that someone had wanted her baby more than she had."[10]

Heterosexual love, too, is furtive, perverse, and often tragic. When heterosexual coupling takes place, it is animalistic such as that between Mel Spain and Rita Golden on the floor of the ruined house conceiving Pearl/Mary, or quick, lusty, and doomed such as that of Rita Spain and Guiseppe Forte in his studio office conceiving Stella. The man and woman who profoundly want a child are Irene and Stanley. Sadly, the distance between virginal Irene and impotent Stanley cannot be measured: "He would lie there, surrendering to her probing, his eyes averted as if she were conducting a humiliating physical examination. . . . Her life's work, the joyless skills of years, were of no use. Stanley Godwin was impotent" (52). When Irene realizes that producing a child with Stanley is impossible, *all* distances become equally measurable. We see Irene equalizing distances when Charlie Piper shows up as a door-to-door salesman. Irene tells him that her and Stanley's daughter, Pearl, is asleep upstairs. There is, of course, no baby girl asleep upstairs, but it does not prevent Irene from measuring one—from connecting the idea of a child with a child for Charlie's benefit:

> "Any kids?" Charlie inquired.
> "Yes," Irene said promptly, "but she's asleep right now."
> She pointed at the ceiling and put a finger to her lips. Alarmed, Stanley made to contradict her. There it was again, out of the blue. A totally brazen lie. (70)

While Stanley thinks of Irene as producing a "brazen lie," Irene looks upon her invention as merely making something meaningful—as measuring the distance. With this lie she begins to measure the distance to a "real" Pearl.

At the very end of the novel, after she has been released from prison and returned to Granitefield to work, Irene is still able to measure the distance between herself and Pearl:

> "Is this your baby?" Clare, the kitchen maid, asked, coming across Irene alone with her treasures. . . ."Yes, but she's a big girl now," Irene told her. "Fully grown."
> "And do you see her often?"
> "Oh, yes," Irene tells her, and for once it is not altogether a lie. She sees her every day, in fact, a child skipping ahead of her on a dusty street. . . . It gives her ease to know that Pearl has an existence, somewhere, even at a distance and with another mother. (281)

In this passage we can see that the "distance" to Pearl is never too far for Irene; meaning is measured even when Pearl is away "out in the world and as long as Irene lives, she is not lost but merely waiting to be found again" (281). However, Pearl, who is now Mary, is alive but quite lost because she is unable to measure the distance between a little girl whose name she cannot remember and a person called Mary. Mary spends her life trying to read—to measure—a past that is and is not there. She, too, wishes to read in the dark of the past, a past that contains the suppressed Pearl.

Instead of finding Pearl the child she was, she invents Jewel, the supposedly dead sister that preceded Mary. In half a fiction, Rita invents a dead baby girl to cope with her returned child; completely an invention on

Mary's part, Jewel stands in as the measured distanced for something that cannot be recovered—namely, her own past as Pearl. And so we can see the repetition of the "invention" from mother to daughter. In fact, both mothers invent a child that was never "real": Irene invents Pearl, while Rita displaces Mary as the rightful firstborn with the invention of the dead sister. Both inventions—both attempts to make meaning or to make sense out of a senseless situation—wreak irrevocable psychological and emotional damage on Mary. Mary cannot recover "Pearl," nor can she make sense of the dead sister, and so she makes her own meaning with Jewel, who stands in for both "daughters." Tragically, the distance to Jewel is measurable, but her distance to her own fetus is immeasurable. When Mary discovers she is pregnant, all she can think about is that the baby will displace her "firstborn" Jewel: "Jewel was fully formed, a child who was part of me, whom I had nurtured and loved. . . . How could I abandon her? She lived and breathed, she stalked my dreams. . . . I could not turn my back on her. She was my firstborn, my only child. No other baby could be allowed to take her place" (273). Similar to Irene's "Pearl of a great price," Mary is searching for herself; this situation can be read as a repetition of Irene's lost self before Granitefield. This mirroring is also an attempt to measure the distance between the adult Irene and the Irene who was healthy years before. In a repetition with difference in deed but repetition of the Same in outcome, Mary recreates the sadness, violence, and loss that Irene created a generation before:

> There is the conjugal bed, steeped in blood, the sheets tormented as if the witness to violent love, a woman clawed by the pangs of birth, screaming. His first instinct is that she had been attacked, that someone has literally tried to slaughter her in her bed. He searches the rooms for evidence of an intruder, a forced lock, rifled drawers, a weapon that could have inflicted such wounds. And finds it in the knitting needle beside the bed. He tries to stem the flow of blood but cannot staunch it. He talks to her through her delirium that has transformed her silence into a kind of exultance of pain. She rides on the waves of it, like someone possessed, exhilarated by the sting of seaspray and the thunderous roar of the sea.
>
> "What have you done?" he shouts at her.
>
> At this stage it is merely a question. Only after the ambulance arrives does he ask again, sorrowfully, the blue light flashing across his face, the scream of a siren drowning out her answer.
>
> "What have you done?" (274)

What Mary has done is measure the distance between Jewel and herself; that distance must not have a new baby as a barrier, wall, or even a detour between Jewel (point A) and Mary (point B). Despite the fact that Jewel comes to Mary in the dark ("she stalked my dreams"), Mary is able to measure the distance to her, similar to Irene's ability to measure the distance to Pearl, when there seems to be "nothing there" to measure. With these examples we see that the ability to make meaning has very little to do with what we might call "reality" or a shared experience of "reality."

Concerning technique and immeasurable distances, I would like to mention briefly Roddy Doyle's 1999 *A Star Called Henry*. *A Star Called Henry* is at one level a fairly realistic tale of a boy born into abject poverty at the turn of the century who eventually becomes part of the Easter Rebellion and Michael Collins's inner circle, but at another level is a story that slips and slides all over the page. Action, events, and situations are liminal—neither completely believable nor completely unbelievable. In a recent reading of the novel, "Roddy Doyle: From Barrytown to the GPO," Brian Donnelly finds this indecidibility to be defect of Doyle's would-be attempt to create a realistic historical novel:

> the problem with the novel as an historical recreation is that it operates uneasily between the modes of naturalism and a kind of magic realism in the person of Henry's father and his wooden leg which serves him as both limb and deadly weapon. After his father's death this leg accompanies the young narrator as talisman and wooden Excalibur throughout the 1916 Rising and the Anglo-Irish war of 1919–1921. However, it increasingly jars against the pervading naturalism of a novel that constitutes a critique of the revolutionary period that seems to owe a good deal to O'Casey's view of those events as well as to much subsequent "revisionist" historical commentary.[11]

On the one hand, Donnelly's view is quite valid *if* Doyle is actually attempting a realistic/naturalistic portrayal in *A Star Called Henry*. On the other hand, Doyle may be deliberately skewing the prose of the text in order to create a different kind of reading experience and a different kind of sense. Perhaps the life of Henry Smart is not intended to be portrayed from a realistic point of view because a realistic, naturalistic common sense view of the events of this story is not possible. In other words, there is no way to measure the distances within Henry Smart's life and actually produce reasonable sense or meaning. Therefore, technique and form are employed to blur and skew our sense-making capabilities.

The reason Doyle may wish to produce an immeasurable distance is evident from the very first lines of the text. Young Henry is sitting with his mother on the steps of their tenement, when she directs his attention to the sky:

> My mother looked up at the stars. There were plenty of them up there. She lifted her hand. It swayed as she chose one. Her finger pointed.
>   —There's my little Henry up there. Look it.

> I looked, her other little Henry sitting beside her on the step. I looked up
> and hated him. She held me but she looked up at her twinkling boy. Poor me
> beside her, pale and red-eyed, held together by rashes and sores. A stomach
> crying to be filled, bare feet aching like an old, old man's. Me, a shocking sub-
> stitute for the little Henry who'd been too good for this world, the Henry God
> wanted for himself. Poor me.[12]

What Donnelly is calling revisionist is in this novel Doyle's persistence in depicting the underside of Dublin at the turn of the century and the league of
self-serving patriots who rebelled and fought against the English and then
each other for personal gain. Henry Smart is the quintessential odd man out.
Poised, skilled, and "smart," despite his miserable beginnings, he never quite
gets the idea until its too late that the new bosses of the potential republic
will be just like the old bosses of the Empire. It is my contention that Doyle
wishes to show that for someone like Henry Smart born into a cruel, cold,
starving world in which you are always already preceded by a dead sibling,
one too good for this world, there is no possibility of measuring the distance
to normal, rational meaning. Indeed, in spite of his intelligence, Henry is
not capable of discerning situations—the rebellion and war, for example—
in the same way others do; he thinks that the rebellion is a class rebellion and
believes that there will be an equality available in the new Ireland not available under British rule. Henry's ability to measure this illusion for what it is
comes late in the novel after Collins puts a contract out on him.

Fictional phantoms populate the last novel I would like to consider in
this chapter, Robert McLiam Wilson's *Ripley Bogle*. In fact, Loreto Todd in
Green English: Ireland's Influence on the English Language notes that the word
bogle is a word retained from planter English: "Although many dialect words
are recessive in Ireland, items such as the following can be heard in the natural speech of Ulster Scots speakers, especially those from rural areas . . .
bogle (spirit, poltergeist)."[13] An image of the narrator Ripley Bogle being a
ghost is not difficult to imagine as Bogle barely exists as a street person in
London during the telling of his supposedly "autobiographical" tale. Bogle's
narrative text is also ghostlike because it imperceptibly slips from one version of a story to another version of the same story. At least one version must
be what Stanley calls a "lie," a "lie" or a non-truthful version that destabilizes the narrative so that all versions of Bogle's story are suspect. This idea
further adds to the bogle of Bogle: as a spirit, we can never be certain that
the narrator is telling us anything concrete—anything that exists or happened in reality. With *Ripley Bogle* we enter into a text that is surprisingly
Beckettesque: a narrator tells us stories about people, including himself, but
the more we read, the more we realize that this narrative is simply a story or
a kind of metanarrative that must "go on" and tell stories.[14]

One difference, however, between Beckett and Wilson is that Wilson's story is place-specific; narrated from London, the text is actually centered in Belfast where Bogle was born and grew up. Even after leaving Belfast, Bogle continues to blame Belfast for his and everyone else's pathologies. After childhood friend Muire Ginchy's crotch is sliced through by barbed wire she had been standing on, he heaps the blame not on the British soldiers or the Troubles, but on the city: "I prefer to blame Belfast. It's all Belfast's fault. Something should be done. Belfast shouldn't be allowed to get away with this kind of thing. Belfast has to be stopped. Its time will come. I hope."[15] Published in 1989, *Ripley Bogle* predates the 1990s revival and celebration of all things Belfast. In 1989 Belfast is still the city of "Belfastards," which unlike the Derry-centered narratives, are full of venom and self-loathing. Evidence of the ever-changing culture in Ireland, the 1990s brought fictional accolades to Belfast. In "Transforming Belfast: The Evolving Role of the City in Northern Irish Fiction" Laura Pelaschiar describes the change as a "redemption and rediscovery of the Northern capital and of its spirit."[16] Pelaschiar elaborates on this change:

> Such a revolutionary change has brought about a most welcome redemption and rediscovery of the Northern capital and of its spirit. Initially portrayed as home to alienation, confusion and violence in the more conservative and pessimistic depictions of the nineteen seventies and nineteen eighties, in the nineteen nineties Belfast has gradually become a new, fertile urban location, no longer a place from which escape is necessary, but rather a laboratory for opportunities, a post-modern place depicted as *the* only space where it is possible to build and articulate a (post)national conscience, the only location for any possible encyclopaedic, multivoiced and multi-ethnic development of Northern society.[17]

Indeed, Wilson's 1996 *Eureka Street* makes fictional love to the northern star, Belfast, and illustrates Pelaschiar's "revolutionary change." *Eureka Street* concludes with Jake's early morning musing on "Belfast . . . a tender frail thing, composite of houses, roads and car parks."[18] In fact, even the elusive Ripley Bogle makes a Belfast appearance in *Eureka Street* shrewdly making good money as a translator for foreign film crews covering the Northern Ireland peace talks.[19]

Nevertheless, the Bogle of *Ripley Bogle* is acerbic in his attitude toward Belfast. According to Bogle early in the text, his Irish mother was a cheap prostitute and his conception occurred during one of her business transactions. Bogle's text actually begins with this event: *(Enter man with money. He waits. Enter woman, misclothed and passionate. They rut. Exeunt.* [1]). While Bogle is not the first author to begin his autobiography with conception, this

rendering is a certain kind of measuring of distance. Bogle's low and inaus-
picious beginning, unlike most coming of age narrative accounts, does not
improve. As a street person in London, barely existing on fellow tramp
Perry's handouts, Bogle has not improved his situation in life. Bogle's mother
marries Bogle senior but apparently he is not the biological father of Ripley.
Yet Bogle states that "I am part Welsh and Irish" (8), attributing the Irish to
his mother and Welsh to his father as he adds, "excuse my candour if I point
out that this is a fucking dreadful thing to be. I can never quite make up my
mind as to whom I loathe most . . . the Welsh or the Irish (the Welsh generally have it by a slim margin)" (8). While Bogle senior is Welsh, it is highly
unlikely that Bogle's mother's business attracted anyone besides the local
Irish Catholics at the infamous Turf Lodge where she plies her trade. So it is
puzzling why Bogle takes on the Bogle Welshness when he is not a Bogle:

> My father is definitely dead. This, I know. Though less physically repulsive
> than my mother, he was much more of a bastard. I remember fondly that he
> once tried to disembowel me with a broken Bass bottle. I think I was eight at
> the time. I would probably have murdered the old shitpot eventually if he had
> not beaten me to it by emptying the majority of his vital organs over the
> kitchen floor one day before I was old enough or big enough to slice him up
> on my own account. I don't know a great deal about his antecedents. They
> were, undoubtedly, rancid Welsh fuckbags like himself. (8)

And so we have another novel bound and tangled in the misread history and
events of the family. The important distinction between *Ripley Bogle* and two
of the novels already considered in this chapter is that it is the *reader* who is
reading in the dark; it is the *reader* who cannot measure distance properly
between events or situations. For most of the text Bogle's style indicates that
he is *not* reading in the dark; that he does not have difficulty measuring the
distance between point A and point B, however ugly, violent, and sad that
distance might be. However, the deeper into Bogle's text we go, the more it
becomes apparent that he is toying with the distances and forcing the reader
into the dark. The narrative presents one version, one measurement, only to
revise that measurement later. For example, the narrator's initial bond with
Bogle senior is put into question when he is a student at Cambridge. In an
italicized passage, Bogle admits late in the novel that he did have trouble
measuring the distance between Bogle and himself. He confesses:

> *I think many of my personal problems stem from the fact that I never knew who
> my father was. My real father that is, the man who paid the halfpenny or what-
> ever it cost in 1963 to shtup my old mother. A lot of men have visited a prostitute
> at some point. It really could have been almost anyone. Soon, every time I saw an
> attractive or admirable man over forty years of age I would begin my extravagant*

chronological calculations other imagined fathers include: Richard Burton, Gerry Fitt, Philip Larkin (!), Anthony Burgess, Robert Mitchum and Pat McGahey, barman in the Sports Bar on the Lower Falls during the early months of 1963. (237–238)

Bogle's italicized passages, the reader assumes, are supposed to function as the truthful version or the coming-clean version of Bogle's story; yet we will discover that this assumption is fallible. The mystery of Bogle's biological patriarch will never be solved, and up to this point in the novel the reader is not aware that Bogle is troubled by this mystery. We now see clearly that the above cited quotation from early in the novel, "I am part Welsh and Irish," is a fabrication, simply a version of the Bogle story.

The blatant inconsistency concerning his father in Bogle's story is particularly telling because of his part in the death of, and his disavowal of responsibility for, his own child with Deirdre. Yet Bogle does not register the inconsistency concerning the competing versions of his "father" story. The three differing versions of the text that he acknowledges, the "three little porkies that I've told you" (316), concern Deirdre's pregnancy, his relationship with Laura, and his account of Maurice's death. In the first account of Deirdre's pregnancy and subsequent miscarriage, Bogle states that he is not the father and that her losing the child has nothing to do with him. Midway through the novel, Bogle states, "I was ignoring the actual fatherhood of her abortion mess. I never seemed to get round to asking the identity of her impregnator" (186). This clear measurement of the distance between Deirdre and Bogle *should* make the reader suspect but probably would not on an initial reading of the novel. However, the text begins to slip off the page when Bogle adds, "the notion that my supposed lover had shown her sexual incontinence in this nasty fashion didn't prey on my mind half enough" (186). Bogle sacrifices a great deal to be with Deirdre, who is Protestant, even ignoring an IRA family member's warning to stay away from her. Therefore, we should be suspicious that the not-said is more important than the said.

Perhaps of the "three little porkies" Bogle tells it is the one concerning Deirdre that least surprises us when we find out that the first version was not true. Near the end of the text he says, "You remember that when I told you about Deirdre's fabulous miscarriage I claimed innocence of the actual impregnation. Well, that was a lie. It was me really" (312). With abortion illegal in Ulster, Bogle decides to attempt the removal the fetus himself, because from what Deirdre tells him, she is not very far along. After studying medical books at the local library, he believes he has a good idea of the basics of the task. Needless to say, Bogle botches the job with his little paint brush, yet defends himself accordingly: "it probably would have been all right if my temporal calculations had proved correct. If she *had* been merely a couple of months gone by my amateur efforts might have done the job without too much fuss. Since she was in reality more than five months along her way, I cocked it up rather. Christ, five months! It must have been a fully formed, recognisably human and bloody huge—football size. And I had tried dislodging it with that barbarous brush of mine!" (314). As Bogle then says, "You can see why I lied about it," and indeed, the reader can see. Yet Bogle fails to measure the distance between himself and his aborted offspring; he concentrates his remorse on the fact that he tried to seduce Deirdre after the fact: "The whole thing was horrible; the brush, the mess, the lavatorial rejection, the grief and all; but by far the worst bit was the fact that I had tried to boff her afterwards. God, I wish I hadn't done that!" (314). Admittedly, while Bogle's trying "to boff" Deirdre afterward is unfeeling and self-centered, it still does not fully account for the loss of the child nor—adequately—for Deirdre. Both topics are abandoned as the narrative quickly moves on to admit the next "little porkie." The next little porkie is the confession that his elaborate story about his relationship with the posh Cambridge Laura was untrue. Bogle states that some of the story was true—the fact that he was obsessed with her—but that he "never made it with Laura" (315).

The third little porkie concerns Bogle's friend Maurice, who becomes involved in the IRA. Maurice, who comes from the middle-class Malone Road area, is, as Bogle states, ironically committed to the Nationalist cause: "It was ironic really. There was me, Ripley Bogle, from out of the less-than-working classes, child of the Falls and son of a gun, breaking my supraspermbound balls to get out of all that and there was Maurice, child of ease, of silvergobbed and pretty posh, trying to be Che Guevara" (102). On the same page, Bogle states that Maurice should have left his politics in the realm of theory, because in the end, "They killed him. I knew they would in the end but what could I do? I was young, a boy. I had problems of my own. It wasn't my fault. There was nothing I could do" (102). Bogle is immediately defensive, which should warn the reader that this account may be missing a few details.

Two hundred pages later the reader gets the full account of the story. Maurice does in fact get himself in over his head; going on the run, he enlists Bogle's help. Unable to turn down his friend in trouble, Bogle helps him hide in Maurice's family boat out in Kilkeel, bringing him cigarettes and food; this act, of course, makes Bogle implicitly "involved," too. Information can be a dangerous thing. After Bogle is picked up by those looking for Maurice, he is beaten and with a gun pressed to his head tells them where his friend is: "the old gun-at-the-head ploy is such a good one . . . it really gets the job done. It's a great incentive scheme" (303). He continues: "I spilt the beans, of course. In a big way. I sobbed and screamed my way to infamy. I told them everything. I told them about Kilkeel, the boat, the gun he was carrying. I told them things they didn't want to know. I just talked and sobbed and begged. I went to work on treachery and accomplished quite a lot" (303). And yet this part is not the worst of the whole ordeal for Bogle; he must take them to the boat and draw Maurice out so that they will shoot him, leaving him to die a purposefully slow death with Bogle adrift on the water in the boat.

All these "lies" that Bogle retells lead the reader to reevaluate each story and the narrator's reliability. The first interpretation of the Maurice story, for instance, seemed plausible enough; the retelling of it *should* seem plausible, but it does not because we no longer trust Bogle's narrative. In the last few pages of the text, Bogle categorizes his lies. The worst lie is the one concerning Deirdre; yet the lie that causes him "the greatest loss of dignity and self-esteem was, surprisingly, that fictional Laura boff" (318). This admission alone seems suspicious; the distance between Bogle's hand in aborting his and Deirdre's child is much farther or much harder to reach than the distance to his failed "boffing" of Laura. This admission comes from a man who seems not to have actually *experienced* the abortion of his own child and the treachery and death of his best friend. And so the "worst lie" may be that nothing is true, including each of the revisions—each of the "porkies." Bogle's lame "greatest loss of dignity and self-esteem" attributed to "that fictional Laura boff" is necessarily a lie because the entire story (both versions) is a lie; yet Bogle ironically may actually believe this to be the fictional event having the most impact on his person and thus "true" from a position of fantasy.

The suspicion that all of Bogle's narrative is fictional is further supported by Bogle's narrative on his fellow street person friend Perry. In fact, Bogle's story actually unravels and reveals its invention-in-the-making in the passages concerning Perry. Bogle's interaction with Perry is supposedly in the present; Perry, like Bogle, is a derelict barely surviving on the streets of London. According to Bogle, Perry was a refugee from Poland during World War II, making him thirty or forty years older than Bogle. Perry has an uncanny ability to survive homelessness; he even builds himself a little shack by the river and shares cigarettes and coffee with Bogle. It is evident that Perry fulfills a father-figure role for Bogle. Perry shows this fatherlike concern for Bogle early in the text:

> The mist gathered and banked around them now. A ponderous curtain of diaphanous fog and subtle drizzle. Mist glitters on the hair of both men, thick and thin. Perry speaks.
> "Why do you do this thing?"
> "What thing is this?"
> "Being a tramp, you know, that thing."
> "Oh yes, that."
> "Well?"

"My career plans are a little uncertain at the minute, Perry."

"Funny."

"Yes."

He strikes another match and lights both paltry cigarettes.

"This is no good for you. You look like a dead man."

He gives the mortal remains of Ripley Bogle another cigarette. The corpse thanks him.

"Get yourself some money. Get a place to live. You could do that easily enough. Couldn't you?"

Ripley's merriment burgeons.

"Oh yes. Not a problem nowhere."

His laughter fades and his face grows bitter with the mild amusement of despair. His future does not trouble him. He'll mix a kind of hope, knead it and bake it in experience.

"Ah, we understand each other, Ripley. There are things we don't have to say." (90–91)

This conversation could easily be between a father and a son; in a typical scenario the father urges the son to get a job or to go back to school. From what Bogle has told us about his family life—basically nonexistent, as his father, Bogle senior, is murdered, and he leaves home as a young teenager in order to be with Deirdre—we can imagine how a lovingly concerned conversation with father-figure Perry might easily be worked into Bogle's story. Bogle measures the distance of a true father-son bond in the form of adopted father Perry.

The reader has no way of knowing if this conversation is "real" or a "lie." The fact that it occurs early in the text and takes place in Bogle's present lends credibility to its verisimilitude. Yet there seems to be something askew with the Perry story, which emerges in one of Bogle's italicized passages later in the text. The italicized text appears after Bogle finds out Perry has died. Bogle is quite upset by his death and sobs openly. For the first time in his life Bogle states that he would like to mourn the dead: "I'd like to mourn Perry but I don't know how" (284). Bogle confesses that he has never properly mourned death in the past: "When my father died I was too young and too stupid to have much of a clue about a suitable reaction. When Maurice died I performed an approximation of mourning. But it was a feeble thing, mainly composed of anger, guilt, hatred, regret and remorse. None of these quick emotions would seem to apply to Perry's demise and I'm too tired and shamed to work on another version" (284). Despite the noble sentiment of mourning Perry's death, the day Perry is found dead Bogle manages to find Perry's stash of cash in his shack before the police or social workers find it. Bogle claims to toss the seventy-five quid found in Perry's shack off the Waterloo Bridge into the Thames; needless to say, this action is a rather odd

thing for a penniless street person to do, no matter how much guilt or shame
he may feel. It is at this point the text provides the suspicious italicized passage in which Bogle claims that Perry told him that he had dreams about becoming a young, healthy man again; when Perry woke from these dreams,
the image of himself as young and healthy fed into his daily old man, tramp
life. His fantasy self afforded him better looks, more brains, and even a larger
penis. For some reason Bogle finds Perry's admissions quite disagreeable and
unbecoming to a man in Perry's stage and station of life. Bogle's comments
on Perry's fantasy tell us much more about Bogle than Perry:

> *For Perry, this longing to be someone else was the most comic disgrace of all. An
> old man with his laughable pipe dreams and improbabilities.*
>
>   *I told him not to worry and all that kind of reassuring and affectionate stuff.
> I told him it was no big deal but I began to worry on my own behalf when I
> started having similar fantasies myself. It was alright for Perry because he was an-
> cient but I was only a kid for chrissakes! I didn't tell him about this. I didn't think
> he'd have been interested.* (285–286)

Bogle does not tell Perry about his fantasy, but the reader wonders: is he
telling us about his own fantasy self in the form of this text? All the elements
of Perry's dreams manifest themselves in Bogle's stories about himself: incredibly good-looking women are fighting each other to "boff" Bogle (all except Laura); despite Bogle's Falls Road upbringing, he wins a scholarship to
Cambridge; when he is sent down from Cambridge he easily gets a construction job in London, proving again his health and fitness, to say nothing of his prowess as a street fighter, skills gained in the rough parts of
Belfast. It is also after this italicized passage that Bogle admits to his "three
little porkies." Therefore, it is at this point late in the novel that the stories,
whether true, partially true, or completely untrue, need to be retold in a
more unflattering manner. Yet, Bogle gives nothing away of his fantasy
image *except* the Laura story, and as he points out this one hurts him personally the most, which makes sense if we believe that both the Deirdre and
Maurice stories are essentially untrue.

    Events and situations in Bogle's story never stabilize, and so it is impos-
sible to measure accurately the distance from one to another; it is impossible to make stable meaning from the text. Interpreting *Ripley Bogle* from the
point of view that all of Bogle's stories are "lies" based on his denials, omissions, and reworked versions is equally as plausible, if not more plausible,
than believing his life story as he presents it, even in the second, altered version. In the end, Bogle's story about Perry could be as fictional as the other
"three little porkies"; the only difference is that he never admits that the
Perry story is fabricated. With no way to the "fix" events in Bogle's story, we

might even imagine that the Perry tale is completely fictionalized, while the "porkies" are true, or at least partially true. In effect, the novel affords us the freedom to measure the distances in whatever way we think most plausible. Ghostlike, Bogle and his stories are as elusive and difficult to "read" as a ghost in the dark. In the next chapter, bodies and stories will become even more difficult to interpret as the velocity and power of the fictional bodies is increased to the point of imperceptibility.

Chapter Five 🔷

Discourse and the Body
Velocity and Power

I n this chapter the body becomes more difficult to chart because fictional bodies whirl out of control and confound customary narrative, and produce another kind of sense. The body blurs the power grid, challenges our ability to understand and makes nonsense out of accepted or normal ways of acting and agency. The idea of velocity and power concentrates on three of the most bizarre, often comic, sometimes violent and unstable narratives in the contemporary Irish novel. These novels are John Banville's *Book of Evidence* (1989), Patrick McCabe's *The Butcher Boy* (1992) and *Breakfast on Pluto* (1998). Politically demarcated, the gauging of velocity of the body is always coupled with the power grid, which attempts to sensor or squelch the very physicality of the body. After our focus on gender and bodies, especially with the topic of bodies over the boundary in chapter 3 and bodies that undergo erasure at the very point we attempt to interpret them in chapter 4, this chapter more exclusively concerns power and bodies, which, perhaps stereotypically, involves male-centered narrative discourses. The unusual and interesting aspect of each of these novels is that the male-dominated discourse is also a discourse outside the boundaries of a male power structure territory. Instead of the narratives reterritorializing power by validating traditional sense-making capabilities, each text utilizes different prose strategies that deterritorializes traditional sense through the movement both mimetically and stylistically. Thus, the novels formally produce a power and velocity that match the events and movement of the narrative mimetically. The combination of impact and movement makes the novels in this chapter exceptional; in order to interpret these novels, we need to open up a different understanding of violence.

In this chapter we move increasingly into a metafictional realm. The body becomes the abstract prose body as well as the literal or mimetic "body" in *The Book of Evidence, The Butcher Boy,* and *Breakfast on Pluto.* As previously delineated in our discussion of Deleuze in chapter 1, the plane of immanence or consistency reads a text for movement, speeds, "haecceities," and breakdowns and rejects typical "sense-making" strategies. Conversely, the plane of organization reads a text for stability, universalizing truths, and totality and rejects texts that are not predictable and easily categorized. The plane of consistency is not an abstraction or universalized entity unrealized concretely. As we saw in chapter 4, the plane of immanence or consistency is not a "place" where we can conduct fixed measurements or categorize stable entities. As opposed to our ordinary assumption that each of us remains the same over a lifetime, or at least with a stable essential core that slowly changes in predictable ways, Deleuze suggests a constantly shifting flow of disconnected, momentary identities. Narratives in these novels enact this constantly shifting flow.

Deleuze provides a reading strategy that "rolls" with the prose and critiques predictable or traditional ways of interpreting texts. This strategy helps us to read the narrator, Freddie Montgomery, in John Banville's novel, *The Book of Evidence.* Freddie's confessional narrative prose drags, stutters, and then flies forward with the torque of someone in a rage wielding a hammer. This narrator cannot make proper "sense" of the world and in fact admits as much at the beginning of the book: "Other people seemed to have a density, a thereness, which I lacked."[1] According to Tony E. Jackson in "Science, Art, and the Shipwreck of Knowledge: The Novels of John Banville," it is Freddie's lack of knowing, of being unable to come into full presence, that allows him to murder Josie Bell.[2] The word "allows" can be interpreted in the sense of permits or sanctions because it is his inability to imagine her fully "there" that makes him indifferent to her death. I agree that Freddie lacks an ability to "appreciate" Josie as valuable or important by virtue of being human, yet I do not agree that it is simply a lack of knowledge or even a lack of imagination. However, Brian Cosgrove would simply characterize Freddie as "postmodern" as he believes that Banville's text denies "Irish socio-political actualities" that allow them "to indulge (if that is the correct term) in postmodern procedures."[3] Banville has received a great deal of critical attention in the 1990s, and one of the critical controversies surrounding Banville's work involves his "Irishness" versus his indebtedness to certain Modernists (notably Joyce and Beckett). Cosgrove is critical of Banville's own stance as an "Irish" writer because, he argues, that one cannot deal with the "realities" of the situation and write in a self-referential manner:

> There has, conversely, been too much "grief" of various kinds to allow the contemporary Irish writer to resort to self-referential "fiction." It is significant that Banville appears to arrive at a possible postmodernism by screening out

those insistent Irish realities that would otherwise compromise a programme of radical fictionality. It is equally notable that Banville, one of the Irish-based writers with the strongest claim to be considered postmodernist, should in a recent interview have concluded on this note: "I stay in this country but I'm not going to be an Irish writer. I'm not going to do the Irish thing."[4]

Contrary to Cosgrove's view, Joseph McMinn points out that it is already well established that "critics offer a version of Banville which suggests that his style of postmodernism is not without precedent, and that the Irish context, especially of a violent, colonial history, has a deep, but unpredictable, impact on his fictions."[5] Further, Banville's "Irish dimension" in relation to "'modernity' may lie in the way he revises, reinvents and redeploys the Irish experience of change and confusion, translating it into elaborate and dramatic metaphor. As so often, he has turned his back towards the example and achievement of classic Irish modernism."[6]

The critic's ability or inability to read from an Irish context or a so-called postmodern perspective may be doing little to open up a reading that actually *reads* Freddie's movement and often erratic behavior. Freddie, the selfish, pompous, and sophisticated world traveler turned drifter, should not fool the reader; his irony and eventually his cruelty advance like lightning and without warning, yet he has the ability to hide under the cover of statements that insinuate a feigned ignorance and even a modesty: "They would speak of whole peoples as if they were speaking of a single individual, while to speak even of an individual with any show of certainty seemed to me foolhardy. Oh, they knew no bounds" (17). Freddie also knows no bounds as he charismatically glides across the prose page. Freddie does not lack knowledge, as Jackson states; what Freddie lacks is an ability to operate on a plane of organization—his statement that he cannot "speak of an individual with any show of certainty" has to do with his behavior rather than with knowledge. Freddie cannot exist on the plane of rational organization and sensible action—Freddie flies apart, stutters, breaks down, and begins again with an erratic velocity. If he could operate in a rational way or could have operated in a sensible manner according to common sense and tradition, then we would not have a book of confessional evidence.

Ostensibly, Freddie's narrative, this book of evidence, is written because he will now go to trial for the murder of Josie Bell, but we cannot be sure of what the narrator tells us. At the end of the book of evidence the inspector asks how much of this text is true: "True, Inspector? I said. All of it. None of it. Only the shame" (220). Whether he is becoming-murderer, becoming-penitent, or becoming-liar, what matters is the series of haecceities—the slowness and quickness—that produces meaning; Freddie's prose produces a disequilibrium, a vibration and a stuttering that rips up our traditional sense-making capacity. The disequilibrium is further accentuated because Freddie claims to recall the past, and therefore his memory is occasionally interpreted by the present: his attorney, Maolseachlainn's visits, or Daphne's weekly visit, which he does not always record. Although a standard narrative technique, Freddie's role as "unreliable narrator" deterritorializes the very technique that makes him unstable. In other words, the unreliable narrator is a major language convention that Freddie deterritorializes by making it hum, stutter, and break down; he lulls us into a referential sense-making mode (though we know as smart readers what he says is not "reliable") as he destroys our very ability to make sense.

There are three discursive assemblages that I would like to examine: Freddie's mother, his father, and his attempt to steal the painting from Binkie Behrens. A discursive assemblage consists of strands and segments of prose that connect and reconnect. Deleuze and Guattari often characterize an assemblage in prose as "machinic": a machinic assemblage works, builds, breaks down much like a machine. Interestingly, the prime machinic function is its ability to break down and dismantle the very thing it has put together. Freddie's discourses produce a machinic assemblage: they are initiated, built up, and then fall apart only to be rebuilt later in the text. Discourse, for example, concerning his father comes out in a series of segments; these segments are often bitterly and abruptly terminated by Freddie, only to begin, end, and reattach to the former narrative segments in the text. Freddie's father becomes an assemblage of memories, lies, and hate all attaching and reattaching without ever providing us with a "man"; instead, his father is a prose machine that cannot be decoded.

It is interesting that the three main assemblages in the text function as a reterritorialization of the nuclear family: mommy, daddy, me. Binkie Behrens occupies several levels of father-figure assemblage: suitor-lover of Freddie's mother, father of Freddie's peer-lover, Anna, and silent provider for Freddie's years of drifting. The oedipalization of this discourse, however, functions as a deterritorialization of traditional discourse, and social and cultural regulator. Freddie decodes the familial discourse at the same point at which he dismantles the sense-making ability of the major language. It is no surprise that Freddie lacks humanistically instilled character traits that the tradition depends upon in order to "make sense"; it is most likely because Freddie lacks certain commonly understood humanistic ways of thinking that the reader finds it easy to loath Freddie as a character or as a "person."

The text, of course, centers on his one act of bodily violence, but all of Freddie is violence: becoming-Freddie is becoming-violent. The first vivid instance is his interaction with his mother concerning his father's collection of paintings. Freddie's account is a grand series of haecceities: he inflates like a rubber balloon, blows out, deflates, begins again. The flow of language in the following passage tells us more about our narrator than what it is he referentially narrates; the scene opens with the spoiled son making a spectacle of himself:

> Well? I said, but she only raised her eyebrows blandly and said, Well what? She was almost smirking. That did it. I shouted, I waved my fists, I stamped about stiff-legged, beside myself. Where were they, the pictures, I cried, what had she done with them? I demanded to know. . . . My anger, my sense of outrage, impressed me. I was moved. I might have shed tears, I felt so sorry for myself. She let me go on like this for a while. . . . Then, when I paused to take a breath, she started. Demand, did I? . . . I fell back a pace. I had forgotten what she was like when she gets going. Then I gathered myself and launched at her again. (60)

The temper tantrum that Freddie enacts here is suspect. Freddie is indeed acting—this scene is staged: performed for the benefit of himself, his mother, his conscience, or, more likely, for the reader's benefit. Freddie's prose jerks, rolls, breaks down, then begins again. Yet the rhythm seems familiar: has Freddie staged this performance? Is he reenacting a scene from a previous drama? "I had forgotten what she was like when she gets going" indicates that Freddie has been through this before. As readers, we have to assume that Freddie is staging this in prose for the reader's benefit; indeed, he even comments on his own histrionics: "My anger, my sense of outrage, impressed me. I was moved. I might have shed tears, I felt so sorry for myself." This consciousness, this awareness that he is performing is further underscored in the passage that follows as Freddie—the confessor—wants to capture the spectacle of his performance. The room vibrates with noise as even the dog joins in the cacophony; then, spinning forward, both Freddie and his mother fly across the page only to dissipate into a pool of sighs and desolate laughter:

> We were like furious children—no, not children, but big, maddened, primitive creatures—mastodons, something like that—tearing and thrashing in a jungle clearing amidst a storm of whipping lianas and uprooted vegetation. The air throbbed between us, blood-dimmed and thick. There was a sense of things ranged around us in a trance of terror and awe. At last, sated, we disengaged tusks and turned aside. I nursed my pounding head in my hands. . . . Time passed. She sighed again. You got the money, she said. . . . Suddenly she laughed. (60)

The allegory of tearing, thrashing jungle beasts is interesting considering that this battle of engaged tusks is merely a domestic spat between mother and son. For some reason Freddie the narrator wants the reader to feel the power, bodies in motion, anger, anguish, desperation, and pain (the pounding hangover) in this scene. The throbbing "blood-dimmed" air is thick, to be sure, thick with pretension. Freddie is preparing his reader.

Battling with his mother may have been a common activity, but apparently Freddie's father was too distant and too removed from his son to bother with him. This aspect of Freddie's narrative unravels slowly as Freddie hooks pieces of several segments of discourse-about-the-father together. Even Freddie scoffs at his bent toward the cliché of the Oedipal, "I did not think unkindly of him—apart, that is, from wanting deep down to kill him, so that I might marry my mother, a novel and compelling notion which my counsel urges on me frequently" (29–30). Maolseachlainn, as Freddie notes, "has a trick of seizing on the apparently trivial in the elaboration of his cases," and is interested in Freddie's obsession—as evidenced in the narrative—with his parents. Yet the "kill the father and marry the mother" plot is too predictable, too reterritorialized to be believed: Maolseachlainn and the community would sincerely like to frame Freddie's actions as a byproduct of a common Freudian desire to supplant the father-figure. Unfortunately, Freddie's prose cannot be so easily reterritorialized.

Still, Freddie is obsessed with details of his father's life and death—Freddie even fabricates a touching deathbed scene in which he is at his father's side at the point of death, but then he negates the narrative by stating that he was not even at the house when his father died. As a boy, on Sundays and school holidays Freddie accompanied his father to town "to visit a poppet he kept there" (28); "town" was "Kingstown," which at that time was no longer called Kingstown but Dun Laoghaire: "My father never referred to the place as anything but Kingstown: he had no time for the native jabber" (27). Freddie's dad, a "Castle Catholic," was a displaced member of the Ascendancy, which believes that "the world, the only worthwhile world, had ended with the last vice-roy's departure from these shores, after that it was all just a wrangle among peasants" (29). Freddie's disdain for his father is evident in the son's fantasy of the father's sexual exploits with his mistress: "I picture him on those Sunday afternoons with his mistress, an ample young lady . . . before whom he kneels, poised trembling on one knee . . . his moist red mouth open in supplication" (29). A few lines later, Freddie breaks off the segment of his father with, "But I digress" (30) which is only a first in a series of "digressions" or what will become "interruptions" that are abruptly ended. This segment of Freddie's father narrative tells us more in its termination—the blockage—than what it actually tells us about the father.

In other words, the blocks or breakdowns in Freddie's discourse concerning his father are more important than the discourse itself. The reader assumes that when Freddie returns home in order to get money to repay Senor Aguirre, he reminisces about his father because he has not been home for ten years. Freddie's memories, however, are so confused with fictionalized accounts that it is difficult to tell if anything he tells us is "true." During dinner the first evening home, Freddie interjects prose segments about his father into the text; after discussing the decline and final period of his father's life, Freddie, striking a note of rare sincerity, tells us:

> He died at evening. The room was still heavy with the long day's heat. I sat on a chair beside his bed in the open window and held his hand. His hand. The waxen feel of. How bright the air above the trees, bright and blue, like the limitless skies of childhood. I put my arm around him, laid a hand on his forehead. He said to me: don't mind her. He said to me—Stop this, stop it. I was not there. I have not been present at anyone's death. He died alone, slipped away while no one was looking. . . . By the time I arrived from the city they had trussed him up, ready for the coffin. . . . Extraordinary: all that anger and resentment, that furious, unfocused energy: gone. (51–52)

Again, Freddie stages a kind of performance for the reader—if it is a performance. The indecidability is so radical that it could swing either way: he was not there for his father and Freddie is a cad; he was there for his father and the loss is too painful to record accurately. The reader asks, along with the inspector, "how much of it is true"? Before the obvious breakdown, "Stop this, stop it," Freddie's prose seems to form a blockage with "His hand. The waxen feel of." The waxen feel of what? We assume his hand, but Freddie's narrative spaces out with "How bright the air . . . limitless skies of childhood." This becoming-distracted, this narrative technique of spinning off the topic and spinning into a completely different mood and tempo may be a feature of Freddie's story that we cannot "colonize" or reterritorialize.

Freddie's supposedly nostalgic mood is shattered, of course, with the present, as he sits in his cell of the prison: "Stop this, stop it." The memory machine again leaves the reader wondering as Freddie ends this segment with "all that anger and resentment," which could be either his father's own anger and resentment "gone" because he is dead; or Freddie's own anger and resentment is "gone" suddenly at his father's death because there is no longer an object for it; or Freddie, sitting in prison, feels that the anger and resentment he felt or he attributes to his father is very distant and minimal now. In less than a half page of prose, Freddie's becoming-nostalgic or becoming-liar suggests multiple omissions—breakdowns and blockages—and calls into question any kind of "reliable" way to interpret our narrator.

One reason for the stories about mommy-daddy-me could be that this confessional, this book of evidence, is indeed looking for evidence to support a motive for the murder. Was it daddy-inspired rage? Mommy-inspired rage? Freddie is preparing us. He does finally confess the motivation, but it is not the motive Maolseachlainn, the inspector, or the thuggish policemen want to hear. Even after his arrest, Freddie keeps telling stories. Still, most of the novel builds a narrative in the traditional way, only to show that the narrative dismantles the tradition in one scene—the becoming-murderer scene.

The becoming-murderer chapter of the book begins with Freddie happily sailing off to Whitewater in the rented Humber Hawk in order to steal a painting from Binkie Behrens's collection. The hammer purchased in the village hardware shop prior to going to Whitewater, part of Freddie's "burglar's kit" (102), and narrated in the previous chapter is most likely the point that Freddie starts spinning into a stuttering becoming-murderer narrator. The hammer itself brings out Freddie's childhood alter ego, which he confusingly states is "not Bunter." At this point in the narrative, the story becomes blocked and confused. Freddie's narration falters, attempts to explain, to go on, but explains nothing:

> Then I spotted the hammer. One moulded, polished piece of stainless steel, like a bone from the thigh of some swift animal, with a velvety, black rubber grip and a blued head and claw. . . . I insist it was an innocent desire, a wish, an ache, on the part of the deprived child inside me—not Bunter, not him, but the true, lost ghost of my boyhood—to possess this marvellous toy. For the first time my fairy-godfather hesitated. There are other models, he ventured, less—a hurried, breathy whisper—less expensive, sir. But no, no, I could not resist it. I must have it. That one. Yes, that one, there, with the tag on it. Exhibit A, in other words. (97)

We have three important blockages in this passage: first, who or what is Bunter? Second, who or what does "my fairy-godfather" symbolize? And third, the chasm opened with "he ventured, less—."

Interestingly, Billy Bunter is a fictional *enfant terrible* created by "Frank Richards," one of dozens of pseudonyms of Charles Harold St. John Hamilton.[7] Because Bunter comes to the surface of Freddie's fiction every time he becomes violent, we have to assume that in some twisted way in Freddie's mind, "Bunter" should "take the blame." Or at least "Bunter made me do it" would be Freddie's refrain. Bunter, therefore, seems connected to the "fairy-godfather" because both are fantastic or fictional characters with whom Freddie communicates. But the "fairy-godfather" could, of course, be a kind of intuition that usually guides Freddie away from trouble. This is a rather comic notion, given Freddie's past. Apparently Freddie's fairy-godfather has done nothing or very little up to this point in Freddie's life to save him from misguided decisions and deeds, and so it is curious that Freddie suddenly evokes a "fairy-godfather."

The third blockage is manifested both referentially and in the actual prose with the dash "—," that draws our attention to the breakdown, to time stopped, and to the immeasurable distance between one event and the next. The "he" in "he ventured," is supposedly the fairy-godfather, but it is questionable why a supernatural being would be interested in the price of the hammer. The candidate for "he" in "he ventured" could be the shop owner, and the reader may be getting a fragment of the conversation between Freddie and the hardware store worker. However we choose to attribute the line, "he ventured, less—a hurried, breathy whisper—less expensive, sir," the breakdown between "less—" and "—less expensive" posits the idea that Freddie becoming-violent is in the gap of "—." Whoever is supposedly speaking, and we may be sure that it is Freddie, wants to say "less murderous" or "less bludgeoning," or simply "less bloody." And so, premeditated or not, something about the sight of that hammer causes Freddie to evoke "Bunter," the brash bad boy of the Billy Bunter novels and television show, and what he reasons is his childhood deprivation. Freddie intertwines power and deprivation into a fantasy of taking control of a life out of control. Bunter in his original formation in Freddie's mind probably wielded a cricket bat that was a mock or toy becoming-sword or a stick that was an imaginary becoming-tomahawk; now, however, an overage and oversized Bunter desires a hammer that is a becoming-murder weapon.

In the next sentence, Freddie's prose fast-forwards to "I stumbled out of the shop with my parcel under my arm, bleared and grinning, happy as a drunken schoolboy." The "drunken schoolboy" continues Freddie's image of becoming-Bunter and his would-be sincere desire for the woman in the painting; still, he warns: "Do not be fooled: none of this means anything either" (108). The placement of this statement is odd. Freddie apparently wants the reader to feel how much he cares for this painting, and according to Jackson, it is only the painting that is real for Freddie; still, Freddie makes this statement and at the end of the chapter abandons the painting he loves so much in a ditch face-up in the rain. Another break in the narrative is evident as Freddie never gives an account of what he is going to do with the painting after the theft. His actions at this point of the narrative do not "make sense" in relation to "good sense" precepts; yet, his series of haecceities are not merely a "mad rage" or some other conventionally understood temporary loss of sense. Rather, Freddie is now freely deterritorializing the Freddie that has always been reterritorialized onto the plane of organization. Freddie, once he threatens and then abducts Josie, leaves the world of rational good sense; yet, the whole time he wonders why the world is so unreasonable. He even asks, "Why did she not run away?" In other words, why did she act so unreasonably and, by implication, "why did she not run away so I would not have to kill her?"

The bludgeoning that occurs as Freddie drives away from Whitewater is kind of macabre comedy because Freddie's self-pitying disbelief and inaptitude as becoming-murderer causes the narrative to stutter and wail. Yet we should be careful because Freddie's prose has such a terrific ability to draw us in, whirl us around, make us lose ourselves so that we could very easily find ourselves in Josie's position: swept along into a strange car before we know quite what is going on. Freddie makes statements that break up the violent trajectory of the scene; for example, he interjects, "We were shouting at each other now, like a married couple having a fight . . . her thumb went up my nose," (113) or "I was dismayed. How could this be happening to me—it was all so unfair. Bitter tears of self-pity squeezed into my eyes" (114). However, in the next sentence the violence and velocity increase as Freddie swings the hammer "in a wide, backhand sweep. The force of the blow flung her against the door . . . a fine thread of blood ran out of her nostril and across her cheek" (114). With the crash of the forged steel into the soft skin and fragile facial bone, the prose skids and flies across the page during the flight from Whitewater for pages until Josie is finally subdued, although not dead. Devoid of concern, Freddie does not check to see if she is alive when he abandons the car, painting, and Josie.

All motivation stemming from childhood traumas or the mommy-daddy-me reterritorializing break down: nothing causes Freddie to bludgeon and abandon Josie except for the fact that he *can*. There is nothing either sensible or non-sensible in his actions. Freddie has no motivation for either killing her or not killing her—both possibilities are the same to Freddie. It is this absolute apathy to the rules of reason and coherence, then, that is the most shocking thing about Freddie's story. Maolseachlainn, the inspector and the policemen are repulsed by Freddie not because he has some horrible story to tell, rather they are appalled because there is no story to tell. Despite the fact that this book of evidence is supposed to present a plausible "story" or a "reasonable" defense for the perpetrator of the crime, Freddie becoming-murderer has nothing to say. All that is left is Freddie's absolute velocity—his imperceptibility.

Interestingly, it only takes a viewing of Neil Jordan's film, *The Butcher Boy,* based on Patrick McCabe's novel, *The Butcher Boy,* to understand the power of the genre of the novel; the techniques available to the novel simply cannot be duplicated by the celluloid image. To be fair, Jordan's film is a noble attempt—the screenplay co-written by Jordan and McCabe—to capture Francie Brady's narrative. Still, even with a "grown" Francie, played by Stephen Rea, who also plays Benny Brady, narrating between scene shifts and delivering some of the novel's passages that could not be rewritten into dialogue (e.g., "The Francie Brady Not a Bad Bastard Anymore Diploma"), the film suffers from the inability to translate some qualities of the prose to film.[8] Francie's narrative, wild, whirling, and lacking punctuation, tells the story in a way that the film's portrayal of a boy with a dysfunctional family cannot. Although Eamonn Owens, the actor from Killeshandra, County Cavan, who plays Francie, is a spirited, tough, and often humorous Francie, he does not—the film does not allow him to—develop the shockingly mad aspects of Francie's narrative. Depth and nuance are lost as the film must present a reasonable story, even if the story is a young man becoming-murderer, so that audiences can "follow" the actions and motivations of the characters.

The problem, however, is that Francie's narrative is not reasonable and cannot be understood from a common-sense viewpoint; Francie is out of control in a way that is as equally savage as Freddie's violence in *The Book of Evidence*. John Scaggs in "Who is Francie Pig? Self-Identity and Narrative Reliability in *The Butcher Boy*" attributes Francie's identity to a psychological malaise: "Constantly unable to say exactly what he means, it follows that he never means exactly what he says. As in Jacques Lacan's suggestive thesis, Francie does not *speak;* he is *spoken*."[9] I disagree with Scaggs's view; Francie *does* say what he means and means what he says. It is quite true that Francie's discourse is skewed, but it is skewed for a purpose. He carries on conversations that the reader cannot tell are "real" conversations or "only" in his head. The assemblage that is most damaging to Francie, that affects him most deeply, is the connection between his own mother and Mrs. Nugent. One could even say that from one perspective, Francie's narrative is dependent upon this connection because in his own mind, according to his own narrative, his mother commits suicide because Francie "betrays" her. He betrays her, he believes, by his running away from home after an ugly row between Uncle Alo and his father and then his father and his mother on Christmas Eve. When he finally returns bearing a special gift for her, he finds out on the street and from Mrs. Nugent that he has just missed his mother's funeral.

While it is true that Francie's troubles with Mrs. Nugent already started after he and Joe took her son Philip's comics, Mrs. Nugent comes to Francie's house and informs his mother that, "she might have known not to let her son anywhere near the likes of me what else would you expect from a house where the father's never in, lying about in the pubs from morning to night, he's no better than a pig" (4), but learning of his mother's death from Mrs. Nugent cements a deep-seated fixation and remorse in Francie. Mrs. Nugent's earlier parting shot, "Pigs—sure the whole town knows that!" (4), reverberates through Francie's mind and begins the sad, truly self-deprecating charade of "The Pig Family!" (5). Although he hates Mrs. Nugent, one half of Francie's betrayal is in the fact that he did not want to be in the "pig family"—he wanted to be a Nugent, to belong to a family in which the mother does not go off to the "garage" because of her breakdowns and the father does not lie about in pubs from morning until night.

Therefore, meeting Mrs. Nugent on the street, fresh from running away, lodges a connection between Mrs. Nugent, his mother, and his own neglect or betrayal into an assemblage that becomes more twisted and convoluted with every segment of prose Francie devotes to Mrs. Nugent. According to Francie, Mrs. Nugent is the sole cause of everything "bad" that happens to him, including, at some level, the very fact that Francie was born into a pig family. And so we do not have a simple binary wherein Francie has replaced his own mother with another woman more worthy of affection; rather, we have an assemblage that includes Francie's mother, Mrs. Nugent, and Francie's own failure to love and to be loyal to the correct woman. Francie's attempt to capture in prose the street scene with Mrs. Nugent falters and breaks down again and again. It is in Francie's narrative omissions, not unlike Freddie's narrative omissions and breakdowns, that the reader can most pointedly commiserate with Francie as he braces himself against the terrible impact of Mrs. Nugent's action and speech on the street: "Then O Francis she says again isn't it a pity you missed the funeral and makes the sign of the cross. Funeral I says funeral and looked around to see was there anyone else with her some trick she was playing. . . . She wouldn't shut up about ma" (45). This segment attaches to the "pig" segment in such a way to render a valid cause and effect for Francie so that his narrative will be constantly infused with either the shadow of "pig" or of "Mrs. Nooge," even though Francie apparently is not fully aware of what Mrs. Nugent is telling him. This fact becomes evident when Francie enters the Brady house to find the place in shambles, "sink full of pilchard tins. Da ate pilchards when he went on a skite. The flies were buzzing round them . . . dogs must have been in" (46). Francie's prose skips and stutters and is finally dislodged with "You, was all he said," (46) coming from his red-eyed and foul-smelling father. Francie's prose is paralogical as it claims two things at the same time: it admits he knows and denies he knows what has happened to his mother: "He meant you did it, what happened to ma. I says what are you talking about what happened to ma. O you didn't hear? he says with a bitter smile. Then he told me they had dredged the lake near the garage and found her at the bottom of it, and says I'm off up to the Tower I might be back and I might not" (46). On the one hand, Francie is recounting what happened and so we have a dual sense of time; yet, on the other hand, Francie's prose suggests, in the above example with Mrs. Nugent, too, that he cannot bear to know what has happened and thus blocks it. The latter scene with his father attaches as a segment, not to his dad, but to Mrs. Nugent. Therefore, the entire trauma of his mother's death in his absence, perhaps because of his absence, and his father's accusation all attach in Francie's mind, and subsequently in his prose, to Mrs. Nugent.

The fact that Francie does not attach any blame or anger to his father is played out in perhaps the most shocking discourse in the entire book. This discourse is with his father and begins after his return home from Bubble's disciplinary school. One day Francie comes home to find Benny Brady in a

typical position, passed out in the armchair, and Francie proceeds to talk to
his father as if he were conscious:

> When I got home there wasn't a whisper in the house only the flies, nothing
> only da in the armchair by the radio. I was talking away to him about Philip
> and how it was better to be straight with people and not keep them hanging
> on. I thought maybe da'd had a Tower bar do you remember the old days party
> for the house was littered with bottles and the trumpet lying over by the skirt-
> ing board so I reckoned he just wasn't fit to answer me. I gave his shoulder a
> bit of shake and when the hankie fell out of his pocket I saw that it was all
> dried blood. Oh, da, I said, I didn't know and I felt his forehead it was cold
> as ice. (126–127)

After this passage Francie begins to converse with his father in Francie's usual
dialogue narrative—one that does not have punctuation. He pulls his dad's
chair up to the fire and offers him tea:

> Da looked at me and when I seen those eyes so sad and hurt I wanted to say:
> I love you da.
> > They said to me. You won't leave me son.
> > I said: I won't da. I'll never leave you.
> > This time its going to be all right—isn't it son?
> > I said it was. We're going to be a happy family son. (127)

This dialogue ends with Francie crying and he and his dad saying how great
it is that they could share their feelings with each other. The next morning
Francie takes charge of the household, cleaning, making tea, going to the
store, and eventually taking a job with Leddy the butcher. For the next several pages Francie records his actions in and out of the house, including his
dialogue with his dad. While the reader may wonder why Benny Brady is
not going to the Tower as usual, it is not until Francie's discourse with Dr.
Roche that we know what is going on in the Brady household.

Dr. Roche stops Francie on the street to inquire about his dad, who has
missed an appointment with him. Francie disdains Dr. Roche and blames
him in part for his mother's suicide, and so, Francie's prose is erratic because
Francie is trying to be civil on the surface while the narrative darts in and
out of his own thoughts. When he lies and tells Roche that his father has
gone to England to see Uncle Alo, Francie knows that the doctor knows that
he is lying: "I see, he says, he was looking me up and down twice as much
now. I had to put my hand in my pocket to stop it shaking for I knew if it
started he'd see it he saw fucking everything didn't he?" (137). As his narrative progresses, Francie frequently attributes others with an omniscience that
they cannot possibly have. If this narrative were about a somewhat "normal"

ten- or twelve-year-old boy, then we could comment on the charming effect through irony this narrative technique produces. But this is not a typical or "normal" prose narrative, and this technique does not show the irony of the situation; rather, it depicts Francie's spinning out-of-control, becoming-paranoid perspective on the world and hence in his prose. In the end, we follow Francie's narrative for weeks as he scurries all over town working and conducting his errands: buying bottles of stout at the Tower and corned beef at the grocery for his dad, peering into the cafe to watch Joe and Philip talking to girls and singing to the jukebox, picking up his pay from Leddy, then going home and talking to his dad about the snowdrops and children playing in the lane.

The narrative completely falls apart when Uncle Alo comes home for the annual Christmas visit; Francie's prose is in a near state of panic, in imitation of his mother's behavior the year before: "I flew round the place chatting to them all and saying more cakes are you enjoying yourselves isn't it great to see Alo home? Ten men under him, I said. I clapped and clapped and cried hooray" (152). Not only is Francie's narrative flying forward without heed, but the reader cannot be sure that Alo has actually returned. Perhaps the scene is Francie's macabre reenactment of the previous year's Christmas: cakes, whiskey, Alo, Mary, songs, and bragging about Alo's job in London:

> Alo said to Mary: Just a minute and came over to me. He reached out and said: Its all right Francie.
> I said Please Alo, can you help me?
> But he couldn't help me because it wasn't Alo. It was Doctor Roche.
> Oh Alo, I didn't see the others leave. They had gone without saying good-bye. I looked around for da but he was gone too. The flies were at the cakes on the piano. (152)

A few lines later, the sergeant says to another policeman, "Maggots—they're right through him," and the policeman replies, "Sweet Mother of Christ" (153). Francie is given an injection by Doctor Roche and then he begins to hallucinate. For weeks, we now know, Benny Brady has been decomposing in his armchair while Francie has not only been conversing with him but caring for him, fetching stout and corned beef for him, "I cut them all up into triangles and put them on a plate and everything. What do you think of the sandwiches da?, I said" (139), battling flies with fly strips, making cakes for the holidays and including his father in his plans. Yet, Francie's text is total blockage: not one word actually verifies his father's death. Francie cannot *measure* this distance—he cannot get to the fact that his dad is dead.

While Francie's segments that concern his mother and his father falter, break down, and are scarred by omissions, the narrative segments that open onto Mrs. Nugent know no bounds: if Francie has succeeded in projecting a voice for his decomposing father, then he is equally successful in projecting narrative, motive, and action onto Mrs. Nugent and to a lesser extent Philip. The power and velocity of the prose transfers, ultimately, to the velocity of the body—to the violence of the body. Francie's prose moves across the page with such speed that it is difficult to track it: he has the reader believing in dialogues that the reader realizes on a second take to be purely imagined. Francie's prose has such velocity that it runs away with even him; on several occasions, Francie states something, then realizes that he is seen to be ridiculous by others or in his own head: "He hadn't moved back too far in case I'd notice it. . . . Then I said: fairly fooled you there Joe. Tiddly! Imagine someone doing the like of that! Tiddly! Rolos—for fuck's sake!" (104).

Indeed it is the episode with "Tiddly," Francie's name for the pederast priest in the boys reform school, that shows the reader that Francie's prose is out of control: it speeds, falters, breaks down, and then attempts to block any thoughts or discourse that will lead to the assemblage known as "mom," even though "mom" for Francie is complex and convoluted idea of Mrs. Nugent's perfect household and his own mom's "pig" sty. Instead of a "catatonic freeze" Francie flies apart as Tiddly continues to prod Francie to tell him "the worst bad thing I ever did" (87). Francie's narrative topples over the scene with Tiddly into a discourse that includes his mother. As Tiddly amorously begs Francie to confess his bad deeds, Francie's narrative spins out of control: "you could never forgive yourself for a terrible thing Francis a terrible thing please tell me I said stop it! But he wouldn't then I heard ma again it wasn't your fault Francie I got a grip of him by the wrist I just grabbed on to it and sank my teeth in he went white and cried out No Francie!, I said stop it don't ever say it again!" (88). This scene, which involves the mother-machine, is the first episode of flying apart and becoming-violent with Tiddly. The next scene with Tiddly compromises the mother-machine by combining Mrs. Nugent. It is in this passage that the reader fully realizes that Francie's guilt is due primarily to the fact that he cannot separate his desire for Mrs. Nugent's house from his love for his own mother. Francie's prose becomes entangled with Tiddly, his mother, and Mrs. Nugent as all occupy the room at the same time. Mrs. Nugent commands the scene: "Do you know what he did? He asked me to be his mother. He said he'd give anything not to be a pig. That's what he did on you Mrs. Brady" (97). When Mrs. Nugent's breast is offered and begins choking Francie, he flies into a rage and attacks Tiddly: "all I could see was ma smiling and saying to me over and over again don't worry Francie no matter what she says about you I'll never believe it I'll never disown you ever not the way I did you ma I said *no son no!* she said I said its's true ma no she says but it was and it always would be no matter what I did" (97–98). The prose tumbles forward at breakneck speed because Francie's inability to present a stabilized narrative; Francie spins into becoming-imperceptible and the leaps from narrative point to narrative point are imperceptible. There is nothing that gets us from Tiddly to his mother to Mrs. Nugent.

The flow of Francie's prose creates a different way of understanding the narrative. Although we could easily dismiss Francie as becoming-mad in terms of referential meaning—that is, in terms of good sense, an easy dismissal would limit our ability to appreciate the impact of Francie's narrative. Because his narrative moves with a velocity that we cannot measure, we cannot universalize and make it reasonable in terms of traditional reading strategies. It is difficult to read Francie's narrative because he logically decides that the only way to end the mother-machine that is complicated by a self-loathing desire for Mrs. Nugent to be his mother is to kill Mrs. Nugent. Francie is utilizing "good sense" logic, but not in a way that the traditional sense-making community wants to recognize. Recognition means that a community can read in a way that matches what it already knows. Therefore, Francie cannot be recognized; he cannot be reterritorialized by the major language. Not allowing himself to be reterritorialized, Francie attempts to deterritorialize the "sense" imposed upon him by all the people in his life: Bubbles, his da, Mrs. Nugent, Dr. Roche, the sergeant, Philip, and even Joe and his ma. Tearing apart their sense-making machine means, in Francie's mind, killing Mrs. Nugent, and not simply killing her but giving her a "pig" treatment: exposing her to the brutal reterritorializations that Francie has experienced. Unable to make sense of the world that he has inherited, Francie offers us a becoming-minor alternative.

From the perspective of good sense, what is most shocking about Francie becoming-murderer is the fact that he operates in a "common sensical" or rational manner in carrying out the murder. In fact, the few "lucid" moments of the narrative may be seen to occur as Francie becomes-murderer. The prose moves rapidly, yet he is methodical: do we then have Francie becoming-parody of good sense? Is this repetition with difference? It would seem that some kind of inversion is occurring. Francie's movement onto the plane of organization—his one true moment of calm, rational planning—consists of his killing Mrs. Nugent. Logically surmising that Mrs. Nugent "did two bad things," Francie states: "You made me turn my back on my ma and you took Joe away from me" (209). Cool and rational, Francie kicks and hits Mrs. Nugent until he cocks the captive bolt: "I lifted her off the floor with one hand and shot the bolt right into her head thlok was the sound it made, like a goldfish dropping into a bowl. If you ask anyone how you kill a pig they will tell you cut its throat across but you don't do it longways. Then she just lay there with her chin sticking up and I opened her then stuck my hand in her stomach and wrote PIGS all over the walls of the upstairs room" (209). As he enters onto the plane of organization, Francie's prose is calm and steady with proper punctuation. If it is true that his only instance on the plane of organization is the murder scene, then do we have a becoming-murderer, or do we have a Francie who is "being" reterritorialized? Is inflicting violence, in other words, the only way that Francie can "make sense" of his world?

Like Freddie, Francie is unable to operate "correctly" on a plane of organization. Francie cannot make sense, and the primary problem in his sense-making capacity is that the assemblage of discourse known as his mother is infiltrated by a "false" image of Mrs. Nugent. He naively and perhaps appropriately desires not to be in a "pig family," which leads him to segment and split open his discourse. The assemblage of the mother is connected to segments he tries to deny: clean kitchens, baking scones, a father who works and, most damaging, a sane mother who looks after her son. Although violent, Francie is able to elicit some sympathy from the reader because of the fact that he is only a boy in a "dysfunctional" family. It is difficult to determine where the reterritorialization begins and ends in *The Butcher Boy* since Francie is so completely an outsider. Francie's narrative is indeed "senseless," yet it reveals the lack of sense in the societal and cultural institutions. Francie is a product of reterritorialization, and his only seemingly rational act is that of murdering a woman with a captive bolt pistol one uses for butchering pigs. Yes, Francie is a butcher boy: his religious and cultural tradition has led him to believe that in effect he butchered his mother, and so as a way of trying to dismantle the tradition, he murders the woman who infiltrated and performed the role of ideal mother.

The mother theme persists in Patrick McCabe's 1998 novel, *Breakfast on Pluto,* another example of the new powerful contemporary Irish novel concerned with gender and sexual constructs. *Breakfast on Pluto* brings us full circle thematically and formally. It is a novel that offers problematic gender constructs and textual undecidability in terms of the body, as well as the body repeatedly brutalized, exploited, and subjected to violence. The prose deterritorializes our ability to make proper sense and narrative closure. The novel is narrated by Patrick "Pussy" Braden, a rather outrageous aging transvestite who, after two short prefaces, begins "The Life and Times of Patrick Braden." The tricky aspect of this novel, as with other McCabe novels, is that we are under the power of an "unreliable" narrator, so much so that it is difficult to tell if *anything* happened in the manner that Pussy presents it. Pussy's narrative "body" is formally innovative, typical of McCabe's sophisticated prose, while it also takes the Irish novel into new spaces by pushing over the threshold of traditional cultural boundaries in regard to gender, sex and the physical body. Dressed like her mother on the ill-fated morning of her conception in 1955, in old housecoat, slippers, and a head scarf, Pussy narrates the suspiciously titled "The Life and Times of Patrick Braden." The old housecoat, head scarf, and hose the color of tea represent the mother assemblage that at one level of the novel is the dominant strain of connections and reconnections. The reader has to wonder why Pussy uses her male nomenclature which was given to *him* by "Whiskers" Braden, the foster-care mother-from-hell, for her autobiographical narrative. One can only surmise that there is a conflict or a kind of playacting going on in the narrative; it does not take one long to realize that in some instances Pussy cannot be telling the truth or cannot possibly be in a position to know the truth concerning certain situations and circumstances of her own past. Pussy's narrative is complicated by yet another factor: the Troubles that erupted in Northern Ireland in the late 1960s. While Pussy provides us with several short narrative interludes that gruesomely describe a sectarian murder or even the longer, knitted-together tale of Irwin's ill-fated involvement with the IRA, she always disassociates herself from any culpability.

McCabe is an expert at making sense slide off the page; two dominate readings coexist at all times in this text: Pussy is an innocent bystander, a "girl" devoted to "Max Factor, Johnson's Baby Oil, Blinkers eyeshadow, Oil of Ulay, Silvikrin Alpine Herb shampoo. Knitted tops in white, purple, lavender, blazing orange, satin-stripe velveteen pants, turtle-neck leotards, flouncing skirts, ribbed stretch-nylon tights," or alternatively, Pussy is posing as a "girl" who is involved with the IRA and thus has a hand in Dummy Teats's murder, the London bombings, and the very opaquely presented Belfast interlude during which women entice British soldiers to their "party" in order for them to be gunned down.[10] These are the two extremes of the novel: on the one hand, extreme black suggests culpability, while on the other hand extreme white symbolizes innocence, with varying shades of gray in between.

The duplicitous nature of the narrative and outrageous gender citations are what make McCabe's novel powerfully engaging. Patrick Braden is sexually (that is, genitally) and culturally conceived as a male, while Pussy Braden enacts, performatively speaking, female citations. Pronoun nomenclature is a problem in this novel because "Patrick" knows that he has been culturally and genitally inscribed male, but "Pussy" is the identity "Patrick" uses throughout the novel, and she is female. Traditionally, one could interpret Pussy's narrative as an attempt to *engender* herself, and certainly this notion corresponds to Pussy's need to narrate, actually invent, her own conception.[11] In order to underscore how McCabe's prose dismantles sense and foils our ability to firmly situate Pussy in the heterosexual matrix as either male or female, my use of pronouns will correspond to the period or situation in Pussy's life; for example, as a child Pussy is Patrick and at the police station in London, Pussy is "Pat," the English pejoratively stereotypical "stage name" ("Paddy") for all Irish *men*. Depending on the context, s/he or she or he will be used accordingly. Ostensibly, Pussy passes as a homosexual man attempting to pass as a woman; yet Pussy is able to ply her trade in London in particular only because those who buy sex from her know that she is a transvestite. We do not have a simple case of what Peggy Phelan calls the "paradox of using visibility to highlight invisibility."[12] Having been socialized in a heterosexual society, we expect lucid gender distinctions because that they represent the norm. According to Phelan, homosexuals attempt to "pass" as heterosexuals: "But this very passing also highlights the 'normative' and unmarked nature of heterosexuality. It is easy to pass as heterosexual because heterosexuality is assumed. In other words, what is made visible is the unmarked nature of heterosexual identity. The one who passes then does not 'erase' the mark of difference, rather the passer highlights the invisibility of the mark of the Same" (96).

To be sure, in many instances in the novel when Pussy is dressed completely as a woman she only serves to highlight the "normality" of everyone else. This idea is best illustrated when Pussy develops an infatuation with a heterosexual man in Tyreelin; she fantasizes that they set up house and have a "normal" heterosexual union:

> It's just that somehow I'd managed to work it all out so perfectly in my mind, with him and me together at last in the house I'd always dreamed of, our *Chez Nous* picture on the wall ("this is our little home") with its lovely twining flowers and everything spotless for him when he'd come home from work, putting his arm around you with a sort of definite-ness that said: 'You belong here! Here and nowhere else!' instead of brown glass marble eyes that bored right through and said: 'Who are you?' No! Said: 'Who or *what* are you?' (193)

In the latter admission, Pussy admits to knowing that hair, clothes and makeup will not let her *pass* as a heterosexual. As Kevin Whelan points out, there is a downside for those who do not conform to small-town expectations: "The very notions of place, territory and identity embedded in the regional construct may well disenfranchise those who have been displaced or alienated from it; it may also have inbuilt gender and generational biases" (12). However, rather optimistically, and as we recall from chapter 1, Judith Butler in *Gender Trouble* proposes that a perverse repetition of gender constructs from a point of difference does achieve a disruption of the category of stable gender. Granted, a parody of the idea of the gender construct of female, therefore, could be enacted by a transvestite; by repeating the clothes, hair, and makeup, gestures and language of a female we can see that all these things that create "femaleness" are superficial props or affectations that sustain the idea of "female." The transvestite is sexed male, and therefore "he" shows us that he can perform the female gender as well as the sexed female; thus, "maleness" is a cultural construct, too. More perversely, in this novel the duplicity goes one step further by not working against constructs, by completely ignoring the very idea of categorization. For example, if Pussy is actually involved in IRA operations, then in her attempt to pass as a representative of the heterosexist matrix she draws more attention to herself, but this attention serves to elude detection as a participant in the war in the North. Thus, Butler's "copy of a copy," or Deleuzian repetition, is truly enacted as Pussy's simulacrum of the heterosexual norm is so perversely subtle in its glaring outrageousness that it unravels the entire system, creating a different kind of sense. This different kind of sense is what makes McCabe's prose exciting and even dangerous. Indeed, it is my contention that intelligibility comes at a level other than the sharply demarcated sexual/gender binary traditionally expostulated by heterosexuality; McCabe's prose—with clearly oscillating gender and textual meanings—creates a different way to think about Irish culture and the Irish novel.

Woven into Pussy's presentation of herself and of her construction of her mother is Foucault's idea that women's bodies were turned into hysterical discourses in the nineteenth century in order to regulate bodies and sexuality. The hysterical female body was thought to be "saturated with sexuality," which caused innumerable pathologies ("female troubles"). Pussy's stereotypical hysterical woman's body is presented in two ways in the novel, and both, it seems, produce an ironic effect. First, Father Bernard, the person Pussy believes to be her biological father, is so overcome by a teenage girl's body, that of Pussy's biological mother, that he rapes her. According to Dreyfus and Rabinow, Pussy's narrative is playing into this idea of the women's body: "a mysterious and pervasive sexuality of the utmost importance resides somewhere and everywhere in the body . . . the personal identity of the woman and the future health of the population are linked in a common bond of knowledge, power, and the materiality of the body."[13] From Pussy's point of view, his mother is victimized by the very materiality of her body as interpreted by Father Bernard who, in Pussy's portrayal of him, *does* believe that women's bodies are "hysterical" because even women wearing "drab old housecoats, shuffly slippers and stockings of cold tea" arouse Father Bernard. The second presentation of the hysterical female body is Pussy herself/himself. In effect, Pussy actually becomes the woman Father Bernard would have been unable to resist. Pussy makes her/his mother a saint and herself/himself a whore. This familiar duality serves to avenge Pussy's mother's innocence and exacerbate Father Bernard's shame: not only an illegitimate child by a teenage village girl, but that male child grows up to be a transvestite prostitute.

McCabe's novel also plays out Foucault's fourth domain issued to regulate bodies and sexuality, namely the designation of normalization through the pathologization of sexual diversity (non-heterosexual activity teleologically meant for procreation) or "perversity." Foucault theorizes that "in the psychiatrization of perversions, sex was related to biological functions and to an anatomo-physiological machinery that gave it its 'meaning,' that is, its finality."[14] Again, not only does Pussy exacerbate his biological father's guilt, she also flies in the face of conventional religion and heterosexual normality and morality. This situation feeds into the novel's form because the novel functions as a "confessional" written by Pussy for her psychiatrist, "Dr. Terence," who, we are told in the Preface to the story, instructed her to write out her life story for therapeutic purposes. Terence leaves the clinic where Pussy receives her treatment before the narrative begins, and thus she laments the loss of Terence throughout the entire book. From Foucault's perspective Terence is a representative of medical authority who encourages Pussy to release her pent up emotions and traumas as a means to dispel them. This practice follows from the nineteenth-century medical and scientific authorities who usurped the territory of the confessional and assigned pathological discourses to sexual behavior. According to Foucault, in regard to sexual pathologies knowledge was constructed so that guidelines for deviants could be established; in turn, the policing of sexual behavior developed an elaborate and multifaceted apparatus.

Similar to the need to confess and create discourse concerning our repression, the fact that an activity or behavior is prohibited and policed gives one the impetus to engage in that activity or behavior; the pleasure was strictly in the transgression itself. This phenomenon is certainly true in Pussy's case: she delights in her confession and relishes the storytelling aspect. Because Terence is no longer her doctor, Pussy imagines Terence's role as interlocutor and invents questions and objections. In this way, Pussy can play both sides of the analyst's couch because, as Foucault noted, pleasure is available for both the confessor and confidante. The new discourses of regulation, therefore, excites and stirs and, according to Foucault, *produces* sexuality. What we realize early in the narrative, however, is that Pussy loves to confess what has up to this point been supposedly repressed. As we recall, Foucault theorizes that we are not sexually "repressed," but that the very claim is an excuse—a ruse—to produce discourse about our terrible, fictional repression. "We 'Other Victorians'" desire nothing more than the opportunity to tell or write our desires: in the confessional, on the analyst's couch, in our memoirs, and now in tabloids and on talk shows. Pussy loves "telling" herself "and another, as often as possible, everything that might concern the interplay of innumerable pleasures, sensations, and thoughts which, through the body and the soul, had some affinity with sex," and in regard to Pussy, money, clothes, makeup, and perfume.[15]

The 1969 Don Partridge song "Breakfast on Pluto," yet another popular song to become the title of a contemporary Irish novel, is significant in regard to the body for readers of McCabe's novel.[16] Don Partridge croons along to a boom-boom beat (á là Rick Springfield's "Speak to the Sky") the inane and saccharine "be happy" message. The theme of the song that one can be happy ("without leaving your chair") in one's mind and experience a kind of weight-lessness. The body can fly up to the stars, drop by Mars, and have "breakfast on Pluto"; thus, the body is no longer bound to the constraints of the earth, from earth's gravitational pull to human society's rules and regulations re-garding clothing or behavior. The body is *free*. Pussy's attachment to the song "Breakfast on Pluto" is partly nostalgia (she was a teenager in the late sixties), partly wishful thinking, and eventually a description of her "reality" when she is finally pushed too far psychologically and physically. The song may refer to one's ability to be cut loose from one's body and, in this narrative, the ability to leave one's body is a useful way to avoid pain; these "out of body" experi-ences are a psychological trick, a survival technique, for Pussy. The physical body is put through a great deal in this novel; it is ridiculed, beaten, aban-doned, blown up, tortured, raped, and occasionally adored.

Psychologically speaking, the most important historical construct that Pussy pens is the narrative of the scene of her conception because quite lit-erally, her existence and all of her pathologies originate in that moment. Or at least this is what Pussy would have us to believe. According to Pussy, Fa-ther Bernard McIvor from the local parish is his/her biological father as the result of McIvor raping a teenage girl, Eily Bergin, who was temporarily fill-ing in for old Mrs. McGlynn, the housekeeper. In an inane yet cynical man-ner, Pussy narrates his own conception which, as far as we know, he has no real knowledge of since he never knew his mother or actually talked to his father about this incident. Pussy tells us she began her siege against Father Bernard as a teenager by leaving Father Bernard suggestive notes and writ-ing inappropriate essays concerning Pussy's parentage for her English class assignments. In the end, Pussy's anger and inability to forgive Father Bernard are played out in fantasy scenes in which she returns to Tyreelin to burn down his church. Pussy creates out of bits of information a Tyreelin local provides about his mother the idea that his mother is a Mitzi Gaynor look-alike who loves, for example, the soundtrack of *South Pacific* and Perry Como as much as Pussy loves them; yet Pussy adds that her/his love for dresses and skirts comes from his father's wearing of the soutane.

If it were not simply an instance of violent rape, then Pussy's narrative about his conception would be comical due to the asides and tone of his/her language. The Mitzi Gaynor look-alike wears to work the costume of the priest's housekeeper, borrowed from Mrs. McGlynn, "the standard uniform, one had no difficulty whatsoever in acquiring a washed-out, pale blue house-coat with a ringpull zip, a pair of stockings the colour of tea kept in the cup for twenty years or thereabouts and an old hairnet which when you squashed your hair under it made it look like irregular handfuls of rabbit's droppings," which is Pussy notes as she writes in the present, "Not entirely unlike my own!" (24). Pussy wishes to make sure that the reader knows that her biological mother wore nothing inappropriate to serve breakfast to Father Bernard, and in fact, if anything, is too young and naive to realize that she was supposed to wear the "uniform" in order not to arouse the priest sexually. According to Pussy, all that her mother has in her mind is the extra money she is earning by filling in for Mrs. McGlynn and that "this extra money will be buying not only Perry Como's latest record but also perhaps—if Mrs. McGlynn ('God forgive me!' she whispers softly.) stays out sick for long enough—the complete, long-playing soundtrack of *South Pacific!*" (25). Supposedly these are Eily's thoughts while serving Father Bernard his breakfast; meanwhile, Father Bernard— according to Pussy, of course—only notices that her housecoat skirt rides up slightly when she leans over to serve him his breakfast.

It is with this scene that "Breakfast on Pluto" begins to take on another level of meaning. Sarcastically, and typically of Pussy's narrative style, she imagines her mother's thoughts: "'Oops! My skirt and housecoat are riding up! Better abort this task at once or we could have an explosive clergyman filling the air with pent-up sexual energy thanks to God know how many years' abstinence!'" (26). Needless to say, a female rural Irish teenager in the 1950s would not use a suggestive (to the situation) word such as "abort" or even know what "pent-up sexual energy" is; Pussy counters with: "O yes— but of course she said that! I mean—what else would you expect? Because, like Father Bernard, thwacking penises and salty sweatbeads running down your face were never off her mind! Well, excuse me, Father, but don't make me laugh—please don't make me fucking laugh—you know? For that sort of thing she doesn't think, actually. That sort of thing she doesn't say. She doesn't say because she doesn't care. She doesn't fucking care, you see!" (26). Pussy adds that "in those days, girls didn't really have any experience of boys and their electric little tootling flutes!" and in this Pussy is probably correct; nevertheless, Eily Bergin is portrayed as the perfect girl whose life revolves around listening to records and going out to dance once a week. Pussy's mother must remain innocent so that Pussy can go on believing that s/he was not actually abandoned by her/his mother, when Eily was cruelly forced to give her/him away and then disappear forever.

The details of the conception and the birth are graphically presented by Pussy partly to depict the horror of the rape and the desolation of the teenager, who has not told anyone she is pregnant and who single-handedly delivers the baby in the middle of a cold November night, and partly to further shame Father Bernard, who apparently did nothing to help Eily, and perhaps most significantly Pussy's graphic language renders his/her own self-disgust. A product of rape, then left in a Rinso box on the doorstep of the baby-farmer, "Whiskers" Braden, Pussy, as is evident from his narrative, feels "abject," totally unwanted since conception, yet alive, however miserable his life and circumstances. As we recall, in *Bodies that Matter* Butler claims that bodies that do not adhere to heterosexual regulatory norms of the body are "abject": "The abject designates here precisely those 'unlivable' and 'uninhabitable' zones of social life which are nevertheless densely populated by those who do not enjoy the status of the subject, but whose living under the sign of the 'unlivable' is required to circumscribe the domain of the subject."[18] It would seem that only the former form of *abject* makes sense: baby "Patrick" is regarded at the level of defecation and slobber, or, as Butler states, Patrick is beyond the boundary of "that which qualifies as the human." To proclaim abjectness for those who are different than the binary (queer versus straight) is not theoretically helpful, because first it requires a position of self-objectivity that is not always available, useful, or even helpful; and second, no matter how you attempt to turn a pejorative word like *queer* or *abject* into something positive, which is a contemporary strategy— you are still operating in the heterosexual paradigm that originally defined the words.

On the contrary, if Pussy is to be viewed as an outcast or abject, then we need to look to something other than her gender construction. More pointedly, Pussy is made abject at birth by a religious and traditional cultural hegemony that protects priests and makes victimized young women unpardonably guilty—literally cast out—and indeed *abject*. In short, the hegemonic control of the Catholic Church in *Breakfast on Pluto* ruins Pussy's life by making his mother and, in turn, her baby abject by the measurement of these traditional standards. McCabe may be touching on raw Irish historical nerve, as Ursula Barry indicates in "Women in Ireland": "This country went through its bitterest battles over issues of State involvement in what the Catholic Church considers the area of 'private morality,' such as the Mother and Child Health Scheme in the 1950s when the Catholic hierarchy opposed a state health scheme for pregnant women and newborn infants."[19] In the late 1980s Barry believes that the Catholic Church still dominates gender, sexuality and power issues: "Pulpits, right across the country, serve as powerful political platforms, used to bolster a narrow and rigid ideology concerning women: compulsory motherhood, guilt ridden sexuality, opposition to birth control, self-sacrifice, and economic dependence."[20] And as a case in point, Barry provides an eerily similar case to Eily Bergin's: "In 1984 in a small provincial town in Ireland, a 16 year old schoolgirl and her baby died as she gave birth in the open, before a religious shrine to the Virgin Mary."[21]

The novel dwells on the abject plight of the unborn or those abandoned after birth with the Martina Sheridan and Tommy McNamee incident. This account of the fifteen-year-old girl being "wooed" by the married McNamee twenty years her senior is strangely interwoven with IRA murders and Pussy's own troubles; it nevertheless keeps surfacing in the narrative because Pussy sees a young Eily in Martina and, needless to say, himself/herself in the unwanted child Martina will have as result of McNamee's seduction. Wishing to intervene, Pussy makes the mistake of confronting Martina who has been heterosexually-socialized: "'Please listen to me, Martina! Stay away from Tommy McNamee! Listen to me, please!' I pleaded, but she wouldn't. 'Let me go,' she said, 'you get your hands off me now and let me go, you fucking queer!'" (105). Obviously, queering the town of Tyreelin is not working so well for Pussy, and this incident does even more to make him an outcast in the village than anything else he had so far done:

> Once—not long after I came back to Tyreelin—I was standing in the shop queue and he (McNamee) lifted up my dress with a bicycle pump. I was sure it was all a joke you see and that the people were well-used to me by now. (I was wrong, of course—I can see that now. The only reason the "Hello, honky tonks" and "Ooh, you are awfuls" had stopped was that they wanted absolutely *nothing* to do with me.) Which I hope explains why I turned and smiled at him. It was just a big completely unoffended smile but when I saw the expression on his face, it frightened me. . . . All I can say is that the eyes seemed dead. (104–105)

The depth of despair Martina causes Pussy is evidenced in her after-dark search for McNamee's semen on the ground behind the creamery where the couple supposedly had sex, "A few groping strokes and stab between the legs behind the dilapidated creamery!" (106). Later Pussy admits that this was "silly and I don't even know what made me do it"; yet, she claims to have found what she was looking for: "Why I broke down after putting my hand directly on some which had spilled on a dockleaf I'm not really sure—I think it was because it seemed so ridiculous that such a minuscule amount of liquid could cause so much heartache" (107).

Although the narrative is achronological, disjointed, and very often the product of Pussy's fantasy, one major assemblage in the narrative, similar to McCabe's previous novel, *The Butcher Boy,* is the mother or the recovery or revalidation of the mother's love. Pussy's pathological behavior seems to center, not unlike Francie Brady's, on the lost mother. In London, for example, Pussy engages in a performance in which she enacts the role of a dead son, Shaunie, for her boyfriend Bertie's landlady, Louise. Louise, who helps Pussy with her hair, convinces her to dress up in "the little grey jacket and the short trousers" in order to facilitate verisimilitude; Pussy begins to enjoy the play-acting: "'O my silly boy, my Shaunie Shaunies!' she'd say, and I'd say: 'Mammy!' After a while I started to really like it, just sitting there on her knee and being engulfed by all this powdery warm flesh, I never wanted to get up in fact" (91). At first, the play-acting is rather innocuous, but, as is typical of McCabe's destablizing prose, the scene soon turns pathological. When Bertie finds Louise and Pussy playing out their mother/son ritual to the fullest, "as well as being in the middle of sucking on her nipple and going: 'Mammy!'" Pussy continues, "all hell broke loose" as Bertie protests, "'It's not fair!' and 'He's my girlfriend, you fucking old cow! Mine!'" (91–92). The gender indecidibity is striking, "*He's* my *girl*friend" shows the text is unrelentless in its destabilization of gender and sexuality, so much so that it no longer is an issue at all. The aftermath of this incident, however, shows us two distinct sides of Pussy's character. First, Bertie portrays Pussy as a young woman/man who should not be manipulated into playing the role of Louise's dead little boy; this view renders Pussy not only vulnerable but a bit pathetic, even somewhat demented, as if Pussy were unable to fend for herself. The second view is shown when Pussy gives up Bertie to continue with Louise; this rendering is more in line with the "gold-digger" Pussy we have come to know:

> We were all in a right old state after that incident. I'm afraid. All I can re-
> member is poor old Bertie coming up the stairs, whimpering: "He's not a
> schoolboy! He's my girl and you have no right to be doing this to him!"
>   It was a hard decision for me to have to make but I'm afraid that Louise
> as part of the bargain had been doing my hair so beautifully—with pins and
> clips and slides, not to mention providing me with creams and lotions for
> your skin that you would absolutely die for, that in the end I had no choice
> but to say to him: "Sorry, Bertie, I really am so sorry."
>   He was heartbroken and left that very night. I never saw him again. Then
> it was straight into Louise's arms to hug her and hug her and hug her. (92)

With this passage we see a twin presentation of Pussy, one vulnerable and the other calculating; furthermore, the calculating Pussy produces hysterical female heterosexual gender citations. The only thing unpredictable about her transvestite heterosexualized behavior is that she does not "stand by her man"; rather, she stands by her surrogate "Mammy."

This scene, however, is only the beginning of Pussy's pathological behavior with Louise. Pussy claims that "somewhere at the back of my mind, I kept thinking: 'You shouldn't be doing this. . . . She's not your mammy. If she wants you to be her son, that's fine. But she's not your mammy. Your mammy was special. Even if she did dump you on Whiskers Braden's step and leave you for ever'" (92). The quest for Eily Bergin continues as Pussy play-acts for Louise. Unknown to Louise, Pussy would go out on the London streets and address strange women as Eily Bergin. A master of creating fissures in prose, McCabe provides less than half a page for all of chapter 26, "'My Name's Not Eily Bergin!'" in which Pussy relays her encounters with women on the street who wore a housecoat or a headscarf:

> I wouldn't be able to help myself and the next thing you'd know, some complete stranger would be standing back going: "What are you on about? My name's not Bergin! Nor Eily neither! Get lost before I call the police!"
> I made more mistakes like that—but there's no point in pretending! I just couldn't help myself! (93)

Pussy has a time and reality warp between the image of her mother and what she could possibly look like or dress like eighteen years later. Throughout the entire novel Pussy maintains the idea that she is the *same;* this sameness, of course, is not even bound to reality because Pussy only imagines what Eily Bergin must have looked in the 1950s, having never seen her or a picture of her. The ubiquitous head scarf and housecoat further point to the gaping aporia in Pussy's mind between reality and a blind desire for his mother.

The fact that the fantasy is more sustainable than reality becomes apparent when Louise decides to play-act for Pussy. One of the most interesting aspects about Pussy's fantasy of her mother is that the entire assemblage is pieced together with snippets of gossip, half-thought-out impressions, and loose associations. The main source of Pussy's knowledge about Eily Bergin is a man in Tyreelin, Benny Lendrum, who supposedly knew Eily. Similar to Francie Brady's building on Mrs. Nugent's "pig family" accusation until it dominates his life, Pussy, too, builds an entire life and history for his supposed mother from snatches of conversation he hears or overhears in town:

> I thought of Eily in that dancehall long ago, the way Benny Lendrum had told me she'd been, with her gorgeous bubble-cut hair, check blouse in yellow and capri pants in white, not a fellow in the place able to take his eyes off her. "The most beautiful girl in the town," Benny said. "The one and only Eily Bergin—give your woman out of *South Pacific* a run for her money any day, they used to say!"
> Which had really excited me when *he* said it for no one could say: "Oh, that's just Braden again—making up stupid fantasies about his mother just because she was rode by a priest and then dumped him on a step in a bloody Rinso box!" That was one thing they couldn't say for as I sat there on the summer seat on that day in 1965, I had heard the words fall right from Benny's lips, one by one watching them fall and sparkle there like gold. (111–112)

This passage seems to be a key to Pussy's mother-narrative and, typical of McCabe's prose, is completely ambiguous as the prose slips and slides off the page; all we have are possibilities: Is ten-year-old Patrick's companion,

Benny, reliable? Why would he tell the supposed offspring of the Bergin and
Father Bernard union about Eily? Is Pussy simply constructing the entire
story about Benny? Does Benny say one thing and Pussy remember something else—pieces that "one by one" "fall and sparkle there like gold"? Does
Benny even exist?

Pussy, like Francie and the pig-family narrative, hears this story from
Benny when he is very young; yet, for Pussy, unlike Francie, it is a positive
situation. The Eily Bergin story grants Pussy the ability to construct a family and a new life out of the shards of Benny's (supposed) memories of a local
girl at a dance over a decade ago. Patrick/Pussy gains endless hours of com-
fort we imagine as chapters such as "Chez Nous" reconstruct an idyllic
Tyreelin village scene where "mammy" and "daddy" love each other and little Patrick; Pussy provides a pathologically inane and sentimental account of
the life he should have or would have had:

—Do you love your mammy? says Daddy then and smiles.
   —I love her millions, Dad, his son replies.
   —And why is that, now tell us!
   —Because she's my mam!
   —Because she's your mammy!
   —Who bakes bread!
   —Bread!
   —And buns!
   —And scrubs the floor!
   —And loves her little Patrick!
   —The finest mam in the whole wide world! (109)

Pussy imagines that this is the stereotypical warm family setting as he enu-
merates all the things he did not have at Whiskers Braden's house: his real
mother, a father, love, fresh baked goods that signify care, a clean house (an
obsession with Pussy), and another unspoken aspect, the fact that Patrick is
an only child in his fantasy, the center of his parents' attention, in contrast
to his reality, being one of six in Whiskers's baby-farming tribe. Despite the
fact that Eily is pure fantasy, this construct is the only thing holding Pussy
together—or keeping her/him on earth.

By the time Louise decides to play-act Pussy's fantasy, Pussy has already
been through the bombing of Dummy Teats, nearly strangled by Silkie while
turning a trick in his car, and through numerous other routine humiliations
and insult-ridden episodes directly in proportion to her transvestite ability
to "pass." But it is Louise, who thinks she is doing something good for Pussy,
who finally causes Pussy's first breakdown or, as Pussy might have it, break-
away from earth. The reader is not, at first, aware of the situation:

When she came into the room first, I didn't believe it was her. I felt my legs turning to string and I moved back against the wall in case I'd collapse. Then my face flushed scarlet and I could feel the saliva in my mouth thickening up into something like jam. "Like me?" she said, and began walking across the floor shaking invisible maraccas and batting her lashes the way she did. All of a sudden it was as if I hadn't washed in weeks as I thought: "Why did I tell her about Mammy? Why did I have to *tell* her?"

Whiskers used to have this habit of lighting cigarette papers and sending them flying up the flue to light, to go spinning off across the stars as far as Pluto or wherever else they wanted to go and that was what I felt like now as I watched the blur of yellow that was the check shirt and the beautifully starched white Capri pants as she ran her hands over them singing: "*I'm gonna wash that man right outa my hair! I'm gonna wash that man right outa my hair!*" (113)

If we believe that Pussy is simply a transvestite who in regard to the Troubles just happens to be in the wrong place at the wrong time, then this episode with Louise is perhaps the most important in the book because it is the most detrimental to Pussy's well being. Once again even when we consider that Pussy's had a murdered lover, is nearly murdered herself during a sexual transaction, and later will even nearly be blown up in a London pub, each of those traumatic situations still do not merit the same reaction as this incident in which Louise plays out Pussy's fantasy of Eily Bergin. The repetition in real life of this mental fantasy creates more than difference: it explodes Pussy's entire mental history. Curiously, Pussy states, "All of a sudden it was as if I hadn't washed in weeks," which is ironic coming from a transvestite who has been enacting the role of a dead little boy so faithfully, from wearing short trousers to sucking Louise's breast. According to Pussy, on hearing about this episode Terence states, "'You've never been quite with us since, have you?'" (114), but Terence also thinks something else happened: "'Why else did you run out that night?' Terence asked me. 'Was there something else she said?'" (114). The reason Pussy runs is the word *breakfast:* "'Yes!' I spluttered through the tears. 'She said "Breakfast." She said: "Please stay for breakfast" or something stupid like that!'" (114). Hence, Pussy provides an assemblage of breakfast links: Eily Bergin was raped serving breakfast, the song "Breakfast on Pluto" connects to the gravity-less feeling Pussy has when reality becomes too much for her/him, a feeling even attributed to Eily while she is being raped by Father Bernard, and lastly, it connects to the film *South Pacific,* which is an iconic image for Pussy and the image that in the end brings the entire fantasy tumbling down. In short, if breakfast had not been served to Father Bernard by Eily Bergin then there would be no Patrick or Pussy, none of his/her pain, and none of this narrative.

If, however, this interpretation is too simplistic (and this *is* a Patrick McCabe novel, after all), then the more complex as well as more troubling interpretation that Pussy is directly involved in the IRA and that she is not simply "an innocent bystander," "caught in the cross-fire" or "at the wrong place at the wrong time" is needed. Deciphering McCabe's tangled prose is not always a straightforward operation, but there seem to be three major incidents that raise questions regarding not only Pussy's involvement with the IRA, but also Pussy's entire narrative and our ability to believe anything she has narrated. Perhaps it is simply a coincidence that the very day Pussy leaves Whiskers's house with "Please, Paddy!" stay (she was getting extra money from Father Bernard for Patrick) dinning in his ears, he is picked up on the road by "Dummy Teats," his sugar daddy: "a Merc pulls up beside me and who is there as the door swings open but the one and only, ladies and gentlemen—His Eminence Mr Dummy Teats! My darling Married Politician Man!" (331). According to Pussy, she did not care anything about his involvement with the IRA: "I understand that there were many who would impugn his good name—importing arms for the IRA and any amount of nonsense!—but, whether the truth or not, the fact is I don't care and didn't" (32). What Pussy was interested in was the fact that he was very clean, perfumed with aftershave, and most important, he lavished money and gifts on Pussy. There was, of course, a concubinage agreement: "But that tootling stick with which he poked—it definitely was a problem. 'You really will have to leave me alone, you know, I simply am exhausted!' I'd try my best to tell him. Always, sadly, to no avail. 'Give me another little chuck-chuck!' he'd say, then, or 'How about a little tune for Dummy?' Then—off I'd go, down on my knees crooning away—but not for fun-time only! O no! Sometimes my Dums, so serious he could be. 'You sweet and darling beauty! How much can I give you to make you mine for ever?'" (32–33). Humorously, we have several things going on all at once in this passage. First, the glaring affront to traditional morality— not only two men engaging in sexual practice, but a married man supporting another man to pose as his "sweet and darling beauty." The bodily negotiation Pussy enjoys with Dummy is materially satisfying, yet there seems to be a limit to or a boredom with Dummy's constant and over-powering concupiscence, which may indicate that Pussy is not such a sexual creature or that she is servicing Dummy's needs for some other purpose. The purpose ostensibly appears to be cash, gifts, and a little bungalow for privacy. Yet, just after the above passage, Pussy's narrative hints that there may be a covert purpose to her favors. In the following passage she attempts to get Dummy to talk about his worries: "Obviously, I knew he was on edge about something. At nights I'd take his tootling stick and say, 'Please tell me, honey. Tell me all your secret troubles.' But he never would. He'd just shed a tear and sigh, then touch me, saying: 'No! Then they'd only come for you!'" (33). Pussy knows her greatest power lies with sexual expertise ("I'd take his tootling stick"), and if she were trying to pry information out of Dummy, then this would be her method. If she wanted only to ease his mind or let him process his troubles, then she would not have to use her body and sex. From the previous passage, we know that Pussy is somewhat bored with Dummy and is only interested in what she can get from him; one reading of this passage would be that she wants information from him.

Although Pussy does not state it lucidly, it appears that her "lover husband" (32) was getting his large supply of cash from two-timing a paramilitary organization: "There are those who say it was the IRA and others the UDA and then some who say it was the two of them together. I didn't know, and didn't fucking care. All I knew was that dear old Dums was gone! Poor old Dummy! Why did you have to immerse yourself in the sinister world of double dealing?" (33). Nonchalantly and perhaps with a trace of malice, Pussy envisions the explosion that killed Dummy; Dummy's "poor little mickey in slo-mo coming back to earth, like a flower pink and bruised, an emblem sent by all the dead men who'd crossed over" (33). From what Pussy tells us about Dummy's "tootling stick," that "at any hour of the day or night, that old tootling stick he had in his trousers would always be ready for action" (31), it would seem that she is happy or at least relieved that in the aftermath of the explosion they had to shovel him up with spades (33). Two other aspects add to Pussy's possible culpability: first, one wonders why Pussy is not with Dummy when the bomb goes off, and, second, she suddenly has a lot of cash to go to Dublin with Charlie which she says is "courtesy of the Dummy Teat Financial Institution" (35).

The subtext that Pussy is a member of the IRA and is used as bait and incidentally a great cover—who would imagine a male transvestite as a member of the IRA?—is further substantiated by an episode that describes a British soldier setup in Belfast. Chapter 28, "Dancing on a Saturday Night," may be the crucial chapter for the reading that argues that Pussy is working for the IRA. A disturbing chapter, "Dancing on a Saturday Night," never names anyone from Pussy's life and she does not narrate herself into the action; it is an anonymous little interlude that happens to be positioned precisely in the middle of the novel, twenty-eighth of fifty-six chapters. Another odd thing about this chapter is that it is set in Belfast; there are no other incidents in the novel that indicate that Pussy was ever in Belfast—the big Irish city she always goes to is Dublin. This omission on Pussy's part is important: had there been any other mention of Belfast, then the reader could much more easily read Pussy into this set-up operation. But with Pussy's (possibly intentional) omission about visits to Belfast, we are less likely to interpret her as one of the girls in this chapter. Yet, Pussy's narrative in describing this scene could lead the reader to believe she is one of the "girls" involved in luring the British soldiers to their deaths. The narrative presents the scene: arrogant British soldiers make their way out on a Saturday night, "All red-cheeked and rosy as out of the barracks they go and down the street they ramble, not giving a toss about the 'facking war!', as one them says while he lights a fag. 'It's the politicians wot facks it ap! Let 'em go and fack 'emselves!'" (98). At the bar, they immediately are attracted to two girls in particular. The interesting aspect of the sentence that describes the girls is that it is straight out of Pussy-speak. Suddenly Pussy comes up from behind the anonymous narrative: "Three pints of Harp and the ultra-violet strobes lighting up them sweet and fancy girls" (98). A possible giveaway, "Three pints of Harp," and then, "The girls they truly look fantastic—done up to the nines in their turtlenecks and wet-look minis, the make-up laid on with a trowel. And the smell of perfume? Phew! And watch them dance now on that floor, despite the high cork wedgies!" (99). This is Pussy's voice laying on the details of the clothes, shoes, makeup and perfume, the music (Barry Blue), and vodka—"How many vodkas did everyone have? No one could re-member!"—which, along with Harp, is Pussy's drink of choice. The "girls" persuade the soldiers to come to an after-hours party—"In literally a matter of seconds the sitting room is just about the last place on earth you would want to hold a party" (100)—where they are simply gunned down, then dumped at a waste site.

The quintessential episode of Pussy's possible IRA involvement is the London disco bombing that targets British soldiers. Pussy claims to have been drinking most of the day, then decides to go dancing, hoping to turn a trick, of course, and spends a lost hour in a public bathroom making her-self up. As soon as she enters the disco a British soldier asks her: "'You fancy a drink or summat?'" (141). The instant she answers him, the bomb goes off: "'Oh, yes!' and look into his eyes when one part of his head and the brains which were inside to the floor pouring like scrambled egg—or so it seemed to Puss. . . . At least a minute had passed before it dawned on her that she wasn't dead too. . . . It was only then she noticed her Christian Dior tights were torn to ribbons. . . . A strip of nylon from Puss's tights had become de-tached and looked for all the world like a scorched piece of skin hanging from the cheek of one of the dead soldiers" (141–142). Pussy is found laugh-ing hysterically among the debris of bodies and body parts. This behavior and her Irish nationality makes her an instant suspect. Although she is abused at the station ("if you weren't whistling Dixie backwards on the far side of Pluto by the time they were finished with you, dearies, then you were made of strong stuff and no mistake—which, sorry to say, Missy Pussy was-n't!"), typical of her attraction to older, authority figures such as Terence, she begins to have a fondness for "Detective Inspector Peter Routledge of Scot-land Yard CID" and colleague PC Wallis. Anxious to nail responsibility for the bombings on someone, Routledge and Wallis interrogate Pussy several times, watch her through the peephole, and even get her to confess. Routledge knows there are two possibilities with the "fairy boy" suspect, and these two possibilities strike the reader as precisely the two interpretive possibilities that the text presents. Perhaps as readers we should feel comforted that Routledge and Wallis, too, vacillate between the two versions of Pussy. Routledge's first interpretation acknowledges his suspicions of Pussy's political agenda: "Why could he not just admit he had dressed up as a woman in an ingenious scheme to disguise himself—for they would stop at nothing, these mad, fanatical bombers—and his plan had gone horribly wrong!" (148). Yet, he questions his initial impression in a second interpretation: "What was at the back of the inspector's mind, of course, gnawing away at him like a cancer, was the nagging suspicion that he might have apprehended the wrong person. What if the callow, fair-skinned youth (David Cassidy—we love you!) was, in fact, as he insisted, nothing more than a drifting transvestite prostitute from the backwoods of Ireland, in search of nothing more than a good time and a reasonable living on the streets of London?" (149). With these two possibilities, Routledge mirrors the novel's duplicitousness; each interpretation—and the possibilities between the two polarities—drives an entirely different reading of the narrative. The fact that Pussy is eventually let go—actually she did not want to go but was pushed out into the London street and told "You stay off the game now, you hear us, Pat?" (181)—leads the reader to believe that Pussy is nothing more than a "drifting transvestite prostitute from the backwoods of Ireland."

Certainly, Pussy wishes the reader to believe this interpretation of the narrative, and we know this through her careful presentation of the events, but she has made her reliability more tainted by the narration of her cell hallucinations—Eily Bergin comes to visit Patrick—and her fantasies of revenge—mostly directed at Father Bernard, the village of Tyreelin, and one odd set-up in which Pussy shoots UDA boss "Big Vicky" in the head and groin area. Pussy also sarcastically fantasizes a short chapter, "'It's Bombing Night and I Haven't Got a Thing to Wear.'" This chapter is deliberately campy and written to be unbelievable. Hammersmith, a London suburb, "and the IRA active service unit was getting ready for another night on the town . . . West End restaurant. . . . First there was the gelignite to be unwrapped. . . . Paddy Pussy, of course, being the undisputed leader of the unit, was well-occupied too, slipping into one of his many luxurious evening gowns"(145). Suddenly, Pussy is Paddy Pussy, and *she* is a male, "slipping into one of *his* many luxurious gowns"; on the next page, however, Pussy is back to being a female:

"Oh, figs!" she exclaimed, casting her fifteenth and final gown to the floor. "Let someone else do it tonight! I can't find a thing to wear!"

"No! No, please!" the other members of the unit pleaded with their adored leader. "We beg you to do it, Puss! After all, you *are* the most feared terrorist in London!"

"Oh, don't I know it, sweetie!" cried Pussy, as she flapped her hands. "Don't I just know it, all you flattering, sweety honey pies!" (146)

Pussy ends this chapter as "she"—"she flapped her hands"—and so we have two different gender citations in one chapter of fewer than three pages.

Yet, two chapters before, "Busy Men Prepare to Blow Up London and Get Pussy into Trouble," we have an odd account of three bombers preparing for their "night on the town": "It was six o'clock—6th November 1974 and Big Joe Kiernan from Offaly was smoking a Player's No. 6 . . . doubled the end of a piece of copper wire from which he had removed the plastic coating and inserted it through the hole he had made in the glass of the pocket watch" (138). There is a "queer" element in this short chapter, "Mayo Jack" who, while he waits for Kiernan to finish, is "absorbed by the photo story which he was reading in a copy of *True Detective* magazine" (138), and the third person from Belfast, "Faigs" McKeever, whose job is to deliver the bomb. "Faigs" supposedly got his name by bumming cigarettes off of people, "as in: 'Have youse any faigs?'" (138). When Faigs is finally ready to deliver the bomb, there is a brief exchange that ends the chapter: "'Don't forget your magazine,' Faigs chuckled as he winked at the *femme deshabillee* on the cover and grabbed his friend between the legs, Mayo Jack hitting him with two well-aimed jabs and laughing: 'Fuck you!' as Big Pat opened the door of the brown Mark 2 Ford Cortina and climbed inside" (139). McCabe puts readers, too, in a position of "true detective" reading strategies by forcing us to play sleuths in order to figure out what is going on—for surely something strange is going on in this chapter. On the one hand, McCabe is perhaps just "having us on" by putting both heterosexual and homosexual innuendos in the text. Sure, the cover of the magazine has a nude female on it, but how many men grab another man "between his legs"? A playful "Fuck you!" does not indicate hostility; rather, it could indicate that either Mayo Jack or Faigs ("fags") is homosexual or they are both homosexual. Narratively speaking, Pussy may be planting a homosexual in the narrative as a disguised self or indicating that there are homosexuals working for the IRA. That they might be friends of Pussy's is borne out by a previously unmentioned "Big Pat" who "opened the door of the brown Mark 2 Ford Cortina." Who is Big Pat? Patrick? And is "Big" an ironic nickname? Also, we might note, he has recently come from Belfast. Reaction to this bombing is contained early in the novel and narrated by a British cockney: "Frowing bombs into restaurants! Wot do they 'ope to gain by that—ai? Bladdy 'ell! They're all cammin' aht nah—screamin' and crying some of 'em, it's like somefink you'd see in a bleedin' 'orror movie! . . . Paddies! . . . Blahdy bog Arabs!" (86). Although presented achronologically, this restaurant bombing was carried out "successfully" and is not the same bombing in which Pussy is injured and interned. In this way, Pussy is becoming-imperceptible. Not only is Patrick/Pussy becoming- insofar as gender is concerned, but also the prose is a imperceptible—the reader's ability to measure the speed of the prose is compromised. We are subjected to both gender and prose undecidability and imperceptibility.

Instead of "true detectives," we may be more like amateur artists attempting to connect the dots in order to draw a reasonable picture—a picture that looks like something familiar. Unfortunately, McCabe does not let his readers off so easily by giving them simplistic and stable readings. One reading, as we have seen, interprets Pussy's narrative as a reliable though embellished story of a transvestite from small-town Ireland whose adventures eventually bring about the breakdown of what little mental stability she had. Pussy is definitely and by her own account *on* Pluto in the London prison, and she never comes down for the rest of the narrative; the story ends where it began, with retired Pussy, "Mrs. Riley" to the local Kilburn boys, wearing a head scarf, housecoat, and slippers. And so, coming full circle at the end of the novel, we realize that Pussy's entire narrative is written "on Pluto" because it is all written after her breakdown in the London prison. The other basic interpretation reads culpability into Pussy's narrative and is much more difficult to stabilize and bring to resolution. At the end of the text, this interpretation may make the reader wonder: Is Kilburn where once-useful but now-mad IRA soldiers are sent out of harm's way to while away their remaining unproductive years? Or in yet another alternative, does Pussy *want* the reader to believe she was involved in IRA operations in order to feel more important and more glamorous or perhaps simply because she is bored? This reading strategy would acknowledge that Pussy's "confessional" is going over the top because she loves the power to narrate to "another, as often as possible, everything that might concern the interplay of innumerable pleasures, sensations, and thoughts which, through the body and the soul, had some affinity with sex," and she is simply too excited by her own narrative to stop. McCabe's radical textual undecidability is made more potent by the irrelevant attitude the text has toward gender and sexual signification. By the end of the novel, McCabe has pushed our sense-making capacity into a new space. There is not—nor should there be—a correct answer or a final interpretation to this slippery novel. To be sure, the undecidability of the narrative is what makes *Breakfast on Pluto* so compelling and offers us a different way to think about Irish culture and the Irish novel.

Afterword

Positioned now in the twenty-first century, we may recall, perhaps in an ironic manner, the words of the early twentieth-century critic, Lionel Johnson: "After all, who is to decide what is, absolutely and definitely, the Celtic and Irish note? Many a time I have shown my English friends Irish poems, which Irish critics have declared to be un-Irish; and the English verdict has constantly been: 'How un-English! How Celtic! What a strange, remote far-away beauty in the music and in the colour!'" Indeed after reading some of the most engaging and outrageous novels from the last decade of the twentieth century, we may be at a loss to name "the Celtic and Irish note," yet fully agree that these novels have "a strange, remote far-away beauty in the music and in the colour." For example, McCabe's characters, Francis and Pussy, certainly challenge Celtic myth and yet have a strange, remote far-away quality. Johnson would probably have some difficulty identifying the homogenous elements in *Hood* or *Crazy Love* that designate them as Irish novels. What Sameness can be accorded?

The 1990s Irish novels interpreted in the previous chapters do not fit into any kind of neat and tidy scheme. While we have been reading for gender construction, body regulation and power dynamics, it should be clear that most of these novels, especially those discussed in chapters 4 and 5, break away from easy definitions and pat interpretations. The only "Sameness" we can accord is that each of the novels was written by an individual born and living primarily in Ireland. Also the social and political context of the '90s contrasts with the stereotype of Ireland. Economics, politics, sexual preference, and lifestyle choices in Ireland in the 1990s are a reflection of a greater European and global awareness. In the Republic of Ireland signs of self-satisfaction were beginning to emerge in the 1990s. In 2001 Ireland rejected a treaty to expand the European Union; in June 2001, the election results were 54 percent against the treaty, while 46 percent supported it. The election results could be construed as self-serving. If the treaty goes through, and EU officials are certain it eventually will, then poor countries like Romania and other former Eastern bloc countries will be admitted to the EU in 2004. Perhaps Irish memory is short; Ireland, too, was rejected prior to its 1973 ratification. The practical consequences of admitting struggling countries into the EU is that the wealthier members must initially subsidize these poorer economies. Not so long ago, in the 1980s, Ireland was considered a peripheral economy along with Spain, Greece, and Portugal, entitled to receive substantial developmental aid and subsistence. Is this vote a sign of the times? What happens to a nation and its national literature when it passes through so many societal, cultural, and economic changes in less than one generation? Also what has happened to the IDA's 1980s campaign to promote the Irish as "We're the Young Europeans"? Perhaps, not unlike Wax Hennessey in Lennon's *Crazy Love,* the young Irish are now older and more concerned with new suburban houses, tax shelters, and foreign investment.

While the so-called Celtic Tiger roars on, another more subtle change is taking place in the Republic and will be an issue of contention in the coming decades. With the wealth of successful economic globalization comes the attraction to Ireland by refugees and asylum-seekers, as well as a migrant work force. An increase in diversity, a multiracial, multiethnic, and multicultural population looms in Ireland's future. The conservative reaction in England to a multiracial and multiethnic society has been extreme. Race riots and politicians' proclamations that England is becoming a "mongrel race" are just two examples of the unpleasant side effects of a global economy. It will be interesting to see how Ireland develops in diversity and how this diversity affects politics, lifestyle, and literature.

Northern Ireland begins the twenty-first century with the old sectarian problems unresolved and the cycle of the violent past threatening to emerge once again. The outcome of the British parliamentary election on June 7, 2001, may signal the beginning of the end of the 1998 Northern Ireland peace accord that set up a power-sharing government. Hardliners on both sides of the aisle gained seats, ousting moderates. With eighteen seats up, Ulster Unionists gained two, but David Trimble's authority was challenged within the ranks of his own party. Sinn Fein achieved a historic victory by winning four seats, doubling its previous two. The Democratic Unionist Party, however, won five seats; its leader, seventy-five-year-old Ian Paisley, promised to work toward the destruction of the power-sharing government. Basking in the glow of victory, Paisley was characteristically outspoken: "David Trimble has destroyed this country with his drip-feed of concessions to the IRA." These election results may indicate that history will repeat itself—yet again. Ian Paisley's 1974 election victory led to the collapse of the last attempt to form a power-sharing type of government with the Catholics. On October 18, 2001, the Ulster Unionist party resigned from the power-sharing government; Trimble claimed that his party had worked hard to hold the coalition together: "For 18 months we have demonstrated every day our willingness to make progress, in terms of this institution and in terms of developing politics in Northern Ireland. For 18 months we have carried the burden." Northern Ireland is in store for a repetition of the Same.

The 1990s may be regarded by historians of Ireland as a hopeful time, a time when the North was on the verge of peace and the Republic saw unprecedented economic and cultural expansion. For the Irish novel, the era must certainly be regarded as a time of great fruition: young writers creating new paradigms that in many instances have virtually no precedent. In this way, the Irish novel in the last decade of the twentieth century did create something new. In chapters 2 and 3 we saw that gender, sexuality, and lifestyle presentations represented life in Ireland in terms of new choices, new situations, and new economic—hence, standard of living—choices. In chapters 4 and 5 the Irish novels we considered opened up new spaces by presenting experience and the ability to capture it in prose. The Irish novel in the 1990s presented readers with great variety—from realistic, domestic novels to bizarre, mosaic-like metafictional novels. Several novelists considered in this text have already published in the twenty-first century, and many young novelists not considered here or just emerging have also published in the last two years. One question, of course, is will this exciting level of productivity and creativity continue? Other questions—how will the Republic's newfound prosperity affect literature, especially the novel, and how will the threatened and perhaps collapsing peace negotiations affect writers in the North? In the Republic, especially in Dublin, racial and ethnic diversity is becoming a reality. Hence, the issues that we have discussed in this text, "gender, bodies and power," are likely to have a new spin in the coming decades. This new spin involves the assimilation of foreigners into Ireland. How will the Irish subaltern "Other" eventually cope with racial and ethnic Otherness within its own borders? In the 1990s we know that traditional ecclesiastical culture continued to diminish as the Church's influence declined. Will the Church be instrumental in the assimilation process? Will traditional Irish Catholics be accepting of those with not only different religious beliefs but also different skin color, language, cultural, and moral beliefs? Entering a global economy may pose its challenges for the future of Ireland.

One thing seems certain: the 1990s novel challenged decades of coagulated thought processes. The 1990s novels forced readers to think differently about the Irish novel and about cultural constructions that have been overly stereotyped in the past. As Lionel Johnson aptly put it a hundred years ago, "After all, who is to decide what is, absolutely and definitively, the Celtic and Irish note?" And now, having fully entered into a new era of economic, cultural, ethnic, and creative production, it is even more difficult to "decide," "absolutely and definitively," what is or what should be "Irish" in the twenty-first century.

Notes

Introduction

1. See Joseph O'Connor, *The Secret World of the Irish Male* (Mandarin, 1995), p. 146.
2. Ibid., p. 152.
3. See Dermot Bolger's introduction in *Invisible Cities: The New Dubliners* (Raven Arts, 1988), p. 9.
4. See Damian Smyth's review, "Dandy Beano Topper," *Irish Review*, no. 15 (Spring1994), p. 134.
5. See "Irish Fiction Writes Itself into a Hole," *The Sunday Times,* Culture section, July 11, 1999, p. 23.
6. See Eamonn Hughes, "Belfastards and Derriers," *Irish Review*, no. 20 (Winter/Spring 1997), pp. 151–152.
7. See *Gender in Irish Writing*, eds. Toni O'Brien Johnson and David Cairns (Open University Press, 1991), pp. 3–4.
8. See "Subalternity and Gender: Problems of Post-colonial Irishness," *Journal of Gender Studies,* vol. 5, no. 3 (1996), p. 370.
9. See "A Fine Old Irish Stew," *New Statesman,* 29 (November 1996), p. 21.
10. See "Poetry and Patriotism in Ireland," in *Post Liminium: Essays and Critical Papers,* ed. Thomas Whittemore (Elkin Mathews, 1911), pp. 172–173.
11. See *Imagined Communities* (Verso, 1991), p. 26.
12. Ibid., p. 119.
13. See "Subalternity and Gender," pp. 363–364.
14. See "The Failure of Economic Nationalism," *The Crane Bag,* vol. 8, no. 1 (1984), pp. 75–76.

Chapter 1

1. See "Part I: Background" in *Lesbian and Gay Visions of Ireland: Towards the Twenty-first Century,* eds. Ide O'Carroll and Eoin Collins (Cassell, 1995), p. 13.
2. Ibid., p. 13.
3. Ibid., p. 17.
4. Ibid., p. 14.

5. Ibid., p. 23.
6. Ibid.; see the Editors' "Introduction," p. 6.
7. Ibid., pp. 6–7.
8. See Pat O'Connor, *Emerging Voices: Women in Contemporary Irish Society* (Institute of Public Administration, 1998) pp. 29–30.
9. Ibid., pp. 24–25.
10. See David Hempton, *Religion and Political Culture in Britain and Ireland: From the Glorious Revolution to the Decline of the Empire* (Cambridge, 1996), p. 90.
11. See Maryann Valiulis, "Neither Feminist nor Flapper: The Ecclesiastical Construction of the Ideal Irish Woman," *Chattel, Servant or Citizen: Women's Status in Church, State and Society*, eds. Mary O'Dowd and Sabine Wichert (Queen's University of Belfast, 1995), p. 176.
12. Ibid., p. 178.
13. See *Emerging Voices*, p. 25.
14. See Ann McClintock, "Family Feuds: Gender, Nationalism and the Family," *Feminist Review*, vol. 44 (1993), p. 66.
15. See Patrick O'Mahony and Gerard Delanty, *Rethinking Irish History: Nationalism, Identity and Ideology* (St. Martin's, 1998), p. 182.
16. Ibid., p. 183.
17. See *Under the Belly of the Tiger: Class, Race, Identity and Culture in the Global Ireland*, eds. Ethel Crowley and Jim Mac Laughlin (Elo Press, 1997), p. 2.
18. See *Regions: Identity and Power*, ed. Proinsias O Drisceoil (Institute of Irish Studies, The Queen's University of Belfast, 1993), p. 7. All subsequent page references will be in the text.
19. See Timothy J. White's "The Changing Social Bases of Political Identity," in *Representing Ireland: Gender, Class, Nationality*, ed. Susan Shaw Sailer (UP of Florida, 1997), p. 116.
20. Ibid., p. 118.
21. Denis O'Hearn is the author of *Inside the Celtic Tiger* (Pluto Press). This quotation is taken from his article, "The Celtic Tiger: The Role of the Multinations," *Under the Belly of the Tiger* (Irish Reporter Publ., 1997), p. 21.
22. Ibid., pp. 22–23.
23. Ibid., pp. 24–25.
24. Ibid., p. 27.
25. Quoted in Dublin Chamber of Commerce publication, *Dublin* (Dyflin Publications, 1999), p. 3.
26. See "In Dublin's Fair Overhyped City . . . ," *The Sunday Times,* feature story, Culture section, July 11, 1999, p. 2.
27. Ibid., p. 2.
28. *The Irish Times,* Saturday, July 17, 1999, p. 11.
29. Broadcast on National Public Radio, September 18, 1999 (5:00 P.M. EST).
30. See *Emerging Voices*, p. 191.
31. Ibid., p. 199.
32. Ibid., p. 243.

33. Ibid., see chapter 8, "Women and Top Jobs: Getting In but Not Getting On," in *Emerging Voices,* pp. 216–243.

34. Quoted in Paul Arthur and Keith Jeffery's *Northern Ireland since 1968* (Blackwell, 1988), p. 34.

35. See Jennifer Todd's "The Limits of Britishness" in *The Irish Review,* no. 5 (Autumn 1988), p. 11–16.

36. *Imagined Communities,* p. 7.

37. I photographed the Loyalist Cuchulainn mural in Belfast, July 1999. A very similar mural is photographed, though on another building in Belfast, by Bill Rolston. See Bill Rolston's *Drawing Support 2: Murals of War and Peace* (Belfast: Beyond the Pale Publications, 1998), p. 17.

38. The Irish Nationalist Cuchulainn mural photo comes from Bill Rolston's *Drawing Support: Murals in the North of Ireland* (Belfast: Beyond the Pale Publications, 1992), p. 39.

39. See Tim Pat Coogan, *The Troubles* (Arrow Books, 1996), p. 81.

40. See Monica McWilliams's "Violence Against Women in Societies Under Stress," in *Rethinking Violence Against Women,* eds. R. Emerson Dobash and Russell P. Dobash (London: Sage, 1998), p. 131.

41. See Megan Sullivan's *Women in Northern Ireland* (University of Florida, 1999), p. 4.

42. See Begona Aretxaga's *Shattering Silence: Women, Nationalism, and Political Subjectivity in Northern Ireland* (Princeton UP, 1997), p. 7.

43. See *The Troubles,* p. 216.

44. Ibid., p. 217.

45. Both quotes from *The Irish Times* report, "Community mourns the deaths of Quinn boys," July 13, 1998.

46. Quoted in *The Irish Times,* Saturday, July 18, 1998.

47. Ibid., Monday, August 17, 1998.

48. Drawn by Chris Riddell, *The Observer,* July 18, 1999.

49. Quoted in *The Irish Times,* Monday, November 29, 1999.

50. See "The Erotics of Irishness," *Critical Inquiry,* vol. 17, no. 1 (Autumn 1990), pp. 1–34.

51. Ibid., p. 6.

52. See Foucault's *Power/Knowledge: Selected Interviews & Other Writings 1972–1977,* ed. Colin Gordon (Random House, 1980), p. 187. All subsequent page references will be in the text.

53. See *Cartographies: Poststructuralism and the Mapping of Bodies and Spaces,* eds. Rosalyn Diprose and Robyn Ferrell (Allen & Unwin, 1991), p. 81.

54. See the *London Review of Books,* May 21-June 3, 1981, p. 5.

55. See Michel Foucault's *The History of Sexuality, Vol. I,* trans. Robert Hurley (Random House, 1978), p. 11. All subsequent page references will be in the text.

56. See Judith Butler's *Gender Trouble: Feminism and the Subversion of Identity* (Routledge, 1990), p. 17. All subsequent page references will be in the text.

57. See *Signs* (1980) vol. 5, no. 4, or *Compulsory Heterosexuality and Lesbian Existence* (Antelope Publications, 1982).

58. See *Compulsory Heterosexuality and Lesbian Existence* (Antelope Publications, 1982), p. 4.
59. See Gilles Deleuze's *Difference and Repetition,* trans. Paul Patton (Columbia UP, 1994), p. 266. All subsequent page references will be in the text.
60. See *Fear and Trembling; Repetition,* eds. and trans. Howard V. Hong and Edna A. Hong (Princeton UP, 1983), p. 150.
61. See Peggy Phelan's *Unmarked: The Politics of Performance* (Routledge, 1993), p. 96.
62. See Judith Butler, *Bodies that Matter: On the Discursive Limits of "Sex"* (Routledge, 1993), p. 9. All subsequent page references will be in the text.
63. See Julia Kristeva, *The Powers of Horror: An Essay on Abjection,* trans. Leon S. Roudiez (Columbia UP, 1982), p. 1.
64. See Butler's *Gender Trouble,* p. 24, quote from Foucault's *Herculine Barbin, Being the Recently Discovered Memoirs of a Nineteenth-Century Hermaphrodite,* trans. Richard McDougall (Colophon, 1980), p. x.
65. See Larry McMurtry's *Buffalo Girls* (Simon and Schuster, 1990), p. 343.
66. Ibid., p. 342.
67. See Biddy Martin, "Extraordinary Homosexuals and the Fear of Being Ordinary," *Differences,* vol. 6 (Summer-Fall 1994), p. 102.
68. Ibid., p. 102.
69. *Buffalo Girls,* p. 342.

Chapter 2

1. See Michel Foucault's article, "The Subject and Power," in *Michel Foucault: Beyond Structuralism and Hermeneutics,* eds. Hubert L. Dreyfus and Paul Rabinow (U of Chicago, 1982), p. 222.
2. Ibid., p. 222.
3. Ibid., pp. 222–223.
4. Ibid., p. 217.
5. See Jo VanEvery, "Heterosexuality and Domestic Life," in *Theorising Heterosexuality: Telling It Straight,* ed. Diane Richardson (Open University, 1996), p. 40.
6. Ibid., p. 40.
7. See, for example, Catharine MacKinnon's *Towards a Feminist Theory of State* (Harvard UP, 1989).
8. See Adrienne Rich's *Compulsory Heterosexuality and Lesbian Existence* (Antelope, 1980), p. 9.
9. See Maureen Gaffney, *Glass Slippers and Tough Bargains: Women, Men and Power* (Attic, 1991), p. 4.
10. Ibid., pp. 4–5.
11. See Rich's *Compulsory Heterosexuality,* p. 15.
12. See Roddy Doyle, *The Woman Who Walked Into Doors* (Viking, 1996), p. 5. All subsequent quotations will be cited in the text.
13. See Lenore E. Walker, *The Battered Woman Syndrome* (Springer, 1984), p. 203.

14. Ibid., p. 11.
15. See Bronwyn F. Bartel, *The British Criminology Conferences: Selected Proceedings, Volume I: Emerging Themes in Criminology,*
16. See Sylvia Walby, *Theorizing Patriarchy* (Blackwell, 1990), p. 128.
17. Ibid., p. 128.
18. See Pat O'Connor, *Emerging Voices: Women in Contemporary Irish Society* (Institute of Public Administration, 1998), pp. 69–70.
19. See O'Connor, pp. 70–71. See also E. Evanson, *Hidden Violence: A Study of Battered Women in Northern Ireland* (Farset Press, 1982).
20. Ibid., pp. 70–71.
21. See the Roddy Doyle *Salon* interview with Charles Taylor at
22. Ibid., p. 3.
23. See Walker, pp. 80–81.
24. See James Ptacek, "Why Do Men Batter Their Wives," *Feminist Perspectives on Wife Abuse* (Sage, 1988), p. 152.
25. Ibid., pp. 152–153.
26. Ibid., p. 155.
27. See Mary Costello, *Titanic Town* (Methuen, 1998), p. 66. All subsequent quotations will be cited in the text.
28. See David Lloyd, *Anomalous States: Irish Writing and the Post-Colonial Moment* (Lilliput, 1993), p. 112.
29. See Laura Pelaschiar, "Transforming Belfast: The Evolving Role of the City in Northern Irish Fiction," *Irish University Review,* vol. 30, no.1 (Summer 2000), p. 119.
30. Unfortunately, I cannot give greater attention to these novels in the context of this book. The issue of space and urban space in particular in the Irish context is an interesting concept and one that needs further exploration.
31. See Sarah Edge, "Representing Gender and National Identity," *Rethinking Northern Ireland,* ed. D. Miller (Longman, 1998), pp. 215–126.
32. See Monica Mc Williams, "The Church, the State and the Women's Movement in Northern Ireland," *Irish Women's Studies Reader,* ed. Ailbhe Smyth (Attic, 1993), pp. 82–83.
33. See Cynthia Cockburn, *The Space Between Us: Negotiating Gender and National Identities in Conflict* (Zed, 2000), p. 59.
34. See Michael Parker, "Shadows on a Glass: Self-Reflexivity in the Fiction of Deirdre Madden," *Irish University Review,* vol. 30, no.1 (Summer 2000), pp. 95–96.
35. See Deirdre Madden, *One by One in the Darkness* (Faber and Faber, 1996), p. 75. All subsequent quotations will be cited in the text.

Chapter 3

1. See *Sex, Nation, and Dissent in Irish Writing,* ed. Eibhear Walshe (St. Martins, 1997), p. 2.
2. Ibid., p. 2.

3. See "Part I: Background" in *Lesbian and Gay Visions of Ireland: Towards the Twenty-first Century,* eds. Ide O'Carroll and Eoin Collins (Cassell, 1995), p. 13.
4. Ibid.; see the Editors' Introduction, p. 6.
5. Ibid., pp. 6–7.
6. See *Sex, Nation, and Dissent in Irish Writing,* p. 12.
7. Fritz Martini claims that Karl (von) Morgenstern used the term as early as 1819–1820. See "Bildungsroman—Term and Theory," in *Reflection and Action: Essays on the Bildungsroman,* ed. James Hardin (University of South Carolina Press, 1991), pp. 1–25.
8. See Wilhelm Dilthey, "The Rise of Hermeneutics," in *The Hermeneutic Tradition: From Ast to Ricoeur,* eds. Gayle M. Ormiston and Alan D. Shrift, trans. Fredric Jameson (SUNY Press, 1990), p. 114.
9. See *Poetry and Experience, Wilhelm Dilthey Selected Works, Vol. V,* eds. Rudolf A. Makkreel and Frithjof Rodi, trans. Joseph Ross (Princeton UP, 1985), p. 335.
10. Ibid., p. 335.
11. Ibid., p. 336.
12. See *The Hermeneutic Tradition: From Ast to Ricoeur,* p. 56.
13. Ibid., p. 56.
14. See Eve Tavor Bannet's essay, "Rewriting the Social Text: The Female Bildungsroman in Eighteenth-Century England," in *Reflection and Action: Essays on the Bildungsroman,* pp. 195–227.
15. Ibid., pp. 205–206.
16. See Sue-Ellen Case, "Tracking the Vampire," *Differences,* vol. 5 (Summer 1991), p. 3.
17. Ibid., p. 4.
18. See Emma Donoghue, *Stir-fry* (Penguin, 1995), p. 27. All subsequent references are to this edition.
19. See Tom Lennon, *When Love Comes to Town* (O'Brien, 1993), p. 82. All subsequent references are to this edition.
20. See Peggy Phelan's *Unmarked: The Politics of Performance* (Routledge, 1993), p. 96.
21. The last verse of the song: "I was there when they crucified my Lord / I held the scabbard when the soldier drew his sword / I threw the dice when they pierce his side / But I've seen love conquer the great the divide" (Chappell & Co., 1988).
22. See Gerry Smyth, *The Novel and the Nation* (Pluto, 1997), p. 161.
23. See Dilthey on Holderlin, p. 137.
24. See Smyth, p. 159.
25. See Carole-Anne Tyler, "Passing: Narcissism, Identity, and Difference," *Differences,* 6.2+3 (1994), p. 212.
26. Ibid., p. 157.
27. See "Swings and Roundabouts: An Interview with Emma Donoghue" *Irish Studies Review,* vol. 8, no. 1 (April 2000), p. 76.

28. Michel Foucault's idea of the four functions of the author-function are detailed in "What Is an Author?" collected in *Language, Counter-memory, Practice: Selected Essays and Interviews,* ed. and trans. Donald F. Bouchard (Cornell UP, 1977).

29. See Monique Wittig, *The Lesbian Body,* trans. David Le Vay (Avon, 1975), and Sue-Ellen Case, "Toward a Butch-Femme Aesthetic," *Making a Spectacle: Feminist Essays on Contemporary Women's Theatre* (U of Michigan, 1992), pp. 282–299.

30. See Marilyn R. Farwell, *Heterosexual Plots and Lesbian Narratives* (New York UP, 1996), pp. 99–100.

31. Quoted by Dilthey in section on Holderlin from Gottfried Keller's novel, *The Green Henry.* See *Poetry and Experience, Wilhelm Dilthey Selected Works, Vol. V,* eds. Rudolf A. Makkreel and Frithjof Rodi, trans. Joseph Ross (Princeton UP, 1985), p. 343.

32. See Gilles Deleuze and Felix Guattari, *Thousand Plateaux,* trans. Brian Massumi (U of Minnesota P, 1980) p. 308.

33. Cited in Case's "Toward a Butch-Femme Aesthetic," in *Making a Spectacle,* p. 290.

34. Ibid., p. 291.

35. Ibid., p. 291.

36. Ibid., p. 291.

37. Ibid., p. 291.

38. See Emma Donoghue's *Hood* (Penguin, 1996), pp. 188–189. All subsequent references are to this edition.

39. See *Cartographies: Poststructuralism and the Mapping of Bodies and Spaces,* eds. Rosalyn Diprose and Robyn Ferrell (Allen & Unwin, 1991), p. 81.

40. Ibid., p. 81.

41. See Walshe's Introduction to *Sex, Nation, and Dissent in Irish Writing,* p. 7. The quotation is from Jonathan Dollimore, "The Cultural Politics of Perversion," *Sexual Sameness,* ed. Joseph Bristow (Routledge, 1992), p. 9.

42. See Adrienne Rich, *Compulsory Heterosexuality and Lesbian Existence* (Antelope, 1982), p. 14.

43. The definition of *hood* as a suffix: "a native English suffix denoting state, condition, character, nature, etc., or a body of persons of a particular character or class, formerly used in the formation of nouns: *childhood; likelihood; knighthood; priesthood,*" p. 918 (*Random Unabridged,* 1987).

44. See Tom Lennon, *Crazy Love* (O'Brien, 1999), p. 51. All subsequent references are to this edition.

45. See *The Irish Times,* Saturday, July 17, 1999, p. 11.

46. The song is "Crazy Love" from Van Morrison's 1970 album *Moondance.* "Crazy Love" was written by Morrison.

47. The only Irish novel to win the Booker Prize was *Paddy Clarke Ha Ha Ha* by Roddy Doyle in 1993. Incredibly enough—or incredulously enough— Irish novelists usually score a nomination that might be viewed as tokenism, but they never win, outside of Doyle's *Paddy Clarke Ha Ha Ha.* In the 1990s

Patrick McCabe, for example, was nominated in 1992 for *The Butcher Boy* and in 1998 for *Breakfast on Pluto* losing to Michael Ondaatje's *The English Patient* (better known as a film), and Ian McEwan's 1998 winner, *Amsterdam,* respectively.

48. Figures available from Factsheet Ireland which accompanied the Owen Metcalfe, Chief Education Officer, Health Promotion Unit, Department of Health, Ireland, the HIV/AIDS report on prevention policies for youth in Europe. Factsheet available online: www.nigz.nl/eie/ireland.

49. RTE, Friday May 19, 2000.

50. See Colm Toibin's *The Blackwater Lightship* (Picador, 1999), p. 47. All subsequent references are to this edition.

51. See the above cited Department of Health, Ireland, HIV/AIDS report, p. 8.

52. Ibid., p. 8.

53. See Patrick Hannon, "AIDS: Moral Issues," *Studies,* vol. 79, no. 314 (Summer 1990), p. 109.

54. Ibid., p. 109.

55. Ibid., p. 106.

56. See "The AIDS-Avenger Scare," *Time,* September 25, 1995, vol. 146, no. 13.

57. Ibid.

58. See Ailbhe Smyth, "States of Change: Reflections on Ireland in Several Uncertain Parts," *Feminist Review,* no. 50 (Summer 1995), p. 24.

59. Ibid., p. 25.

60. First reported by the *Kansas City Star* on January 31, 2000, and subsequently picked up by Reuters and Associated Press; a full account can be found on a website for survivors of clergy sexual abuse: www.thelinkup.com/aids.

61. For example, in February 2000 the *Irish Times* reported that Robert Keoghan, a former Fransciscan brother, was sexually abused by his confessor when he went to confess his own sexual abuse of boys. As it turns out, Keoghan was abused from the age of thirteen by brothers in the seminary who were older, mostly in their twenties. Keoghan is serving an eighteen-month sentence after he pleaded guilty to eight charges of indecently assaulting eight boys between nine and sixteen years of age.

62. See "Swings and Roundabouts: An Interview with Emma Donoghue," *Irish Studies Review,* vol. 8, no. 1 (April 2000), p. 76.

63. See Sue-Ellen Case, "Tracking the Vampire," *Differences,* vol. 5 (Summer 1991), p. 3.

Chapter 4

1. See Eamonn Hughes, "Belfastards and Derriers," *The Irish Review,* no. 20 (Winter/Spring 1997), pp. 151–157.

2. See Liam Harte, "History Lessons: Postcolonialism and Seamus Deane's *Reading in the Dark,*" *Irish University Review,* vol. 30, no. 1 (Spring/Summer 2000), pp. 149–162.

3. Ibid., pp. 151–152.

4. Ibid., p. 152.
5. Ibid., p. 159.
6. Catholic preoccupation with building an educated Catholic middle class in the North is evident also in the generation that follows Deane's. In *One by One in the Darkness,* Helen, discussing her university plans with Sister Benedict in the 1970s is aware that the North needs to educate and establish a Catholic middle class:

> "And why law?"
> "We need our Catholic lawyers in this society," Helen said, and Sister Benedict looked up sharply at her. She thought Helen was being sarcastic, repeating the words Sister Philomena was constantly repeating to them: "Our educated Catholics have a role to play in this society. We need our Catholic teachers and doctors and nurses and lawyers." (158)

7. See Seamus Deane, *Reading in the Dark* (Knopf, 1997), p. 29. All subsequent quotations will be cited in the text.
8. See Anne Fogarty, "Uncanny Families: Neo-Gothic Motifs and the Theme of Social Change in Contemporary Irish Women's Fiction," *Irish University Review,* vol. 30, no. 1 (Spring/Summer 2000), pp. 59–81.
9. Ibid., p. 68.
10. See Mary Morrissy, *Mother of Pearl* (Scribner, 1995), p. 160. All subsequent quotations will be cited in the text.
11. See Brian Donnelly, "Roddy Doyle From Barrytown to the GPO," *Irish University Review,* vol. 30, no. 1 (Spring/Summer 2000), pp. 17–31.
12. See Roddy Doyle, *A Star Called Henry* (Jonathan Cape, 1999), p. 1. All subsequent quotations will be cited in the text.
13. See Loreto Todd, *Green English: Ireland's Influence on the English Language* (O'Brien, 1999), p. 62.
14. My comparison with Beckett is most easily understood if we consider *Molloy* or *Malone Dies* in relation to *Ripley Bogle.* The most obvious connection is each novel is titled after the narrator who is in some way a derelict, and later in the text will beat to near-death another derelict. More striking is the tone that Bogle assumes and the narrative he frames. Each novel begins in a similar manner. Molloy begins his narrative: "Here's my beginning. Because they're keeping it apparently. I took a lot of trouble with it. Here it is. It gave me a lot of trouble" (8). Near the beginning of Bogle's narrative: "This for what my story is. This the sly map from which I shall exhume my goal, my task and treasure. This is where we are all going. You, me and my story (such as it is)" (9). I am merely suggesting a few similarities; proper critical work needs to done on the connections between Beckett and Wilson.
15. See Robert McLiam Wilson, *Ripley Bogle* (Vintage, 1998), p. 38. All subsequent quotations will be cited in the text.
16. See Laura Pelaschiar, "Transforming Belfast: The Evolving Role of the City in Northern Irish Fiction," *Irish University Review,* vol. 30, no. 1 (Spring/Summer 2000), pp. 117–131.

17. Ibid., p. 117.
18. See Robert McLiam Wilson, *Eureka Street* (Minerva 1997), p. 396.
19. When Wilson was asked by Richard Mills in "'All Stories Are Love Stories':
    Robert McLiam Wilson Interviewed by Richard Mills," *Irish Studies Review,*
    vol. 7, no. 1 (1999), "Why did Ripley Bogle turn up in *Eureka Street?*" Wil-
    son replied, "I think that was more for me. This was the first book where
    anyone had a conversation. I'd written two novels about solitary characters,
    who lived alone and didn't talk much" (76).

Chapter 5

1. See John Banville, *The Book of Evidence* (Warner: New York, 1991), p. 16.
   All subsequent page references are to this edition.
2. See Tony E. Jackson, "Science, Art, and the Shipwreck of Knowledge: The
   Novels of John Banville," *Contemporary Literature,* vol. 38, no. 3, 1997, pp.
   510–533.
3. See Brian Cosgrove, "Irish/Postmodern Literature: A Case of Either/Or?"
   Studies, vol. 88, no. 352 (Winter 1999), pp. 381–388.
4. Ibid., p. 387. The interview was conducted by Hedwig Schall, "An Interview
   with John Banville," *The European English Messenger,* vol. VI, no. 1 (Spring
   1997), pp. 13–19.
5. See Joseph McMinn, "Versions of Banville: Versions of Modernism," in
   Contemporary Irish Fiction: Themes, Tropes Theories, eds. Liam Harte and
   Michael Parker (St. Martin's, 2000). See also McMinn's *John Banville: A
   Critical Study* (Gill and Macmillan, 1991) and *The Supreme Fictions of John
   Banville* (Manchester UP, 1999), along with Rudiger Imhof's *John Banville:
   A Critical Introduction* (Wolfhound Press, 1989).
6. Ibid., p. 82.
7. "Frank Richards" wrote the Billy Bunter and Magnet series books, first published from 1908 to 1940. Cassell issued editions during the period between
   1950 and 1965 called "The Billy Bunter Series." Billy Bunter also inspired
   a 1950s British television program: "The series starred Gerald Campion . . .
   and was based on the books written by Frank Richards. At one time it was
   so popular that it was transmitted at 5:25 P.M. for children and again two
   hours later for the their parents!" See:
8. See Patrick McCabe's *The Butcher Boy* (Warner: New York,1997), p. 75. All
   subsequent page references are to this edition.
9. See John Scaggs, "Who is Francie Pig? Self-Identity and Narrative Reliability in *The Butcher Boy.*" *Irish University Review,* vol. 30, no. 1 (Spring/Sum-
   mer 2000), pp. 51–58.
10. See Patrick McCabe's *Breakfast on Pluto* (Picador: London, 1998), pp.
    35–36. All subsequent page references are to this edition.
11. In "Engendering and the Erotics of Editing" Mary Ann Caws discusses the
    way in which certain female authors have been engendered by subsequent
    editors, e.g., Virginia Woolf by Leonard Woolf, and, more tellingly, Sylvia

Plath by Ted Hughes. Caws states that "the voice of all women adjusting our memory to our truth is an *engendering voice*" (59), but she does not indicate how a metafictional, in this case, male transvestite engendering herself /himself female might be interpreted. See Caws's article in *The Poetics of Gender,* ed. Nancy K. Miller (Columbia UP, 1986), pp. 42–61.

12. See Peggy Phelan's *Unmarked: The Politics of Performance* (Routledge, 1993), p. 96.

13. See Hubert L. Dreyfus and Paul Rabinow's *Michel Foucault: Beyond Structuralism and Hermeneutics* (U of Chicago, 1982), p. 171.

14. See Michel Foucault's *The History of Sexuality, Vol. I,* trans. Robert Hurley (Random House, 1978), p. 153.

15. Ibid., p. 20.

16. While McCabe's previous novel *The Butcher Boy* is also a song title, Tom Lennon, too, for example, titled both his novels after popular songs, *When Love Comes to Town* (U2) and *Crazy Love* (Van Morrison).

17. "Breakfast on Pluto" written by Don Partridge and Alan Young, 1969, Onward Music Ltd. (London).

18. The idea of the abject is discussed at length in chapter 1.

19. See Ursula Barry's "Women in Ireland," in the special issue of *Women's Studies International Forum,* "Feminism in Ireland," ed. Ailbhe Smyth, vol. 11, no. 4 (1988), pp. 317–322.

20. Ibid., p. 318.

21. Ibid., p. 318.

Bibliography

Anderson, Benedict. *Imagined Communities*. London: Verso, 1991.

Aretxaga, Begona. *Shattering Silence: Women, Nationalism and Political Subjectivity in Northern Ireland*. Princeton: Princeton UP, 1997.

Arthur, Paul, and Keith Jeffrey. *Northern Ireland since 1968*. Oxford: Basil Blackwell, 1988.

Aughey, Arthur, and Duncan Morrow. *Northern Ireland Politics*. New York: Longman, 1996.

Banville, John. *The Newton Letter*. New York: Time Warner, 1982.

———. *The Book of Evidence*. New York: Warner, 1991.

———. *Mefisto*. London: Paladin, 1987.

———. *The Untouchable*. New York: Knopf, 1997.

Bardon, Jonathan. *Belfast; An Illustrated History*. Belfast: Blackstaff, 1982.

Barry, Sebastian. *The Whereabouts of Eneas McNulty*. London: Picador, 1998.

———. *The Engine of Owl-Light*. Manchester: Carcanet, 1987.

Barry, Ursula. "Women in Ireland." *Women's Studies International Forum,* vol. 11, no. 4 (1988), pp. 317–322.

Beale, Jenny. *Women in Ireland: Voices of Change*. Bloomington: Indiana UP, 1987.

Beckett, Samuel. *Three Novels: Molloy, Malone Dies, and The Unnamable*. New York: Grove, 1958.

Bell, Desmond. "Contemporary Cultural Studies in Ireland and the 'Problem' of Protestant Ideology." *The Crane Bag*, vol. 9, no. 2 (1985), pp. 91–95.

Bell, Ian A., ed. *Peripheral Visions: Images of Nationhood in Contemporary British Fiction*. Cardiff: U of Wales, 1995.

Bennett, Ronan. "Don't Mention the War: Culture in Northern Ireland." In *Rethinking Northern Ireland*. Ed. D. Miller. London: Longman,1998.

Bensyl, Stacia. "Swings and Roundabouts: An Interview with Emma Donoghue." *Irish Studies Review,* vol. 8, no. 1 (2000), pp. 73–81.

Bolger, Dermot, ed. *Invisible Cities: The New Dubliners*. Dublin: Raven Arts, 1988.

Bourke, Angela. *The Burning of Bridget Cleary*. London: Pimlico, 1999.

Bradley, Anthony, and Maryann Gialanella Valiulis, eds. *Gender and Sexuality in Modern Ireland*. Amherst: U of Massachusetts Press, 1997.

Brewster, Scott, Virginia Crossman, Fiona Becket, and David Alderson, eds. *Ireland in Proximity: History, Gender, Space*. London: Routledge, 1999.

Butler, Judith. *Gender Trouble*. New York: Routledge, 1990.

———. *Bodies that Matter*. New York: Routledge, 1993.

Byrne, Sean. *Growing Up in a Divided Society: The Influence of Conflict on Belfast Schoolchildren.* Cranbury, NJ: Associated UP, 1997.

Cairns, David, and Shaun Richards, eds. *Writing Ireland: Colonialism, Nationalism, and Culture.* Manchester: Manchester UP, 1988.

Case, Sue-Ellen. "Tracking the Vampire." *Differences,* vol. 3, no. 2 (1991), pp. 1–20.

Caws, Mary Ann. "The Conception of Engendering: The Erotics of Editing." In *The Poetics of Gender.* Ed. Nancy K. Miller. New York: Columbia UP, 1986.

Cleary, Joe. "'Fork-Tongued on the Border Bit': Partition and the Politics of Form in Contemporary Narratives of the Northern Irish Conflict." *The South Atlantic Quarterly,* vol. 95, no. 1 (Winter 1996), pp. 227–276.

Cockburn, Cynthia. *The Space Between Us: Negotiating Gender and National Identities in Conflict.* London: Zed Books, 1998.

Connolly, Sean. "Approaches to the History of Irish Popular Culture." *Bullan: An Irish Studies Journal,* vol. 2, no. 2 (Winter/Spring 1996), pp. 83–100.

Conrad, Kathryn. "Occupied Country: The Negotiation of Lesbianism in Irish Feminist Narrative." *Eire-Ireland,* vol. 31, nos. 1–2 (Summer 1996), pp.123–136.

———, and Darryl Wadsworth. "Joyce and the Irish Body Politic: Sexuality and Colonization in *Finnegans Wake.*" *James Joyce Quarterly,* 31:3 (Spring 1994), pp. 301–313.

Coogan, Tim Pat. *The Troubles.* London: Arrow, 1996.

Cosgrove, Brian. "Roddy Doyle's Backward Look: Tradition and Modernity in *Paddy Clarke Ha Ha Ha.*" *Studies,* vol. 85, no. 339 (1996), pp. 231–242.

———. "Irish/Postmodern Literature: A Case of Either Or?" *Studies,* vol. 88, no. 352 (Winter 1999), pp. 381–388.

Costello, Mary. *Titanic Town.* London: Methuen, 1992.

Crone, Joni. "Lesbian Feminism in Ireland." *Women's Studies International Forum,* vol. 11, no. 4 (1988), pp. 343–347.

Crowley, Ethel, and Jim Mac Laughlin, eds. *Under the Belly of the Tiger: Class, Race, Identity and Culture in the Global Ireland.* Dublin: Irish Reporter Publications, 1997.

Curtain, Chris, Pauline Jackson, and Barbara O'Connor, eds. *Gender in Irish Society.* Galway: Galway UP, 1987.

Daly, Mary E. *Dublin: The Deposed Capital.* Cork: Cork UP, 1984.

Dawe, Gerald, and Edna Longley, eds. *Across a Roaring Hill: The Protestant Imagination in Modern Ireland.* Belfast: Blackstaff Press, 1985.

Deane, Seamus. *Reading in the Dark.* New York: Knopf, 1997.

———. *Strange Country: Modernity and Nationhood in Irish Writing since 1790.* Oxford: Clarendon Press, 1997.

———. "Society and the Artist." *Studies,* vol. 79, no. 315 (Autumn 1990), pp. 247–256.

Deleuze, Gilles. *Difference and Repetition.* Trans. Paul Patton. New York: Columbia UP, 1994.

———. *Essays: Critical and Clinical.* Trans. Daniel W. Smith and Michael A. Greco. Minneapolis: U of Minnesota, 1997.

———, and Felix Guattari. *Kafka: Toward a Minor Literature.* Trans. Dana Polan. Minneapolis: U of Minnesota, 1986.

———. *Thousand Plateaux.* Trans. Brian Massumi. Minneapolis: U of Minnesota, 1987.

———. *What Is Philosophy?* Trans. Hugh Tomlinson and Graham Burchell. New York: Columbia UP, 1994.

de Man, Paul. *Blindness and Insight.* Minneapolis: U of Minnesota, 1983.

Dempsey, Patrick John. "Dublin: Gentrification or Urban Rival?" *Studies,* vol. 81, no. 321 (Spring 1992), pp. 71–79.

De Paor, Liam. "Ireland's Identities." *The Crane Bag,* vol. 3, no. 1 (1979) pp. 22–30.

Dillon, Michele. *Debating Divorce: Moral Conflict in Ireland.* Lexington: U of Kentucky Press, 1993.

Diprose, Rosalyn, and Robyn Ferrell, eds. *Cartographies: Poststructuralism and the Mapping of Bodies and Spaces.* North Sydney: Allen & Unwin, 1991.

Docherty, Thomas. "Initiations, Tempers, Seductions: Postmodern McGuckian." In *The Chosen Ground: Essays on the Contemporary Poetry of Northern Ireland.* Ed. Neil Corcoran. Chester Springs, PA: Dufour, 1992.

Donnelly, Brian. "Roddy Doyle: From Barrytown to the GPO." *Irish University Review,* vol. 30, no. 1 (Spring/Summer 2000), pp.17–31.

Donoghue, Emma. *Stir-fry.* London: Penguin, 1995.

———. *Hood.* London: Penguin, 1996.

———. *Kissing the Witch.* London: Penguin, 1998.

Doyle, Roddy. *The Barrytown Trilogy.* New York: Penguin, 1993.

———. *Paddy Clarke Ha Ha Ha.* New York: Penguin, 1993.

———. *The Woman Who Walked Into Doors.* New York: Viking, 1996.

———. *A Star Called Henry.* London: Jonathan Cape, 1999.

Dublin Chamber of Commerce. *Dublin.* Dublin: Dyflin Publications, 1999.

Edge, Sarah. "Representing Gender and National Identity." In *Rethinking Northern Ireland.* Ed. D. Miller. London: Longman,1998.

———. "Women are the trouble did you know that Fergus: Neil Jordan's *The Crying Game.*" *Feminist Review* 50 (Summer 1995), pp. 173–185.

Enright, Anne. *The Wig My Father Wore.* London: Minerva, 1996.

Evason, Eileen. *Against the Grain: The Contemporary Women's Movement in Northern Ireland.* Dublin: Attic Press LIP Pamphlet, 1991.

Farwell, Marilyn R. *Heterosexual Plots and Lesbian Narratives.* New York: New York UP, 1996.

Fearon, Kate. *Power, Politics, Positioning: Women in Northern Ireland.* Democratic Dialogue Report Number 4. Belfast, 1996.

———. *Women's Work: The Story of the Northern Ireland Women's Coalition.* Belfast: Blackstaff, 1999.

Feldman, Allen. *Formations of Violence.* Chicago: U of Chicago Press, 1991.

Fogarty, Anne. "Uncanny Families: Neo-Gothic Motifs and the Theme of Social Change in Contemporary Irish Women's Fiction." *Irish University Review,* vol. 30, no. 1 (Spring/Summer 2000), pp. 59–81.

Foster, John Wilson. *Fictions of the Irish Literary Revival: A Changeling Art.* Syracuse: Syracuse UP, 1987.

Foster, R. F. *Modern Ireland: 1600–1972.* London: Penguin, 1988.

Foucault, Michel. *Power/Knowledge: Selected Interviews & Other Writings 1972–1977*. Ed. Colin Gordon. New York: Random House, 1980.

———. *The History of Sexuality, Vol. I*. Trans. Robert Hurley. New York: Random House, 1978.

Gaffney, Maureen. *Glass Slippers and Tough Bargains: Women, Men and Power*. Dublin: Attic Press LIP Pamphlet, 1991.

Geary, James. "The Aids-Avenger Scare." *Time*, vol. 146, no. 13 (September 25, 1995).

Gibbons, Luke. *Transformations in Irish Culture*. Notre Dame: U of Notre Dame, 1996.

Giddings, Robert. *Literature and Imperialism*. New York: St. Martin's Press, 1991.

Goodby, John. "Bhabha, the Post/Colonial and Glenn Patterson's *Burning Your Own*." *Irish Studies Review*, vol. 7, no. 1 (1999), pp. 65–72.

Graham, Colin. "'Liminal Spaces': Post-Colonial Theories and Irish Culture." *The Irish Review*, no.16 (Autumn/Winter 1994), pp. 29–43.

———. "Subalternity and Gender: Problems of Post-colonial Irishness." *Journal of Gender Studies*, vol. 5, no. 3 (1996), pp. 363–373.

Gray, Breda. "Longings and Belongings–Gendered Spatialities of Irishness." *Irish Studies Review*, vol. 7, no. 2 (1999), pp. 193–210.

Grosz, Elizabeth. *Volatile Bodies: Toward a Corporeal Feminism*. Bloomington: Indiana U Press, 1994.

Haberstroh, Patricia Boyle. *Women Creating Women: Contemporary Irish Women Poets*. Syracuse: Syracuse UP, 1996.

Hamilton, A., L. Moore, and T. Trimble. *Policing a Divided Society: Issues and Perceptions in Northern Ireland*. University of Ulster: Centre for the Study of Conflict, 1995.

Hannon, Patrick. "Aids: Moral Issues." *Studies*, vol. 79, no. 314 (Summer 1990), pp. 103–115.

Hardin, James, ed. *Reflection and Action: Essays on the Bildungsroman*. Columbia: U of South Carolina Press, 1991.

Hart, Lynda, ed. *Making a Spectacle: Feminist Essays on Contemporary Women's Theatre*. Ann Arbor: U of Michigan Press, 1992.

Harte, Lara. *Losing It*. London: Phoenix House, 1999.

Harte, Liam. "History Lessons: Postcolonialism and Seamus Deane's *Reading in the Dark*." *Irish University Review*, vol. 30, no. 1 (Spring/Summer 2000), pp. 149–162.

Hawley, John C., ed. *Cross-Addressing: Resistance Literature and Cultural Borders*. Albany: SUNY Press, 1996.

Hempton, David. *Religion and Political Culture in Britain and Ireland: From the Glorious Revolution to the Decline of the Empire*. Cambridge: Cambridge UP, 1990.

Herr, Cheryl. "The Erotics of Irishness." *Critical Inquiry* 17 (1990), pp. 1–34.

Holland, Janet, Caroline Ramazonoglu, Sue Sharpe, and Rachel Thomson. "Pressured Pleasure: Young Women and the Negotiation of Sexual Boundaries." *The Sociological Review*, vol. 40, no. 4 (November 1992), pp. 645–674.

Hughes, Eamonn, ed. *Culture and Politics in Northern Ireland 1960–1990*. Buckingham: Open University Press, 1991.

———. "Belfastards and Derriers." *Irish Review,* no. 20 (Winter/Spring 1997), pp. 151–157.

Humphreys, Alexander J. *New Dubliners: Urbanization and the Irish Family.* New York: Fordham UP, 1966.

Imhof, Rudiger. *John Banville: A Critical Introduction.* Dublin: Wolfhound Press, 1989.

Innes, C. L. *Women and Nation in Irish Literature.* London: Harvester, 1993.

Jackson, Ellen-Raissa. "Gender, Violence and Hybridity: Reading the Postcolonial in Three Irish Novels." *Irish Studies Review,* vol. 7, no. 2 (1999), pp. 221–231.

Jacobs, Susie, Ruth Jackson, and Jen Marchbank, eds. *States of Conflict: Gender, Violence, and Resistance.* London: Zed Books, 2000.

Jacobson, Ruth. "Women and Peace in Northern Ireland: A Complicated Relationship." In *States of Conflict: Gender, Violence and Resistance.* Ed. Susie Jacobs, Ruth Jacobson, and Jen Marchbank. London: Zed Books, 2000.

Jeffers, Jennifer M., ed. *Samuel Beckett: A Casebook.* New York: Garland, 1998.

Johnson, Toni O'Brien, and David Cairns, eds. *Gender in Irish Writing.* Buckingham: Open University Press, 1991.

Joyce, P. W. *English as We Speak It in Ireland.* London: Longmans, Green & Co., 1910.

Kavanagh, Patrick. *Tarry Flynn.* New York: Viking Penguin, 1978.

Keane, Molly. *Good Behaviour.* London: Abacus Books, 1982.

Kearney, Richard. *Postnationalist Ireland: Politics, Culture, Philosophy.* London: Routledge, 1997.

———. "Faith and Fatherland." *The Crane Bag,* vol. 8, no. 1 (1984), pp. 55–66.

Keatinge, Patrick. *Ireland and EC Membership Evaluat*ed. New York: St. Martin's, 1991.

Kirkland, Richard. *Literature and Culture in Northern Ireland Since 1965: Moments of Danger.* London: Longman, 1996.

Kristeva, Julia. *The Powers of Horror: An Essay on Abjection.* Trans. Leon S. Roudiez. New York: Columbia UP, 1982.

Laffan, Michael. "Two Irish States." *The Crane Bag,* vol. 8, no. 1 (1984), pp. 26–40.

Leith, Linda. "Subverting the Sectarian Heritage: Recent Novels of Northern Ireland." *The Canadian Journal of Irish Studies,* vol. 18, no. 2 (December 1992), pp. 88–106.

Lennon, Tom. *When Love Comes to Town.* Dublin: O'Brien, 1993.

———. *Crazy Love.* Dublin: O'Brien, 1999.

Leonard, Dick. *Guide to the European Union.* London: Profile Books, 1998.

Lloyd, David. *Anomalous States: Irish Writing and the Post-colonial Moment.* Durham: Duke University Press, 1993.

MacKinnon, Catharine. *Sexual Harassment of Working Women: A Case of Sex Discrimination.* New Haven: Yale UP, 1979.

———. *Towards a Feminist Theory of State.* Cambridge: Harvard UP, 1989.

MacLaverty, Bernard. *Cal.* London: Jonathan Cape, 1983.

Madden, Deirdre. *The Birds of the Innocent Wood.* London: Faber & Faber, 1988.

———. *One by One in the Darkness.* London: Faber and Faber, 1996.

Maddox, Brenda. "A Fine Old Irish Stew." *New Statesman*, vol. 29 (November 1996), pp. 21–24.

Mahony, Christina Hunt. *Contemporary Irish Literature: Transforming Tradition*. New York: St. Martin's, 1998.

Makkreel, Rudulf A., and Frithjof Rodi, eds. *Wilhelm Dilthey: Poetry and Experience. Selected Works, Vol. V.* Princeton: Princeton UP, 1985.

Martin, Biddy. "Extraordinary Homosexuals and the Fear of Being Ordinary." *Differences*, vol. 6, no. 2+3 (Summer-Fall 1994), pp. 100–125.

Mathews, P. J. *New Voices in Irish Criticism*. Dublin: Four Courts, 2000.

McCabe, Patrick. *Carn*. New York: Delta, 1989.

———. *The Dead School*. New York: Delta, 1995.

———. *The Butcher Boy*. New York: Delta, 1997.

———. *Breakfast on Pluto*. London: Picador, 1998.

McCarthy, Conor. *Modernisation, Crisis and Culture in Ireland, 1969–1992*. Dublin: Four Courts, 2000.

McClintock, Anne. "Family Feuds: Gender, Nationalism and the Family." *Feminist Review*, vol. 44 (1993), pp. 61–81.

McGahern, John. *The Dark*. New York: Penguin, 1966.

McMichael, Gary. *Ulster Voice: In Search of Common Ground in Northern Ireland*. Boulder, CO: Roberts Rinehart Publishers, 1999.

McMinn, Joseph. *John Banville: A Critical Study*. Dublin: Gill and Macmillan, 1991.

———. *The Supreme Fictions of John Banville*. Manchester: Manchester UP, 1999.

McMurtry, Larry. *Buffalo Girls*. New York: Simon & Schuster, 1990.

McWilliams, Monica. "Violence Against Women in Societies Under Stress." *Rethinking Violence Against Women*. Ed. R. Emerson Dobash and Russell P. Dobash. London: Sage, 1998.

———. "The Church, the State and the Women's Movement in Northern Ireland." *Irish Women's Studies Reader*. Ed. Ailbhe Smyth. Dublin: Attic, 1993.

———, and J. McKernan. *Bringing It Out Into the Open–Domestic Violence in Northern Ireland*. Belfast: HMSO, 1993.

Michasiw, Kim. "Camp, Maculinity, Masquerade." *Differences*, vol. 6, no. 2+3 (Summer-Fall 1994), pp. 146–173.

Miller, D. A. *The Novel and the Police*. Berkeley: U of California, 1988.

Miller, David, ed. *Rethinking Northern Ireland: Culture, Ideology and Colonialism*. London: Longman, 1998.

Miller, R. L. R. Wilford, and F. Donoghue. *Women and Political Participation in Northern Ireland*. Aldershot: Avebury, 1996.

Mills, Lia. *Another Alice*. Dublin: Poolbeg, 1996.

Mills, Richard. "'All Stories Are Love Stories': Robert McLiam Wilson Interviewed by Richard Mills." *Irish Studies Review*, vol. 7, no. 1 (1999), pp. 73–77.

Morrissy, Mary. *Mother of Pearl*. New York: Scribner, 1995.

Mullen, Molly. "Representations of History, Irish Feminism, and the Politics of Difference." *Feminist Studies* 17, no. 1 (1991), pp. 29–50.

Murphy, Gavin. "'Keaning the North': The Paintings of John Keane and Political Conflict in Northern Ireland." *Irish Studies Review*, vol. 7, no. 3 (1999), pp. 359–370.

Neary, Peter. "The Failure of Economic Nationalism." *The Crane Bag,* vol. 8, no.1 (1984), pp. 68–77.

Ni Dhuibhne, Eilis. *The Dancers Dancing.* Belfast: The Blackstaff Press, 1999.

Norris, David. "Homosexual People and the Christian Churches in Ireland–A Minority and its Oppressor." *The Crane Bag,* vol. 5 (1981), pp. 31–38.

O'Brien, George. "Goodbye to All That." *The Irish Review,* no. 7 (Autumn 1989), pp. 89–92.

O'Carroll, Ide, and Eoin Collins, eds. *Lesbian and Gay Visions of Ireland.* London: Cassell, 1995.

O'Connor, Joseph. *Cowboys and Indians.* London: Flamingo, 1992.

———. *The Secret World of the Irish Male.* London: Mandarin, 1995.

———. *The Salesman.* London: Vintage, 1999.

O'Connor, Pat. *Emerging Voices: Women in Contemporary Irish Society.* Dublin: Institute of Public Administration, 1998.

O'Dowd, Mary, and Sabine Wichert. *Chattel, Servant or Citizen: Women's Status in Church, State and Society.* Belfast: The Queen's University of Belfast, 1995.

O Drisceoil, Proinsias, ed. *Religions: Identity and Power.* Belfast: The Queen's University of Belfast, 1993.

O'Flaherty, Liam. *Insurrection.* Dublin: Wolfhound, 1988.

O'Gaora, Colm. *Giving Ground.* London: Jonathan Cape, 1993.

O'Glaisne, Risteard. "Irish and the Protestant Tradition." *The Crane Bag,* vol. 5, no. 2 (1981), pp. 33–45.

O'Mahony, Patrick, and Gerard Delanty, eds. *Rethinking Irish History: Nationalism, Identity and Ideology.* New York: St. Martin's Press, 1998.

O'Riordan, Kate. *Involved.* London: Flamingo, 1995.

———. *The Boy in the Moon.* London: Flamingo, 1997.

Ormiston, Gayle L., and Alan D. Schrift, eds. *The Hermeneutic Tradition: From Ast to Ricoeur.* Albany: SUNY Press, 1990.

O'Toole, Fintan. "Going West: The Country versus the City in Irish Writing." *The Crane Bag,* vol. 9, no. 2 (1985), pp. 111–116.

Parker, Michael. "Shadows on a Glass: Self-Reflexivity in the Fiction of Deirdre Madden." *Irish University Review,* vol. 30, no. 1 (Spring/Summer 2000), pp. 82–102.

Patterson, Glenn. *Burning Your Own.* London: Minerva, 1993.

———. *Fat Lad.* London: Minerva, 1992.

Pelaschiar, Laura. "Transforming Belfast: The Evolving Rose of the City in Northern Irish Fiction." *Irish University Review,* vol. 30, no. 1 (Spring/Summer 2000), pp. 117–131.

Pettitt, Lance. "G(ay)uinness is Good for You." *The South Atlantic Quarterly,* vol. 95, no. 1 (Winter 1996), pp. 205–212.

Pittock, Murray G. H. *Celtic Identity and the British Image.* Manchester: Manchester UP, 1999.

Phelan, Peggy. *Unmarked: The Politics of Performance.* New York: Routledge, 1993.

Rich, Adrienne. *Compulsory Heterosexuality and Lesbian Existence.* Denver, CO: Antelope, 1980.

Roche, Anthony. "Introduction: Contemporary Irish Fiction." *Irish University Review,* vol. 30, no. 1 (Spring/Summer 2000), pp. xii-xi.

Rolston, Bill. *Drawing Support: Murals in the North of Ireland.* Belfast: Beyond the Pale Publications, 1994.

———. *Drawing Support 2: Murals of War and Peace.* Belfast: Beyond the Pale Publications, 1998.

Sailer, Susan Shaw, ed. *Representing Ireland: Gender, Class, Nationality.* Gainesville: U Press of Florida, 1997.

Sales, Rosemary. *Women Divided: Gender, Religion and Politics in Northern Ireland.* London: Routledge, 1997.

Scaggs, John. "Who is Francie Pig? Self-Identity and Narrative Reliability in *The Butcher Boy.*" *Irish University Review,* vol. 30, no. 1 (Spring/Summer 2000), pp. 51–58.

Scally, Robert James. *The End of Hidden Ireland: Rebellion, Famine, and Emigration.* Oxford: Oxford UP, 1995.

Shannon, Catherine. "Recovering the Voices of the Women of the North." *Irish Review* 12 (1992), pp. 27–33.

Sherry, Ruth. "How is Irish Writing Reviewed?" *Cyphers* 31 (1991), pp. 5–11.

Smyth, Ailbhe. *Women's Rights in Ireland: A Practical Guide.* Swords: Ward River, 1983.

———. "The Floozie in the Jacuzzi: Intersextual Inserts." *Irish Review* 6 (1989), pp. 7–24.

———. "'A Great Day for the Women of Ireland': The Meaning of Mary Robinson's Presidency for Irish Women." *The Canadian Journal of Irish Studies,* vol. 18, no. 1 (July 1992), pp.61–75.

———. "States of Change." *Feminist Review,* no. 50 (Summer 1995), pp. 24–43.

———, ed. *Irish Women's Studies Reader.* Dublin: Attic, 1993.

———, ed. "Introduction." *Wildish Things: An Anthology of New Irish Women's Writings.* Attic: Dublin, 1989.

———, ed. "Feminism in Ireland." *Women's Studies International Forum,* vol. 11, no. 4.

Smyth, Damian. "Dandy Beano Topper." *Irish Review,* no. 15 (Spring 1994), pp. 134–142.

Smyth, Gerry. *The Novel and the Nation.* London: Pluto, 1997.

———. *Decolonisation and Criticism: The Construction of Irish Literature.* London: Pluto, 1998.

———. "Irish Studies, Postcolonial Theory and the 'New' Essentialism." *Irish Studies Review,* vol. 7, no. 2 (1999), pp. 211–220.

———. "Shite and Sheep: An Ecocritical Perspective on Two Recent Irish Novels." *Irish University Review,* vol. 30, no. 1 (Spring/Summer 2000), pp. 163–178.

St. Peter, Christine, and Ron Marken. "Women and Irish Politics." *Canadian Journal of Irish Studies,* vol. 18, no. 1 (1992).

Strongman, Luke. "Toward an Irish Literary Postmodernism: Roddy Doyle's *Paddy Clarke Ha Ha Ha.*" *The Canadian Journal of Irish Studies,* vol. 23, no. 1 (July 1997), pp. 31–40.

Sullivan, Megan. *Women in Northern Ireland.* Gainesville: UP of Florida, 1999.

Thompson, Spurgeon. "The Commodification of Culture and Decolonisation in Northern Ireland." *Irish Studies Review*, vol. 7, no. 1 (1999), pp. 53–63.

Todd, Jennifer. "The Limits of Britishness." *Irish Review*, no. 5 (Autumn 1988), p. 11–16.

Todd, Loreto. *Green English: Ireland's Influence on the English Language*. Dublin: O'Brien, 1999.

Toibin, Colm. *The Blackwater Lightship*. London: Picador, 1999.

———, ed. *New Irish Writing*. London: Bloomsbury, 1993.

———, ed. *The Penguin Book of Irish Fiction*. London: Viking, 1999.

Tyler, Carole-Anne. "Passing: Narcissism, Identity, and Difference." *Differences*, vol. 6, no. 2+3 (Summer-Fall 1994), pp. 212–248.

Vance, Norman. *Irish Literature: A Social History*. Dublin: Four Courts, 1999.

Viney, Ethna. *Ancient Wars: Sexuality and Oppression*. Dublin: Attic Press LIP Pamphlet, 1989.

Walby, Sylvia. *Theorizing Patriarchy*. Oxford: Basil Blackwell, 1990.

Walker, Lenore E. *The Battered Woman Syndrome*. New York: Springer Publishing Co., 1984.

Wall, Eamonn. "The Living Stream: John McGahern's *Amongst Women* and Irish Writing in the 1990s." *Studies*, vol. 88, no. 351 (Autumn 1999), pp. 305–314.

Walshe, Eibhear, ed. *Sex, Nation, and Dissent in Irish Writing*. New York: St. Martin's Press, 1997.

Ward, M., ed. *A Dangerous, Difficult Honesty: Ten Years of Feminism in Northern Ireland*. Belfast: Women's Book Collective, 1986.

Weekes, Ann Owns. *Irish Women Writers: An Uncharted Tradition*. Lexington: U of Kentucky Press, 1990.

Whelan, Kevin. *The Tree of Liberty*. Notre Dame: University of Notre Dame, 1996.

White, Padraic, and Ray Mac Sharry. *The Making of the Celtic Tiger: The Inside Story of Ireland's Boom Economy*. Cork: Mercier, 2000.

Wilson, Robert McLiam. *Ripley Bogle*. London: Vintage, 1989.

———. *Eureka Street*. London: Minerva, 1996.

Wolfe, Susan J., and Julia Penelope. *Sexual Practice/Textual Theory: Lesbian Cultural Criticism*. Cambridge: Blackwell, 1993.

Wondrich, Roberta Gefter. "Exilic Returns: Self and History Outside of Ireland in Recent Irish Fiction." *Irish University Review*, vol. 30, no. 1 (Spring/Summer 2000), pp. 1–16.

Yllo, Kersti, and Michele Bograd, eds. *Feminist Perspectives on Wife Abuse*. New York: Sage, 1988.

Index